Official Guide to Texas State Parks and Historic Sites

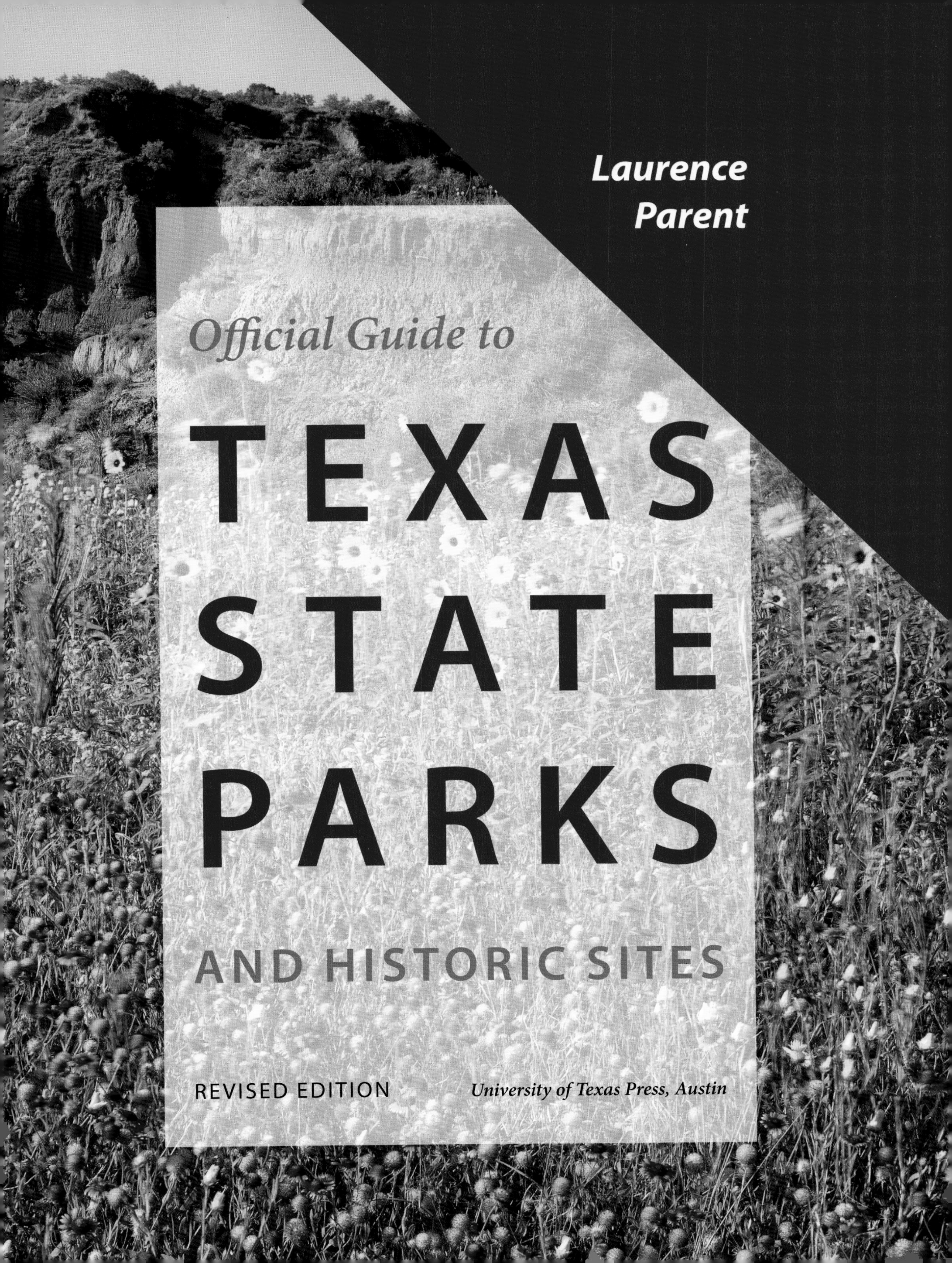

Laurence Parent

Official Guide to

TEXAS STATE PARKS

AND HISTORIC SITES

REVISED EDITION

University of Texas Press, Austin

I would like to thank Patricia Parent, Patsie and James Caperton, Liz Carmack, Patrick Fischer, Lora Hufton, Sienna Jones, Shannon Justice, Dale and Delilah Linenberger, Frank Moster, Andy Skiba, Todd Skinner, Murty and Teniece Sullivan, Keri Thomas, and Amy Whisler for their hospitality and help with the photos. I am grateful to many employees of the Texas Parks and Wildlife Department, in particular Mike Crevier and Robert Cook, for their assistance with my photos and information.

PAGE i
Lost Maples State Natural Area

PAGES ii–iii
Caprock Canyons State Park

PAGES viii–ix
Caddo Lake State Park

Printed in China
Third printing, 2013

♾ The paper used in this book meets the minimum requirements of ANSI/NISO Z39.48-1992 (R1997) (Permanence of Paper).

LIBRARY OF CONGRESS
CATALOGING-IN-PUBLICATION DATA

Parent, Laurence.
Official guide to Texas state parks and historic sites / by Laurence Parent. — 2nd ed. ; Rev. ed.
p. cm.
Includes index.
Rev. ed. of: Official guide to Texas state parks. 1st ed. 1997.
ISBN 978-0-292-71726-8 (pbk. : alk. paper)
1. Parks—Texas—Guidebooks. 2. Texas—Guidebooks. I. Parent, Laurence. Official guide to Texas state parks. II. Title.
F384.3.P36 2008
919.76404'64—dc22 2007043029

doi:10.7560/717268

Contents

Hill Country 57

Panhandle Plains 87

Pineywoods 107

Prairies and Lakes 131

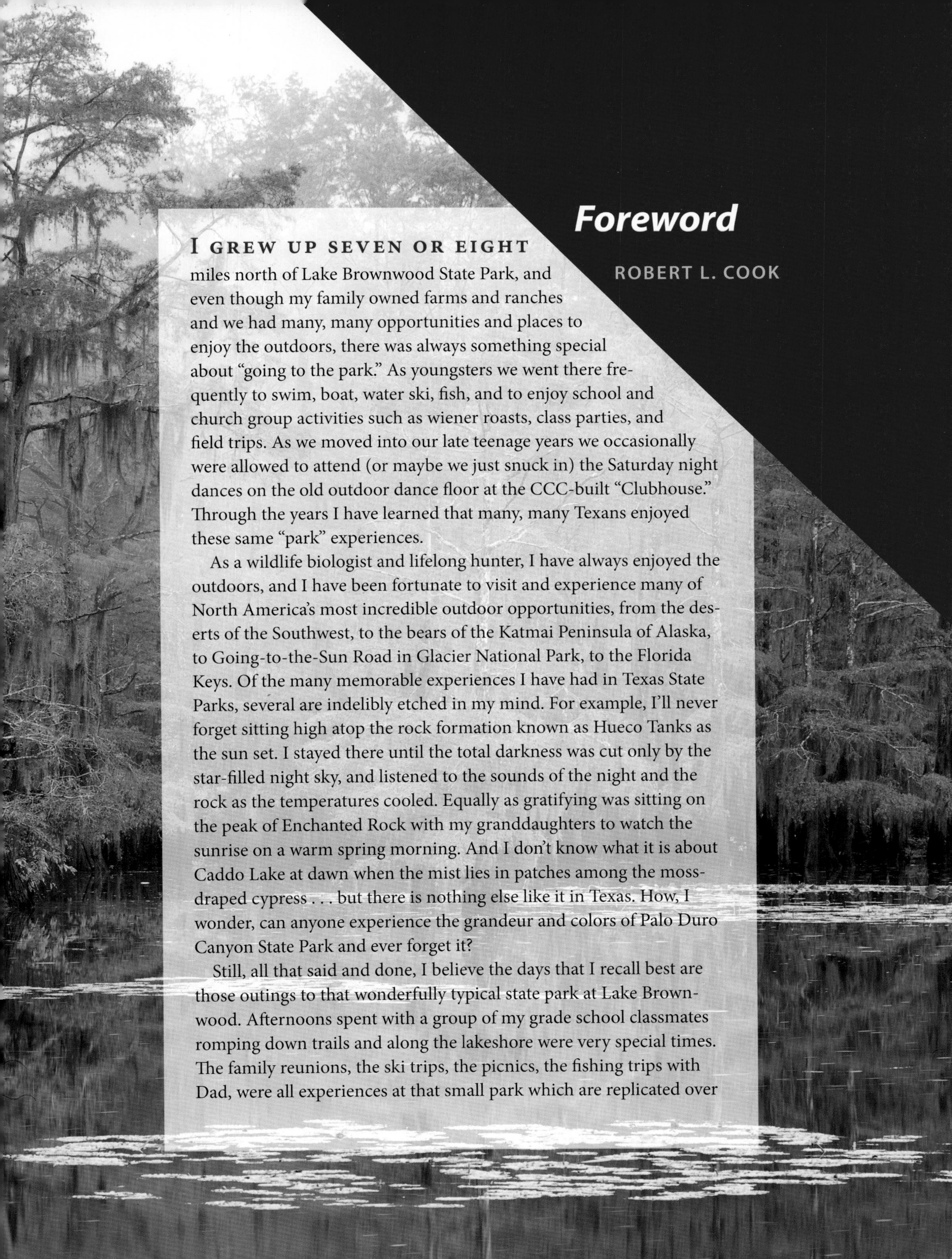

Foreword

ROBERT L. COOK

I GREW UP SEVEN OR EIGHT miles north of Lake Brownwood State Park, and even though my family owned farms and ranches and we had many, many opportunities and places to enjoy the outdoors, there was always something special about "going to the park." As youngsters we went there frequently to swim, boat, water ski, fish, and to enjoy school and church group activities such as wiener roasts, class parties, and field trips. As we moved into our late teenage years we occasionally were allowed to attend (or maybe we just snuck in) the Saturday night dances on the old outdoor dance floor at the CCC-built "Clubhouse." Through the years I have learned that many, many Texans enjoyed these same "park" experiences.

As a wildlife biologist and lifelong hunter, I have always enjoyed the outdoors, and I have been fortunate to visit and experience many of North America's most incredible outdoor opportunities, from the deserts of the Southwest, to the bears of the Katmai Peninsula of Alaska, to Going-to-the-Sun Road in Glacier National Park, to the Florida Keys. Of the many memorable experiences I have had in Texas State Parks, several are indelibly etched in my mind. For example, I'll never forget sitting high atop the rock formation known as Hueco Tanks as the sun set. I stayed there until the total darkness was cut only by the star-filled night sky, and listened to the sounds of the night and the rock as the temperatures cooled. Equally as gratifying was sitting on the peak of Enchanted Rock with my granddaughters to watch the sunrise on a warm spring morning. And I don't know what it is about Caddo Lake at dawn when the mist lies in patches among the moss-draped cypress . . . but there is nothing else like it in Texas. How, I wonder, can anyone experience the grandeur and colors of Palo Duro Canyon State Park and ever forget it?

Still, all that said and done, I believe the days that I recall best are those outings to that wonderfully typical state park at Lake Brownwood. Afternoons spent with a group of my grade school classmates romping down trails and along the lakeshore were very special times. The family reunions, the ski trips, the picnics, the fishing trips with Dad, were all experiences at that small park which are replicated over and over thousands of times every year throughout our state park system. These special places frequently provide some of the most memorable outdoor and personal experiences in our lives. For many of us, we have several of our "firsts" at Texas state parks. For example, I saw my first Texas Longhorns at Ft. Griffin State Park. Several dozen birds on my "life list" were initially recorded at Bentsen–Rio Grande Valley State Park. My first true "sand dunes" were experienced at Monahans Sandhills State Park, my first pictographs at Big Bend Ranch. Where else can you walk beside the 100-million-year-old tracks of *acrocanthosaurus* other than at Dinosaur Valley State Park, or stand on the battlefield where Sam Houston declared victory over Santa Anna on that April afternoon in 1836?

Welcome to Texas State Parks. Enjoy.

Robert L. Cook
Executive Director
Texas Parks and Wildlife

Using This Guide

Guidebook organization

This guide is divided into seven geographic regions within Texas. Each section begins with some general information about the region, followed by descriptions of every park within that region listed alphabetically. The state map and table of contents in the front of the book will aid in finding specific parks. In addition, color-coded symbols appear at the top of each page, with a different color used for each region.

Park descriptions

A short essay provides some historical, biological, and geological background on each park, along with park highlights and recreational opportunities. The Depression-inspired Civilian Conservation Corps (CCC) is frequently mentioned as having been responsible for the skillful construction of many of the buildings and other facilities that are still in use today at numerous parks. A short Visitor Information section at the end of each description gives a brief summary of park size and operating schedule, camping availability, and facilities. It also lists the nearest town with services such as gas stations, restaurants, and lodging. The park's address and phone number allow you to call or write for more information. The Texas Parks and Wildlife Department's website, www.tpwd.state.tx.us, gives additional information. Before visiting a park, checking the website for park schedules and recent changes is highly recommended.

Camping

At campgrounds described as having partial hookups, water and electricity are available. Those described as having full hookups also have sewage connections. Most parks with campgrounds have a dump station even if no sewage connections are available.

Camping reservations are not necessary at the state parks. However, on spring, summer, and fall weekends, campgrounds at many parks often fill up, so reservations are advisable at those times. Campgrounds can sometimes fill up on summer weekdays, particularly at some popular water-oriented parks on lakes, rivers, or the coast. All camping reservations are handled through a central reservation number, (512) 389-8900, in Austin. Be sure to call that number, not the individual state parks, to reserve a site. Reservations can also be made online via the Internet address in the section above.

Park hours

Most parks, especially those with campgrounds, are open every day all year. Some parks, particularly state historic sites, may have more limited days and hours. An effort has been made to give some idea of operating times in the description of these parks. However, schedules sometimes change, both seasonally and for operational reasons. Before driving long distances, you may want to call ahead for a current schedule. In winter, a few of the larger parks with campgrounds may close for a short time to allow public hunts.

Rules and regulations

Regulations are aimed at both protecting the park and providing a pleasant experience for visitors. To preserve the parks, please refrain from removing plants—including wildflowers—as well as minerals and artifacts. Firewood gathering is not allowed, but many parks sell bundles at headquarters. Otherwise, bring your own.

Please don't litter, damage park facilities, or leave fires unattended. Firearms and hunting are not allowed except during special hunts. Public display and consumption of alcohol are prohibited. Be courteous to your campground neighbors and keep music and voices low at night.

Official Guide to Texas State Parks and Historic Sites

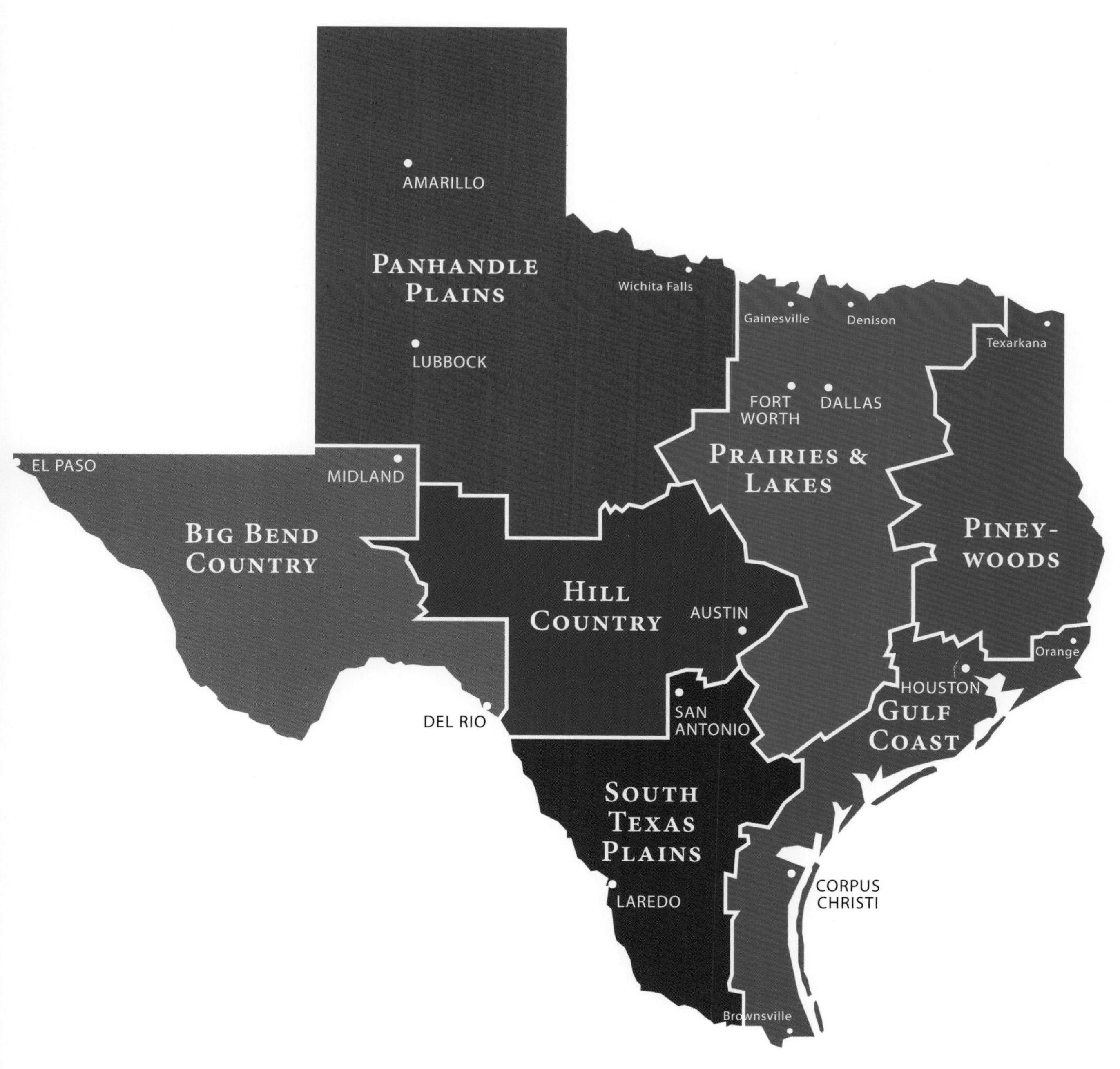

Big Bend Country

Most state parks in the Big Bend Country lie west of the Pecos River, in what is often called the Trans-Pecos region. The area is a land of superlatives. It contains the largest county, the largest state park, the deepest canyons, and the only mountains in the state. It has the hottest and driest country in Texas, right next to mountains with some of the coldest, snowiest, and windiest weather. One of the longest rivers in North America, the Rio Grande, bounds West Texas along its southern and western flanks. The Trans-Pecos contains the most spectacular scenery in Texas and harbors two national parks.

Most of the area lies within the Chihuahuan Desert, a vast province of North America that stretches from deep inside Mexico, across West Texas, and into southern New Mexico. Low elevation areas of the desert usually receive less than ten inches of rain annually, allowing only sparse, hardy vegetation to grow.

Many desert plants have defenses that allow them to survive in the harsh, dry environment. Leaves tend to be small and waxy to limit transpiration, while cacti do away with them altogether. Plants such as the ocotillo, which usually looks like a bundle of dead, upright, spiny sticks, grow leaves only after receiving sufficient rain. Annuals grow, bloom, and die quickly during short wet spells. Many plants grow spines or thorns and secrete chemicals that make their foliage toxic or bad-tasting to deter grazing animals.

Like the plants, animals have also adapted to the hot, dry conditions of West Texas. During the heat of the day, animals retreat into their burrows, crawl under ledges, or seek shade under trees and shrubs. At dusk, the dry air cools quickly and the desert comes to life as many animals come out to feed and hunt.

Mountain ranges are sprinkled across this dry desert country, seeming to float like islands on a vast desert sea. On an absolute scale, the mountains are not especially large; the highest peak, found in the Guadalupe Mountains, rises to only 8749 feet above sea level. However, some of the mountains rise as much as 5000 or 6000 feet above the low-lying desert, making them appear quite impressive.

These large changes in elevation cause moving air masses to rise and cool over these mountain ranges, condensing out additional precipitation. The highest ranges, such as the Guadalupe and Davis mountains, can receive as much as ten or fifteen inches more rain than the surrounding desert lowlands. In stark contrast to the desert below, forests grow on the moist, cool slopes of the ranges, and grasslands cloak the foothills. Oaks, junipers, and pinyon pines cloak the middle slopes of the mountains. Tall pines and even a few aspens can be found in the Guadalupe, Davis, and Chisos mountains, the three highest ranges.

Except for the area around El Paso, West Texas is very lightly populated. The Spaniards largely avoided the Trans-Pecos, calling it *el despoblado*, or the unpopulated land. Only a few small, widely spaced towns dot the empty region. Oil and gas fields lie on the eastern edge of the area; otherwise, only sprawling ranches and parks cover the land.

In the undeveloped country, large predators have been able to survive better than in the rest of the state. Only in West Texas are mountain lions relatively common. Black bears, after having been exterminated throughout Texas, have been recolonizing the Chisos and Guadalupe mountains after migrating from Mexico and New Mexico.

Humans have lived in West Texas for at least 10,000 years. Unlike the Anasazi in the Southwest, the early Texas cultures did not leave large masonry villages and cliff dwellings to mark their passing. However, they did create panels of painted and carved artwork on the walls of remote canyons and caves throughout the region. Notable examples of their work can be found at Hueco Tanks and Seminole Canyon state historic sites. Examples of homes and military outposts dating from the region's frontier days may be found in three state historic sites—Fort Lancaster, Fort Leaton, and Magoffin Home.

Fittingly, three of the largest state parks and several large wildlife-management areas lie in the wide open spaces of West Texas. Big Bend Ranch State Park contains 299,000 acres and borders on Colorado Canyon, one of the most spectacular segments of the Rio Grande. Devils River State Natural Area lies on the far eastern fringe of the Big Bend Country and has a mixed ecosystem of West Texas and Hill Country species. Franklin Mountains State Park encompasses almost the entire Franklin Mountains, creating an island of wilderness in the heart of urban El Paso. From the cool mountain heights of Davis Mountains State Park to the deep canyons of Big Bend Ranch, West Texas contains some of Texas's most notable state parks.

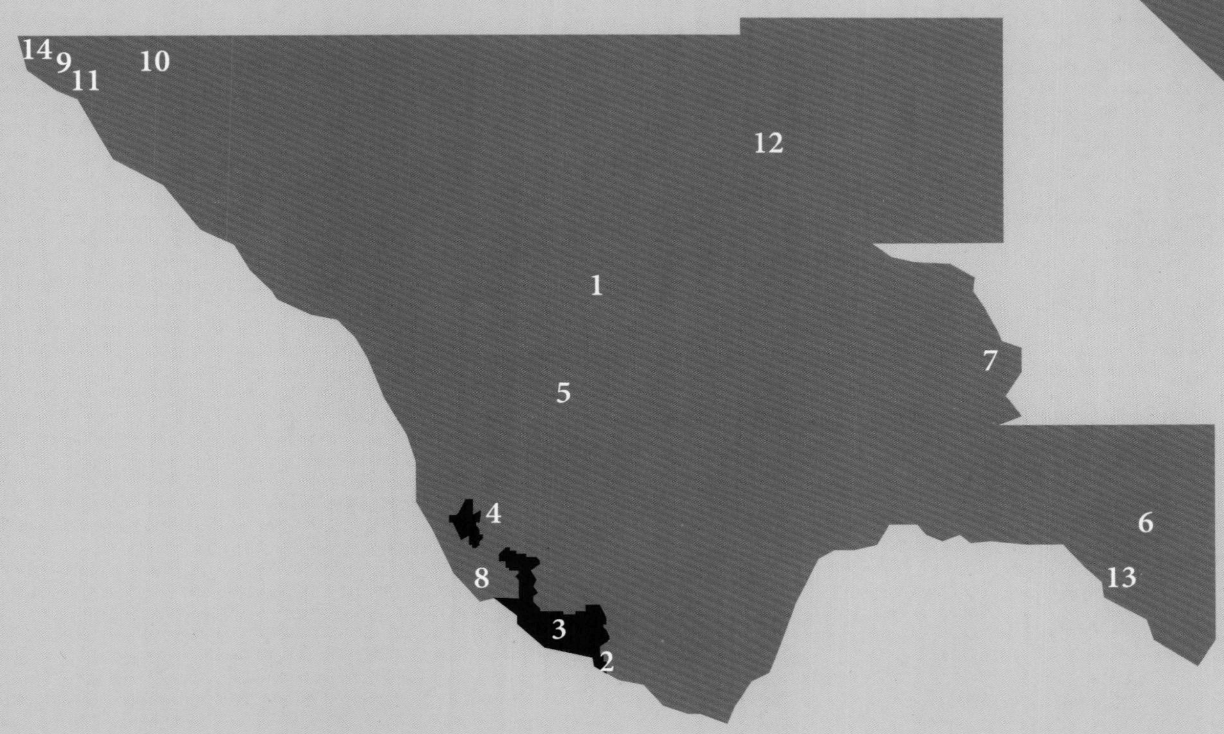

1 Balmorhea State Park

2 Barton Warnock Environmental Education Center

3 Big Bend Ranch State Park

4 Chinati Mountains State Park

5 Davis Mountains State Park • Indian Lodge

6 Devils River State Natural Area

7 Fort Lancaster State Historic Site

8 Fort Leaton State Historic Site

9 Franklin Mountains State Park

10 Hueco Tanks State Historic Site

11 Magoffin Home State Historic Site

12 Monahans Sandhills State Park

13 Seminole Canyon State Park and Historic Site

14 Wyler Aerial Tramway

Balmorhea State Park

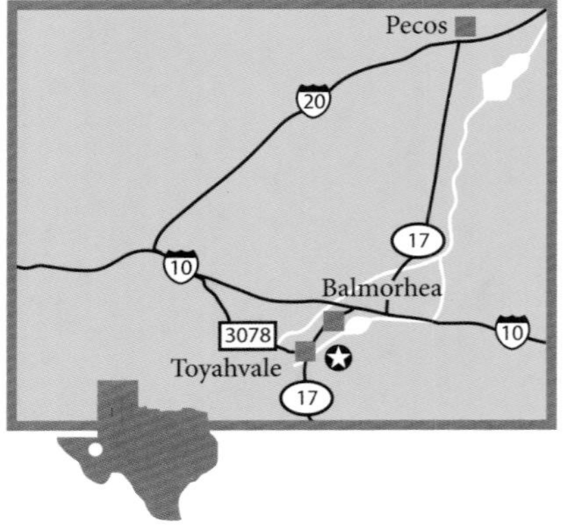

In the dry desert flatlands on the north side of the Davis Mountains, the clear, cold waters of San Solomon Spring gush forth, creating a startlingly green oasis of fields and tree-lined canals for many miles downstream. The spring produces between 15 and 26 million gallons per day from a deep pool in Balmorhea State Park. Its waters irrigate 10,000 acres in the farming towns of Balmorhea, Saragosa, and Toyahvale, and even form a small lake.

Most of the spring's water comes from precipitation falling on the Davis and Apache mountains. The water seeps underground, then flows slowly through subsurface faults and porous rock layers, known as aquifers, to several springs in the Balmorhea area. San Solomon Spring, an artesian spring, is the largest. Artesian springs are under pressure and flow out above the water table, whereas gravity springs flow from below the water table.

Unfortunately, heavy groundwater pumping has lowered area water tables and dried up many West Texas springs. Comanche Springs in Fort Stockton had flow rates comparable to San Solomon and irrigated more than 6000 acres before it stopped flowing in 1961. Two artesian springs near San Solomon Spring, Phantom Lake and Giffin, still flow, although at much reduced rates. Additional groundwater pumping could cause these two springs, and possibly even San Solomon, to fail.

These desert springs are effectively islands, separated from each other by miles of desert. Unique species of plants and animals evolved in the highly localized spring environments. Two endangered species, the Comanche Springs pupfish and the Pecos mosquito fish, live only in the park and a few other West Texas springs.

For thousands of years, San Solomon Spring provided water to early peoples. Later, the spring was a watering hole for Spanish explorers, gold-seekers, and other West Texas travelers. Some Mexican farmers built the first irrigation canals in the mid-1800s. Other more elaborate systems were added over the following years. During the Depression, the Civilian Conservation Corps built the pool around the spring, bathhouse, residences, and motel units. The huge pool is 1.75 acres in area and 25 feet deep, and has a capacity of 3.5 million gallons. With a constant fresh inflow, chlorination of the constant 72- to 76-degree water is unnecessary.

San Solomon Spring has drawn people for thousands of years and still does today. People from near and far flock to the pool during the hot summers for swimming and relaxation. Scuba divers come from all over to dive in the clear, deep pool. They swim

by perch and schools of minnows and hunt for reclusive catfish hiding under rock ledges. The spring itself boils up through the sandy bottom in the deepest part of the pool.

The Texas Parks and Wildlife Department, in partnership with local groups and federal agencies, has restored part of the original San Solomon Spring Ciénega, a desert wetland at the park. Visitors can enjoy some of the ciénega's unique aquatic inhabitants through an underwater viewing window.

VISITOR INFORMATION

46 acres. Open all year. Hot in summer. Pool is open all year from 8 AM until a half hour before sunset. Swim at your own risk. Open to certified divers and classes. Small campground with partial hookups and showers. Motel units, some with kitchenettes, are popular; reserve ahead. Limited visitor services available in Balmorhea. All visitor services available in Fort Davis, Pecos, Fort Stockton. For information: Balmorhea State Park, Box 15, Toyahvale, TX 79786, (432) 375-2370.

OPPOSITE PAGE
The pool at Balmorhea
BELOW
Swimmer at Balmorhea
RIGHT
Barton Warnock Center

Barton Warnock Environmental Education Center

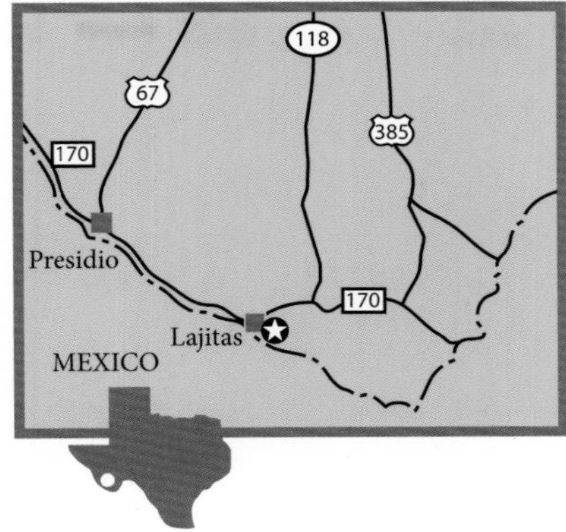

The Barton Warnock Environmental Education Center offers an extensive interpretive museum and desert botanical garden, and acts as a visitor center for Big Bend Ranch State Park. The Lajitas Foundation built the center in 1982, naming it the Lajitas Museum Desert Gardens. The Texas Parks and Wildlife Department purchased the museum in 1990 and renamed it for Dr. Barton Warnock, a longtime professor at Sul Ross State University in Alpine, author of several wildflower books, and probably the most noted botanist in West Texas. Dr. Warnock died in 1998.

The Warnock Center offers extensive exhibits on the human and natural history of the Big Bend region. It covers the history of the area, from the early Indian inhabitants, through the arrival of the Spaniards, to the mining and ranching done by Anglo settlers. Natural-history exhibits cover everything from the ancient geology of the Big Bend area to the biology and climate of the Chihuahuan Desert. A short, easy trail winds through the two-acre outdoor botanical garden, which features many cacti and other dryland plants characteristic of the Chihuahuan Desert, plus a small pond and riparian area. The Warnock Center also has a bookstore with an extensive list of titles relevant to the Big Bend area, as well as a gift shop.

The center acts as one of the visitor centers for nearby Big Bend Ranch State Park, the state-run sister park to Big Bend National Park. It offers information and permits for the massive state park; with nearly 300,000 acres, it is by far the largest state park in Texas. Big Bend Ranch has numerous recreational activities, such as hiking, mountain biking, and camping.

VISITOR INFORMATION

100 acres. Open all year. Very hot from late spring through early fall. Primitive car camping in nearby Big Bend Ranch State Park; no water or hookups. Primitive backpacking campsites at Big Bend Ranch. Extensive museum and bookstore, desert botanical garden. All visitor services available in Lajitas and Terlingua. For information: Barton Warnock Environmental Education Center, HC 70, Box 375, Terlingua, TX 79852, (432) 424-3327.

Big Bend Ranch State Park

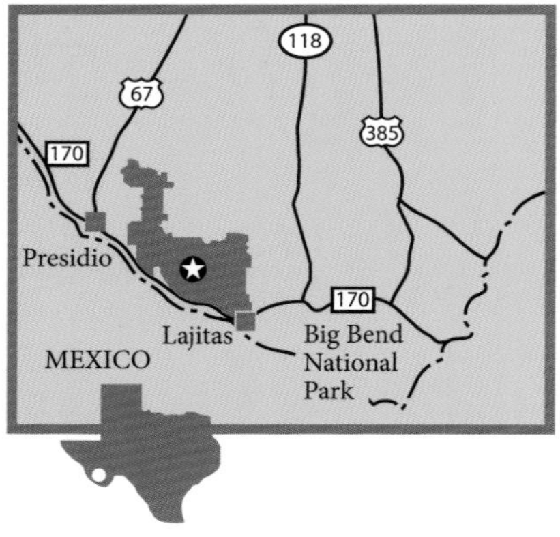

Deep in a remote corner of West Texas lie more than a quarter-million acres of Chihuahuan Desert that invite exploration. The Parks and Wildlife Department purchased the enormous tract in 1988, roughly doubling the size of the state-park system. Big Bend Ranch State Park fronts the Rio Grande between Lajitas and Presidio, and contains a rugged mix of desert mountains, canyons, and grasslands.

The Rio Grande flows through the sheer-walled Colorado Canyon and forms the southern boundary of the state park. The reddish-brown, iron-stained walls of the canyon were carved by the Rio Grande through the Bofecillos Mountains of Texas and the Sierra Rica of Mexico. Between 25 and 40 million years ago, massive volcanoes exploded on both sides of the river, spewing forth dark lava and layers of white ash to form the mountain ranges. Texas Highway FM 170 follows the canyon, squeezed between mountains and the river. To the north of the highway is the Solitario, a huge dome of rock, called a laccolith, pushed upward from below by intruding igneous rocks.

The highway traverses one of the most scenic sections of Big Bend Ranch; it may be the most spectacular drive in Texas. The entire state park lies within the Chihuahuan Desert. Except for small riparian areas along the Rio Grande and around springs and small permanent watercourses, desert vegetation dominates. Dryland grasses, such as blue, side oats, and black grama, and chino are common where they have not been heavily grazed. Lechuguilla is prolific; it is an indicator plant of the Chihuahuan Desert, meaning that it lives nowhere else. It grows in a compact rosette of stiff, green blades tipped with sharp spines. Many an unwary hiker has speared an ankle on the omnipresent lechuguilla.

Other common desert plants include the sotol, ocotillo, creosote,

TOP
Madrid Falls in fall
LEFT
Colorado Canyon

mesquite, and many cactus species. Much of the wildlife is centered around water sources, where reeds, willows, salt cedar, cottonwood, and ash create a lush habitat. Commonly seen animals in the state park include mule deer, javelina, and many species of lizards. Lucky visitors might spot rare or reclusive animals such as the mountain lion, golden eagle, bobcat, peregrine falcon, or zone-tailed hawk. The western mastiff bat, with a wingspan of more than two feet, is one of the most interesting residents of Big Bend Ranch.

Humans arrived in the area at least 10,000 years ago, living in nomadic groups that hunted game and gathered edible fruits, nuts, berries, leaves, and roots. The earliest groups left few traces of their passing, other than projectile points and other stone tools. The remains of later groups, including campsites, rock art, burials, and stone artifacts, dot Big Bend Ranch. By AD 1200, some groups were practicing primitive agriculture along the Rio Grande upstream from Big Bend Ranch. They lived in organized villages and were influenced by the Pueblo cultures of New Mexico. The Spaniards arrived about 400 years ago, but made

TOP
Las Cuevas area in last light
RIGHT
Mountain bikers
BELOW LEFT
Yucca silhouetted against sunrise below Bofecillos Mountains
BELOW RIGHT
Rock-nettle (Eucnide bartonioides)

only sporadic efforts to control and settle the Big Bend area north of the Rio Grande. They called it *el despoblado*, or the uninhabited land. The presence of Comanches and Apaches limited settlement of the area until the late 1800s. Ranchers moved into the area after the Indian threat ended in the late 1800s, and silver mining began at Shafter, just north of the state park, at the same time. Extensive mercury mining developed on the east side of the park around Terlingua. Profitable ore eventually ran out in both mining districts; most operations ceased by the 1940s. Until tourism developed, ranching and farming along the Rio Grande floodplain remained the chief economic activities.

The scenic route of Texas Highway FM 170, the River Road, provides an excellent introduction to Big Bend Ranch. Before starting, stop in at the Barton Warnock Environmental Education Center in Lajitas. It has an extensive museum describing the human and natural history of the region, an elaborate desert garden, a bookstore, plus information and permits. Fort Leaton State Historic Site near Presidio also has information and permits, along with historical exhibits and a bookstore. Big Bend Ranch's administrative headquarters, across Texas FM 170 from Fort Leaton, handles reservations for programs, camping, and lodging at Sauceda, in addition to permits and information.

Popular activities include hiking and backpacking trails ranging in length from 1.5 miles to more than 20 miles. Boating the Rio Grande through Colorado Canyon is one of the most popular pursuits in the state park. The deep, spectacular canyon has long calm stretches punctuated by occasional moderate rapids, floatable by both rafts and canoes when river levels are high enough. First-time floaters may want to consider taking a trip with outfitters based in Lajitas, Terlingua, and Study Butte.

Big Bend Ranch State Park is one of the crown jewels of the state-park system. Its spectacular scenery and large size provide worthy competition to its better-known neighbor, Big Bend National Park.

VISITOR INFORMATION

299,640 acres. Open all year. Very hot from late spring through early fall, particularly in lower elevations along river. Most popular during Thanksgiving, Christmas, and spring-break holidays. Primitive car camping with composting toilets along the river; no water or hookups. Fourteen additional car camping sites in the interior, with showers and restrooms available at the Sauceda Ranch Headquarters Visitor Center. Group accommodations with meals at Sauceda Ranch by reservation. Primitive backcountry camping for backpackers. The Barton Warnock Environmental Education Center in Lajitas has a museum and bookstore. During extended hikes or river trips, it is advisable to use shuttle services available at Terlingua outfitters rather than leaving a car unattended for long periods of time. Scenic drive along paved TX 170 is very steep, winding, and narrow in places and may not be suitable for large RVs or trailers. Dry water crossings can flood rapidly during heavy rains. This is lightly traveled, desert wilderness country. Be prepared with adequate water, food, sunscreen, clothing, and other items before attempting hikes or river trips. All visitor services available in Lajitas, Presidio, and Terlingua. For information: Big Bend Ranch State Park, P.O. Box 2319, Presidio, TX 79845, (432) 229-3416.

Chinati Mountains State Park

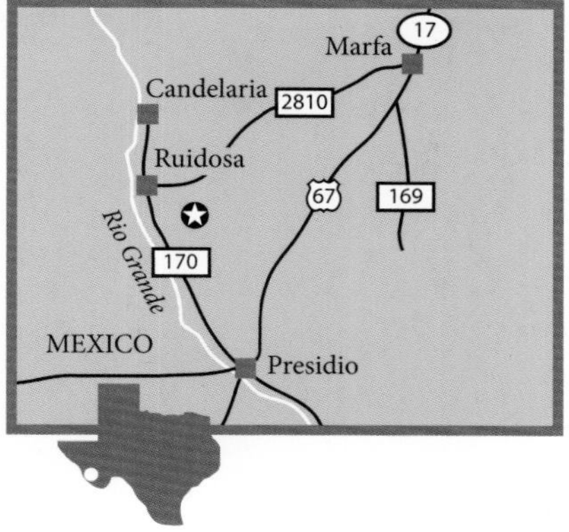

One of the state's largest parks lies deep in West Texas in the Chinati Mountains northwest of Presidio. The igneous mountain range is the fourth highest in Texas, exceeded in height only by the Guadalupe, Davis, and Chisos mountains. The rugged mountains offer everything from dry desert hills to lush, spring-filled canyons. Craggy peaks and sheer granite bluffs tower over the sprawling park.

The land was donated to the state by the Mellon Foundation as part of its effort to secure nationally significant sites as gifts to the people of the United States. The Chinati donation

OPPOSITE PAGE
Moonset over volcanic tuff formations
RIGHT
Hiker on rocky peak in Chinati Mountains foothills

was the largest ever for the Texas Parks and Wildlife Department. The Mellon Foundation not only gave the land to the state, it also set up an endowment for the county to offset the loss in property taxes.

Like the rest of the Trans-Pecos area, the Chinati Mountains are in the Chihuahuan Desert, a vast area that stretches from southern New Mexico through West Texas and deep into Mexico. Like all deserts, it is characterized by an average annual rainfall of less than ten inches at lower elevations. However, mountain areas, such as the Chinati range, trap additional moisture when air masses rise and cool as they push over high-elevation areas. Thus, in contrast to the lowland desert areas, the upper levels of the park have grasslands and even some areas of scrub woodland.

The former owners built an unpaved, but maintained, road system and several simple stone cabins to enhance their enjoyment of the property. Development will probably eventually include campsites and hiking trails, plus renovation of some of the existing buildings. At present the park is not open to the public.

VISITOR INFORMATION

Approximately 40,000 acres. Hiking, mountain biking, wildlife observation. The park is closed pending development. Full visitor services in Presidio. For information: Chinati Mountains State Park, c/o Big Bend Ranch State Park, P.O. Box 2319, Presidio, TX 79845, (432) 229-3416.

TOP
Stone cabin porch in foothills
ABOVE
Sunset over mountain peaks

Davis Mountains State Park • Indian Lodge

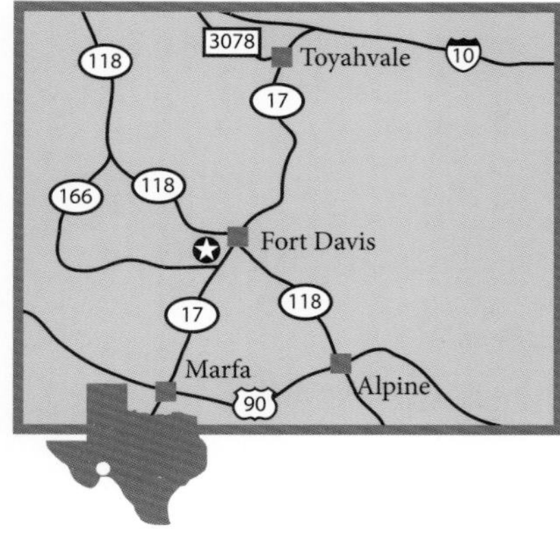

Indian Lodge

To find mountains in Texas, you have to go to the far western part of the state, often called the Trans-Pecos region. Only six counties in Texas, big counties admittedly, have mountain ranges. The Trans-Pecos is dotted with mountains, most small in extent, not exceptionally high, and vegetated with desert plants. The three highest ranges, the Guadalupe, Davis, and Chisos mountains, are exceptions. They are large enough and high enough to create their own weather. As winds blow over the mountains, the air rises and cools and condenses out additional precipitation, sometimes as much as ten inches more than the surrounding desert receives. The extra moisture and coolness of the higher elevations fosters the growth of forests on the mountain slopes. Davis Mountains State Park lies in the largest and most lush range of the three.

The Davis Mountains are the second highest range in Texas, reaching their high point on 8382-foot Mount Livermore, but they encompass the largest area. The mountains were named for Jefferson Davis, the U.S. Secretary of War who ordered construction of the frontier military installation Fort Davis.

Between 35 and 39 million years ago, volcanoes erupted violently, spewing ash and lava across the land that would become the Davis Mountains. During this time, volcanic activity was occurring all along a wide belt

between Montana and Mexico. The Davis Mountains were in one of the largest centers; the eruptions were centered around two large areas, the Paisano volcano west of Alpine and the Buckhorn Caldera northwest of Fort Davis. Today erosion has rounded off the rough edges of the mountains and vegetation has covered the slopes, but dark cliffs of ancient lava flows still mark the mountains' violent past.

The extra precipitation that falls on the Davis Mountains spurs the growth of lush vegetation, in contrast to the surrounding sea of dry desert. The lower slopes are blanketed with rich grasslands that foster large numbers of pronghorn antelope. In the middle elevations, Emory and gray oak and one-seed junipers cloak the hills. Slightly higher, pinyon pines appear, and finally, on the highest slopes, tall ponderosa and southwestern white pines grow, mixed with a few aspens.

Davis Mountains State Park and Indian Lodge lie in the mountain foothills, with a mix of grassland and juniper-oak woodland. The park's mix of habitats draws a large number of bird species; one of the most interesting is the Montezuma quail. The bird has a very limited range in North America; the state park is the only place in Texas with public access where it can be seen.

Fort Davis National Historic Site, the best preserved frontier fort in the Southwest, adjoins the state park's eastern boundary. The fort was established in 1854 to protect travelers and settlers in West Texas from attacks by Apaches and Comanches. It was garrisoned in part with black troops, known as buffalo soldiers by the Indians. Except for interruptions during the Civil War, the military post was occupied by troops until 1891. A scenic hiking trail connects the state park to the old fort.

Historic Indian Lodge, tucked into a bucolic setting in Keesey Canyon in the state park, draws many people. It was built in the 1930s, during the Depression, by the Civilian Conservation Corps (CCC). The architecture was modeled after southwestern Indian pueblos, and has adobe walls more than 18 inches thick and exposed roof beams. Some of the original furnishings made by the CCC are still used in the lobby and some of the rooms. A swimming pool, cool summer evenings, and mountain views add to the lodge's attractions.

The park's scenic drive leads to a high ridge above Limpia Creek where views stretch for miles. To the east lie the town of Fort Davis, the old fort, and sprawling grasslands dotted with mountains. To the west rise the high wooded peaks of the mountains, one of which, Mount Locke, is crowned with the white domes of McDonald Observatory. In late summer, afternoon thunderstorms march across the mountains, trailing curtains of rain. The temperature falls, and the fresh scent of moist earth permeates the air. Rainbows dance across the broad sweep of grasslands at the base of the mountains as the sun sets in the western sky. Davis Mountains State Park and Indian Lodge provide cool, scenic retreats during the long, hot Texas summers.

VISITOR INFORMATION

2709 acres. Open all year. Warm days, cool nights in summer make the park very popular that time of year. Can be cold in winter, with occasional snows. Moderate-sized campground with partial and full hookups. Primitive backpacking and equestrian campsites are available in the park area north of Texas Highway 118. Indian Lodge has 39 rooms, swimming pool, restaurant. Lodge is very popular; reserve well in advance. Scenic drive, hiking and nature trails, picnicking. Interpretive center. All visitor services available in Fort Davis. For information: Davis Mountains State Park, P.O. Box 1707, Fort Davis, TX 79734, (432) 426-3337. Indian Lodge, P.O. Box 1707, Fort Davis, TX 79734, (432) 426-3254.

ABOVE
Stone pavilion, Davis Mountains
OPPOSITE PAGE, TOP
Canoeists on Devils River
OPPOSITE PAGE, MIDDLE LEFT
Mountain biker
OPPOSITE PAGE, MIDDLE RIGHT
Dolan Creek, rocky creek bottom
OPPOSITE PAGE, BOTTOM
Dolan Creek, windmill

Devils River State Natural Area

The dirt road winds endlessly through the dry, dusty hills north of Del Rio, giving little hint of the oasis ahead. After 18 miles, the county road enters Devils River State Natural Area, a remote 20,000-acre preserve. The hilly terrain is dry and treeless near headquarters, but a surprise awaits visitors. Downstream from headquarters, located at the bottom of the dry canyon of Dolan Creek, springs gush out of the bedrock. The first spring encountered is José María Spring and its oases of pecans, live oaks, and sycamores. A short distance further downstream, just above Dolan Creek's confluence with the Devils River, more springs pour into the creek on private land and The Nature Conservancy's Dolan Falls Preserve. Along the Devils River, just above the confluence with the creek, massive springs pour a flood of clear, cool water into the river within the natural area. The clear, rushing waters of Dolan Creek and the Devils River exist in sharp contrast to the steep, dry, treeless hills above.

Over the course of millions of years, Dolan Creek, the Devils River, and their tributaries have carved deep canyons into the thick limestone beds of the western part of the Edwards Plateau. Vegetation of three ecological areas converges here, with the Chihuahuan Desert to the west, the Edwards Plateau/Hill Country to the east, and the Tamaulipan brushlands of northern Mexico to the south. Most of the natural area is dry, with grasses,

shrubs, and cacti dominating. At permanent sources of water, lush groves of trees and other plants thrive.

Humans have lived in the area for at least 12,000 years, leaving pictographs painted in rock shelters, as well as artifacts and campsites. In historic times, Apaches controlled the region, followed by Comanches, Kiowas, and Kickapoos. Because of conflict between settlers and various Indian groups, the area was little explored until the mid-1800s. In 1881, the railroad was built through the country to the south, opening the Devils River area to settlement. In 1883, Erasmus Fawcett settled the area now occupied by the natural area and The Nature Conservancy preserve, and established a sprawling sheep and goat ranch.

The area is still very lightly settled today, with large, widely scattered ranches. The Texas Parks and Wildlife Department and The Nature Conservancy purchased their land from some of these ranchers, including some of the descendants of Erasmus Fawcett. Unfortunately, much of the land has been greatly altered by man's activities. Dolan Creek and the Devils River were once lined by continuous stands of pecans, oaks, and sycamores. Overgrazing of much of the watershed speeded erosion and water runoff, contributing to massive floods in the 1930s and 1950s. The muddy torrents washed away much of the woodland areas, along with vast quantities of topsoil. With proper management and years of healing, the two preserves may one day recover more of their original character.

Bring all necessary food, water, gas, and other supplies to Devils River State Natural Area; this is one of the remotest areas of Texas. The Nature Conservancy's adjoining preserve, with its impressive Dolan Falls, is generally open only to conservancy members on guided field trips.

VISITOR INFORMATION

19,989 acres. Hot in summer. River access requires 1.5-mile hike or bicycle ride. Primitive camping and bunkhouse space available. Dining hall may be rented. Canoe shuttle. Hiking, mountain biking, canoeing, pictograph tours. All visitor services available in Del Rio. For information: Devils River State Natural Area, HCR 1, Box 513, Del Rio, TX 78840, (210) 395-2133. The Nature Conservancy of Texas is based in San Antonio and can be reached at (210) 224-8774.

Springs along Devils River

Fort Lancaster State Historic Site

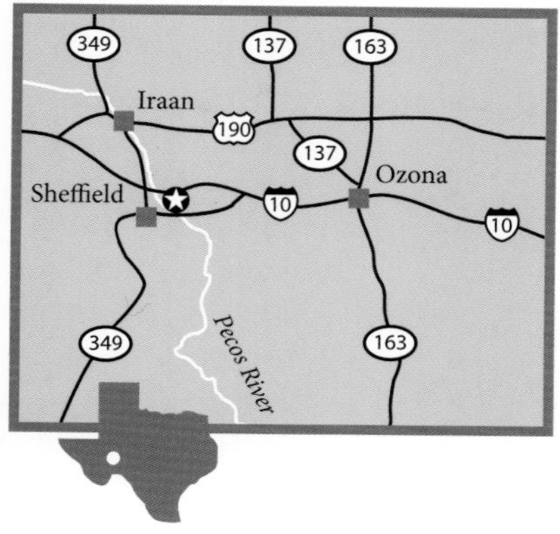

Fort Lancaster is almost lost in the vast emptiness of West Texas, tucked into the valley of the Pecos River and its tributaries. Even with today's paved highways and air-conditioned automobiles, the landscape seems harsh and desolate. To the soldiers who occupied the fort, it must have seemed like the remotest place in the world.

The post was established as Camp Lancaster in August 1855 on the east bank of Live Oak Creek about a half mile above its confluence with the Pecos River. A year later, it became Fort Lancaster. The site was located near an important ford of the Pecos River on the military road between San Antonio and El Paso. The fort was one of four built to protect the route from attacks by Apaches and other Indian tribes. Initially the fort consisted of tents and other temporary structures, but, as time allowed, the troops constructed more durable stone and adobe quarters out of native materials gathered nearby—wood from oak trees, adobe mud, and limestone—and finished lumber from Fort Davis. By 1860, the fort had some 25 permanent buildings and an average complement of 72 men and four officers.

The isolated garrison faced difficult odds in its battles with the Apaches. In the empty country, the Apaches, who knew the terrain intimately, could roam at will and raid parties of travelers. The Apaches were some of the best guerrilla fighters the world has ever seen, attacking swiftly and withdrawing before an opposition could organize. With so few troops and so much country, scouting and punitive expeditions were rarely productive. The soldiers' principal duty became that of escort to mail carriers, gold miners, wagon trains, and settlers. One high point for the troops, in the midst of this dangerous, difficult duty, came when the experimental camel train of Secretary of War Jefferson Davis stopped for the night in July 1857.

Although the Apache threat remained serious, the Civil War brought the fort's short history to an end. When Texas joined the Confederacy, the fort was abandoned, and the troops marched to San Antonio to surrender on March 19, 1861. The Confederacy attempted to garrison the fort for a few months in 1861–1862, but it was soon abandoned to the elements. Travelers still used it as a stopping place and, after the war, U.S. troops used it briefly as a bivouac in 1867 and 1871, but the fort's glory days were over.

The park's visitor center contains interpretive displays and artifacts of

Ruins of Fort Lancaster

the old fort and provides a good introduction to its history. After viewing the exhibits, walk out onto the quiet site. Stone chimneys reach skyward, and mesquite grows over tumbledown walls, but the American flag still flies over the parade ground. Listen closely; maybe you'll hear the sound of distant gunfire, the clatter of horses' hooves, or the sound of a lonesome bugle. More than 100 years later, the ruins of Fort Lancaster still stand guard over the valley of the Pecos River.

VISITOR INFORMATION

82 acres. Open all year except Christmas Day, Thursday through Monday, 8 AM to 5 PM. Hot in summer. Historic buildings, interpretive center, nature trail, picnicking. Limited food and gas available in Sheffield. All visitor services available in Iraan and Ozona. For information: Fort Lancaster State Historic Site, P.O. Box 306, Sheffield, TX 79781, (432) 836-4391.

Fort Leaton State Historic Site

With the end of the Mexican-American War in 1848, Mexico ceded disputed parts of Texas and most of the Southwest to the United States. On August 8 of that year, Benjamin Leaton and three American partners crossed the Rio Grande into Texas at Presidio del Norte. His party had been employed by the governments of Sonora and Chihuahua as bounty hunters and paid to hunt down Indians. He was notorious for terrorizing Chihuahua; one contemporary called him a "noble desperado" in his journal.

Leaton acquired a tract of land on a low bluff on the north side of the Rio Grande, just downstream from the town of Presidio, and built a massive adobe fortress to house his family, employees, and business and to protect them against Indian raids. Leaton farmed the floodplain and began trading with bands of Apaches and Comanches. Both Mexican and American authorities accused him of encouraging the Indians to raid Mexican settlements for livestock that they could trade for guns and ammunition. Even today, some local residents recall him as *un mal hombre*—a bad man.

After Leaton died in 1851, the violence associated with him seemed to linger. His widow married Edward Hall, a local customs agent. Hall moved into Leaton's home, from which he operated a freight business. He later borrowed a large sum of money from John Burgess, one of Leaton's bounty-hunting partners. Hall put up the adobe fortress as collateral and was foreclosed upon in 1864 when he failed

ABOVE RIGHT
Interior room of old fort
RIGHT
Interior courtyard of old fort

to repay Burgess. Hall refused to leave the fort and was murdered shortly thereafter.

Burgess and his family moved into Fort Leaton and established a successful freighting business on the busy San Antonio–Chihuahua Trail. In 1875, Burgess was murdered by Bill Leaton, Ben Leaton's youngest son, in revenge for the murder of his stepfather, Edward Hall, but the Burgess family continued to live in the fort until 1926.

After the fort was abandoned, it deteriorated rapidly under the assault of the elements and vandals. In the 1930s, local residents partly restored the historic structure, but it again fell into disrepair. It was finally donated to the state and was restored by the Parks and Wildlife Department.

The walls of Fort Leaton still loom over the fertile farmlands downstream from the confluence of the Rio Grande and the Rio Conchos, called La Junta de los Rios by the Spaniards. Exhibits document the cultural history of the area, from the Indians who first farmed the floodplain, to the Spanish explorers, to the arrival of Ben Leaton and other Americans.

VISITOR INFORMATION

23 acres. Open all year, 8 AM to 4:30 PM, except Christmas Day; day use only. Historic building, interpretive exhibits, picnicking, nature trail. All visitor services available in Presidio. Also serves as a visitor center for Big Bend Ranch State Park. For information: Fort Leaton State Historic Site, P.O. Box 2439, Presidio, TX 79845, (432) 229-3613.

Franklin Mountains State Park

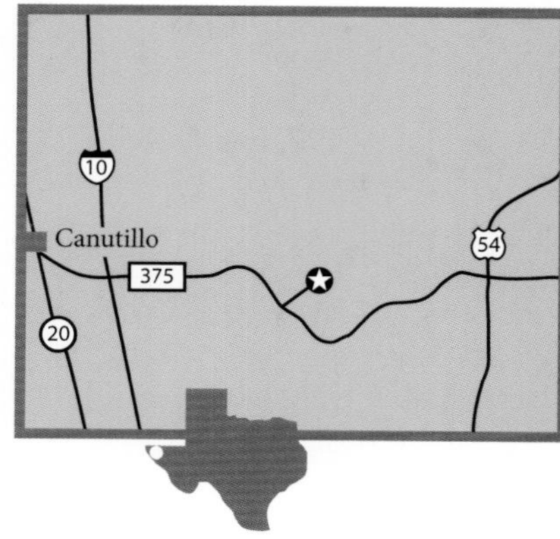

The massive fault-block of the Franklin Mountains rises abruptly from the broad cultivated valley of the Rio Grande on the west and the flat desert basin of the Hueco Bolson to the east. The river cuts through the mountains on the south side, separating the Franklins from mountains lying across the river in Mexico. In that cut, or river pass, sprawls the heart of El Paso. Two horns of the city curve up to the north, flanking the mountains on both east and west, forming a large horseshoe-shaped urban area. Within that urban horseshoe is the wild, rugged terrain of Franklin Mountains State Park.

To Anglo-Americans who visited the Franklins early in the nineteenth century, the mountains were full of menace and hidden dangers. The Franklins were a "chain of frowning mountains" to George Kendall, who was taken prisoner by Mexicans along with 300 others when the Republic of Texas sent them on an expedition to Santa Fe in 1841.

In 1951, noted artist and author Tom Lea wrote of the mountains: "Mount Franklin is a gaunt, hardrock mountain, standing against the sky like a piece of the world's uncovered carcass. The plants that grow along Mount Franklin's slopes are tough plants, with thirsty roots and meager leaves and sharp thorns that neither hide nor cover the mountain's rough rock face. Mount Franklin is a lasting piece of our planet, unadorned."

Although a small range, the Franklins still rise an impressive 3400 feet above El Paso, reaching the highest point on the summit of North Franklin Peak at 7192 feet above sea level. The desert mountains follow a long ridge running north from El Paso to the New Mexico state line. Due to the low precipitation and steep slopes, sparse Chihuahuan Desert vegetation cloaks the mountains.

All desert plants adapt to survive in

Snow and prickly pear cactus below North Franklin Peak

ABOVE
Hiker on snowy trail below North Franklin Peak
BELOW
View from Aztec Cave entrance

harsh, dry environments. Many plants have small, waxy leaves to reduce water loss through transpiration and thorns to discourage browsing animals. The barrel cactus, common in the Sonoran Desert of Arizona, finds its easternmost outpost in the United States in Franklin Mountains State Park. The distinctive cactus grows into ponderous individual stems up to four feet tall and two feet in diameter. Many of the very old plants have been damaged or destroyed by people cutting into them, hoping to find a nonexistent reservoir of water. Many others have been stolen from the park for use in gardens. Consequently, they are becoming quite rare in the Franklins.

Desert vegetation does not completely dominate the mountains. Here and there, tucked into hidden canyons, lie cool oases of trickling water and deep shade. The Franklins are too dry to have any large springs, but even the tiny trickles of water support lush stands of cottonwood, velvet ash, and hackberry.

These permanent waterholes are invaluable to desert wildlife. Mule deer, rabbits, and ground squirrels frequent the springs for water, browse, nuts, and berries. Hummingbirds come for flower nectar, while other birds search for wild grapes growing at the springs. Predators such as bobcats, foxes, and coyotes come, drawn by water and higher concentrations of prey animals. Even an occasional mountain lion appears in the park.

Early people visited the mountains, too. At Mundy's Spring, ancient mortar holes in the rock remain from the grinding of mesquite beans and acacia pods. Members of the Jornada branch

of the Mogollon Indians inscribed petroglyphs on canyon walls in the Franklins between AD 900 and 1400.

Cabeza de Vaca may have been the first European to pass through the area in 1536. In 1541, the Espejo/Chamuscado Expedition was known to have come through. Juan de Oñate, in 1598, was the first Spaniard to attempt to colonize the Rio Grande Valley and northern New Mexico. Since then, the El Paso area has been governed by Spain, Mexico, the Republic of Texas, the Confederacy, and ultimately the United States.

At the turn of the century, tin ore was found and mined on the east side of the range. The mines are small and have been gated off to prevent entry because of the risk of collapse. Additionally, visitors disturb the bats that have set up house in the dark tunnels.

Today, the state park encompasses most of the mountains and is one of the largest state parks in Texas. Part of Fort Bliss, the Castner Range, takes a large bite out of the east side of the mountain range. The old artillery range, no longer used by the Army, includes some of the most scenic parts of the mountains. The federal government may eventually turn it over to the state for the park, but because unexploded ammunition is still probably scattered across the area, a thorough cleanup would be necessary before it could be opened to public use.

Wilderness dominates the park at present, with little in the way of developed-use areas. A picnic area with tables and shelters and a small number of tent and RV campsites, but no water, lies in the Tom Mays area off the Trans-Mountain Highway on the west side. El Paso operates a similar park in McKelligon Canyon on the southeast side within the park boundaries. The Wyler Aerial Tramway, just outside the park, provides an easy route to the top of the mountains. It is also operated by the Texas Parks and Wildlife Department and is covered elsewhere in this book.

Many good hiking and mountain-biking trails exist. From the Tom Mays picnic area, trails lead to East and West Cottonwood springs, Mundy's Spring, Indian Peak, the old tin mines, and various loops. Because the springs are very small and delicate, use care not to trample the vegetation. Other park trails lead off the Trans-Mountain Highway.

One trail climbs from the Tom Mays area all the way to the summit of North Franklin Peak, the top of the range. The spectacular view stretches from mountains far south in Mexico to the 12,000-foot Sierra Blanca Peak, 100 miles north in New Mexico. From the top, El Paso and Juarez seem silent and far away. Amid the craggy peaks and cactus-covered canyons, solitude awaits the hiker.

VISITOR INFORMATION

24,248 acres. Open all year. Hot in summer, rare snows in winter. Extensive hiking and mountain-biking trails, picnicking, limited camping, no water. All visitor services available in El Paso. For information: Franklin Mountains State Park, 1331 McKelligon Canyon Road, El Paso, TX 79930, (915) 566-6441.

ABOVE LEFT
Montain bikers
ABOVE RIGHT
North Franklin Peak with storm and rainbow at first light

Hueco Tanks State Historic Site

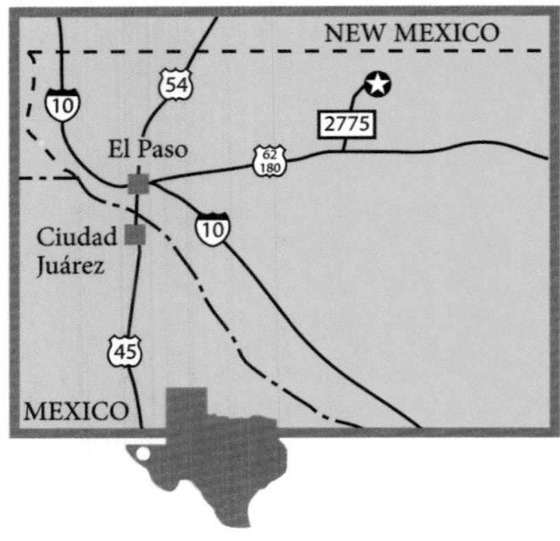

BELOW
Natural stone arch
OPPOSITE PAGE, ABOVE
Rock climber on "Klingon Warship"
OPPOSITE PAGE, BELOW
Pictographs

Although Hueco Tanks is nationally famous today as a winter rock-climbing center, humans have been visiting the site for at least 10,000 years. The rocks of Hueco Tanks have been the attraction all along, either directly or indirectly. The park centers around three small, rocky mountains that tower several hundred feet above the gentle alluvial slope of the Hueco Mountains. The hills are tumbled-down piles of boulders, interlaced with cliffs and caves.

Geologists believe the three mountains originated as magma, or molten rock, that intruded into layers of sedimentary rocks that had been laid down by an ancient sea. The magma cooled and hardened into a low-grade granite called syenite porphyry. Over time, the softer sedimentary rocks were eroded away, leaving the syenite standing alone, like islands floating on the desert.

Although the syenite was harder than the sedimentary rocks, the forces of erosion slowly shaped it, too. Rain and wind wore down the rocks; freezing and thawing of water split off pieces. Even plants took their toll. Lichen slowly ate away at the rock surface, while roots widened cracks. The weathering process created holes and depressions in the rock, called *huecos* in Spanish, which led to the park's name. These *huecos* trapped rainwater that attracted wildlife and humans to the rocky hills.

The bare rocks not only collect pools of rainwater, they also funnel extra water into canyons and cracks filled with soil. The extra water, combined with the coarse igneous soil, enables a relict oak-juniper woodland to survive in the midst of the dry Chihuahuan Desert. During the cooler, wetter period of the last ice age, woodlands dominated the Hueco Tanks area. As the climate warmed and dried, the trees disappeared except in special habitats like Hueco Tanks. Analysis of ancient pack-rat nests shows that there were still pinyon pines at Hueco Tanks 13,000 years ago, but today the most prominent trees are one-seed juniper, Arizona oak, and hackberry.

The first people known to appear at Hueco Tanks were those of the Folsom culture. Evidence indicates that 10,000 years ago they relied heavily on now-extinct animals such as giant bison, camels, and mammoths. They left few signs other than their distinctive projectile points.

As the climate became drier, later nomadic groups relied on smaller game and harvesting edible plants. The water available in the natural rock tanks became more important. Additionally, the many caves and overhangs eroded from the syenite provided shelter from the elements. During this time, called the Early Archaic period (between 8000 and 5000 years ago), the first rock art, consisting of abstract designs, was created in the area that now forms the park. Later, during the Middle and Late Archaic periods (from 5000 to 1500 years ago), the rock art consisted of hunting scenes with stylized humans and animals. Around AD 1000, an agricultural culture appeared in the area, allowing a less nomadic lifestyle. The people of this culture, called the Jornada branch of the Mogollon, left a stunning array of rock art in many parts of the park. Most of their works were pictographs, which are painted onto the rock rather than carved. The art included distinctive geometric shapes, stylized animals, many "masks," and figures reminiscent of classic Pueblo Indian motifs.

The Mogollon had vanished by the time the Spaniards arrived in the 1500s. They found hunter-gatherer groups that they called the Sumas and Mansos along the Rio Grande, and the Apaches. The last Indian rock art at Hueco Tanks may have been done by the Apaches, although dating pictographs is difficult. Some of the most recent paintings include men on horses, indicating encounters with horse-mounted Europeans.

Because the Apaches dominated Hueco Tanks, the Spaniards and Mexicans avoided the area. The United States acquired the Southwest in 1848 after the Mexican-American War, and the California Gold Rush of 1849 spurred a large westward migration. Because of its water, one of the early emigrant routes passed by Hueco Tanks. Later, the Butterfield Overland Mail used the same route from 1858 to 1859. The ruins of the stage stop can still be seen in the park.

In the late 1800s, the tanks became part of a ranch. In the 1960s, a massive land development was started at Hueco Tanks but failed. For a brief time it was operated as a county park, before becoming a state park in 1969. Since that time, the Parks and Wildlife Department has worked to restore natural drainage systems within the park, reseed overgrazed areas, and protect the rock art from vandalism.

People no longer come to Hueco Tanks for the water; the rocks themselves attract visitors. Most people cannot resist scrambling up the rock slopes and boulders of the three mountains. Observant hikers will find many ancient pictographs, along with stone-grinding holes. The rock art is very old and fragile and should not be touched or disturbed in any way.

Because the syenite of Hueco Tanks is very durable, rough-surfaced, and non-crumbly, and also forms towering cliffs and challenging overhangs, the park attracts many rock climbers. In winter, when popular climbing sites such as Yosemite are cold and snowed in, climbers from all over the country descend on Hueco Tanks. They come to the rocks of Hueco Tanks, as people have done for thousands of years.

VISITOR INFORMATION

860 acres. Open all year. Hot and dry in summer, except for occasional late summer thunderstorms. Busiest in winter. To prevent vandalism of the rock art and protect the natural environment, the park has stricter entrance requirements than most state parks. Requirements include visitor registration, fees, locked gates at night, and limits on the number of people allowed in the park at any one time. Advance reservations may be advisable during winter and weekends for day use. Campfires and charcoal fires prohibited throughout park. Small campground with partial hookups and showers. Hiking, picnicking. Rock climbers must register. Climbing is prohibited in rock art areas. Bolts, pitons, and other rock-destroying aids are not allowed. All visitor services available in nearby El Paso. For information: Hueco Tanks State Historic Site, 6900 Hueco Tanks Road #1, El Paso, TX 79938, (915) 857-1135.

Magoffin Home State Historic Site

The Magoffin Home was built in 1875 by Joseph Magoffin, a son of one of the first Anglo settlers in the El Paso area. His father, James Wiley Magoffin, was born in Kentucky in 1799, but went to Mexico in search of adventure and business opportunities. He became a merchant and U.S. consul in Saltillo and then moved to Ciudad Chihuahua. He married a Mexican woman, the daughter of a former governor of the state of Coahuila. Joseph was their second son.

After the Mexican-American War ended, James Magoffin settled on the banks of the Rio Grande across from Paso del Norte, Mexico, today known as Juarez, in 1849. To conduct his trading business, he built a store, warehouses, and an adobe home, which slowly grew into a small settlement known as Magoffinsville. Important visitors to the area were usually entertained by the Magoffins, and the first Fort Bliss was built at Magoffinsville in 1854. A devastating Rio Grande flood destroyed much of the settlement in 1868, the same year that James Magoffin died.

James Magoffin's son Joseph had come to Magoffinsville to help with his father's business in 1856. During the Civil War he left the area and joined the Confederate cause. Afterward, he returned and worked as a bookkeeper until he managed to reclaim the family property that had been confiscated at the end of the war. He became a business and civic leader and, in 1873, helped incorporate the city of El Paso. He was elected mayor of El Paso several times in the succeeding years and continued to work at various businesses before dying in 1923. During his life, El Paso changed from a rough frontier town into a busy sprawling city.

Joseph Magoffin built his home in 1875 using adobe brick and the Territorial style of architecture. It was a mix of the Pueblo Indian style with Greek Revival details on doors and windows. Originally the home had six rooms flanking a central hall, but additions were slowly built, creating a central patio and ultimately 19 rooms. Members of the Magoffin family lived in the house until 1986, when Octavia Magoffin Glasgow died. Because of its historical value, the home had been purchased a few years previously by the City of El Paso and the State of Texas. Many of the Magoffin family furnishings still fill the house and give a view of early life on the western frontier.

VISITOR INFORMATION

1.5 acres. Open Thursday through Sunday, 9 AM to 4 PM, for guided tours, and Wednesday by appointment. Historic home on landscaped grounds. All visitor services available in El Paso. For information: Magoffin Home State Historic Site, 1120 Magoffin Avenue, El Paso, TX 79901, (915) 533-5147.

LEFT
Magoffin home
OPPOSITE PAGE, TOP
Cloud effects
OPPOSITE PAGE, BOTTOM
Wind-sculpted dunes

Monahans Sandhills State Park

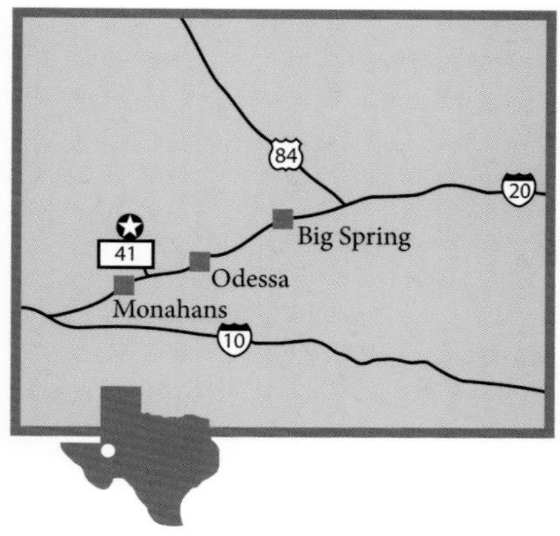

Like bits of the vast Sahara Desert, fields of sand dunes lie tucked away in parts of windswept West Texas. The most well-known is a huge field of dunes in the Permian Basin, a small part of which lies in Monahans Sandhills State Park. Much of the huge dune field has been stabilized by vegetation, but the state park contains an area with many active dunes. These dunes, some as tall as 70 feet, constantly move and change in shape in response to the wind. The dune field is about 200 miles long and stretches from southern Crane County far into southeastern New Mexico.

Originally derived from Triassic period sandstone to the west, winds have deposited sand in a narrow belt on the west side of the caprock that bounds the High Plains. The first major dune-building period began about 25,000 years ago as the climate became dryer.

Miniature oak trees, usually less than three feet tall even when mature, cover much of the stabilized dunes. The shin oaks, *Quercus havardii*, are well-adapted to the arid, windy climate, with roots as long as 70 feet reaching down to the shallow groundwater. In contrast to the oak's small stature, the acorns on the trees are quite large.

The shallow groundwater tapped by the oaks attracted humans to the dunes as long as 12,000 years ago. Indians found abundant freshwater beneath the sands, as well as plentiful game, acorns, and mesquite beans. More than 400 years ago, Spanish explorers became the first Europeans to visit the dunes. But even with the shallow groundwater, most travelers avoided the area because of difficulty crossing the dunes.

The dunes' relative isolation ended in the 1880s when the Texas and Pacific Railroad chose Monahans as a water stop between Big Spring and the Pecos River. In the 1920s, discovery of oil beneath the sand hastened the area's development.

Present-day visitors find easy access to the park from Interstate 20. The park road winds through the dunes, some vegetated and others active. Children love the steep slopes of the dunes and ski, roll, and tumble down the slopes. Campgrounds and picnic areas are hidden away in valleys between the dunes, along with mesquites and desert willows.

Climb a dune and look out on the vastness of the Permian Basin. Dunes stretch to the horizon under the endless blue sky. The wind will soon erase your tracks, leaving the dunes untouched for the next visitor.

VISITOR INFORMATION

3840 acres. Open all year. Hot in summer. Moderate number of campsites with partial hookups. Interpretive center, picnicking, nature and equestrian trails. Use care not to get lost when hiking in the dunes. Park store, sandsurfing disk rental. All visitor services available in Monahans. For information: Monahans Sandhills State Park, P.O. Box 1738, Monahans, TX 79756, (432) 943-2092.

Seminole Canyon State Park and Historic Site

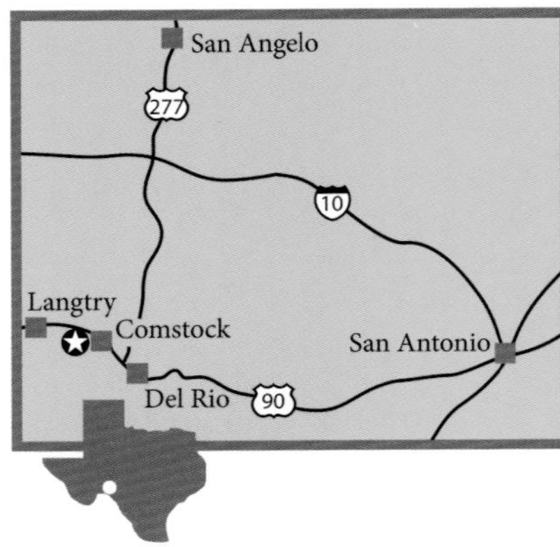

For thousands of years, early peoples lived in the large rock shelters tucked into deep canyons near the confluence of the Pecos River and the Rio Grande. Smoke from their cooking fires blackened the ceiling, and large, flat rocks were polished smooth from years of use as worktables. Striking panels of rock art were painted, the most prominent remnants of these peoples' existence. Bold geometric shapes, shaman-like figures, and stylized animals dance across rock faces, protected from the elements by shelter roofs and walls. Seminole Canyon State Park contains some of the best of these ancient pictographs.

The area around the state park is stark, rocky, and dry. The sparsely vegetated terrain contains a mix of plants and animals from the Chihuahuan Desert, the Hill Country, and the South Texas brushlands. Most of the land is relatively flat, but the Pecos River, the Rio Grande, and their tributaries have carved surprisingly deep canyons through the underlying limestone. The cream-colored rock was created during the Cretaceous period when ancient seas covered the area.

Humans are believed to have first lived here at least 12,000 years ago, at the end of the last ice age. The climate was cooler and wetter, with dense woodlands in the canyons and lush grasslands cloaking the uplands. These early peoples hunted now-extinct animals such as the mammoth and giant bison, but left no rock paintings.

By about 7000 years ago, a new culture appeared that depended on gathering foodstuffs and hunting much smaller game than their predecessors. The dry, rocky terrain seems inhospitable, but they learned how to survive. Fruits gathered from prickly pear and strawberry cacti were eaten

Lake Amistad in canyon

raw or used in other foods. Other fruits included those of the Texas persimmon and the yucca. The hearts of agaves and sotol plants were roasted for eating. Acorns and beans from the mesquite and catclaw acacia were ground into flour. Hunting added fat and protein to their diet.

They made projectile points, awls, scrapers, and knives by chipping them out of chert and flint. The tough fibers of the lechuguilla plant, the yucca, and the sotol were used to make twine, sandals, baskets, and many other items. When time permitted or religious ceremony required, these people painted rock shelter walls using paints made from crushed iron ores and other substances mixed with animal fat. Starting about 7000 years ago, they created their artwork, some of the oldest pictographs in North America.

The dry air and deep shelters protected the rock art, leaving much of it still colorful and fresh after thousands of years. Many pictograph sites are known in the Lower Pecos area, some with a single painting, others with panels hundreds of feet long. Unfortunately, some sites have been damaged by vandals, and other sites were flooded by the creation of Lake Amistad. The state-park staff conducts tours to one of the best locations, Fate Bell Shelter, in Seminole Canyon. The canyon was probably named for Seminole-Negro scouts stationed at Fort Clark in Brackettville during the 1870s. The moderately strenuous hike descends into the canyon to an enormous rock shelter containing hundreds of pictographs.

Another site, Panther Cave, can be reached only by boat, at the confluence of Seminole Canyon and the Rio Grande, now part of Lake Amistad. One of the paintings is an impressive 15-foot-long panther. The cave can also be viewed from a distance by hiking or mountain biking a three-mile trail to a bluff overlooking the confluence. The trail crosses the abandoned grade of the Southern Pacific Railroad along the way. The railroad line was built to link El Paso with San Antonio. Crews worked from both ends of the line and reached the park area in 1882. Crossing the Pecos River Canyon presented a serious problem. Tons of black powder were used to blast tunnels and grades down to river level, where a low bridge was built over the Pecos. The track was subject to numerous rockfalls and collapses, so it was abandoned in 1892 when a bridge spanning the entire Pecos River Canyon was completed. At the time, the 321-foot-high span was the tallest in the world. The modern highway bridge on US 90, located just downstream from the railroad bridge, is the highest vehicle bridge in Texas.

The hiking trail ends at an impressive bluff 200 feet above the Rio Grande, a stark contrast to the flat, dry country that the rest of the trail crosses. Panther Cave lies across the lake waters of the mouth of Seminole Canyon, the large painted panther easily visible even to the naked eye. Take a good flashlight and watch the sunset from the overlook. As the last golden rays of sunlight move up the canyon walls, try to imagine a prehistoric artist hard at work painting the stone walls of Panther Cave.

Panther Cave, pictographs above Amistad Reservoir

VISITOR INFORMATION

2173 acres. Open all year. Hot in summer. Guided tours of Fate Bell Shelter are conducted Wednesday through Sunday, 10 AM only from June 1 to August 31, and 10 AM and 3 PM the rest of the year. A boat is necessary to reach Panther Cave. Small campground with partial hookups and showers. Hiking, mountain biking, picnicking, excellent interpretive exhibits at visitor center. Very limited visitor services in Langtry and Comstock (no lodging). Full services in Del Rio. For information: Seminole Canyon State Park and Historic Site, P.O. Box 820, Comstock, TX 78837, (432) 292-4464.

Wyler Aerial Tramway

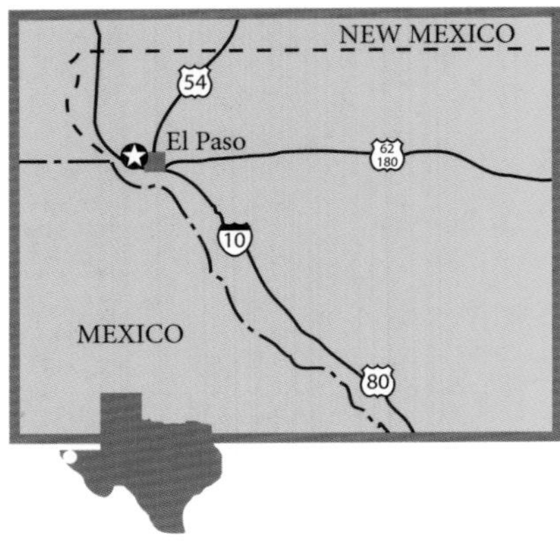

The Wyler Aerial Tramway was originally built to haul people and equipment up to the television and radio towers perched on the summit of Ranger Peak, a high point on the southern end of the Franklin Mountains. To open it to the public, the Texas Parks and Wildlife Department spent several years improving and modifying the tramway to make it safe and comfortable for park visitors.

To ride the tramway, visitors drive up steep McKinley Avenue to a parking area perched high on the eastern slopes of the Franklin Mountains. Views of the east side of El Paso from the parking lot are extensive even without riding the tramway. Chihuahuan Desert cacti surround the parking lot and tramway terminal. The nearly vertical slopes of the mountains tower above. Hardy plants, such as sotol, yucca, and catclaw, cling to the rocky slopes, eking out a living in the dry country.

To ride to the summit, visitors board a small gondola at the lower terminal. Some of the heavy winch and other equipment is visible in the terminal buildings. The gondola rides on a 1.375-inch-diameter steel cable that is 2600 feet long. As visitors ride upward, suspended hundreds of feet above the rocky canyon below, the gondola attendant talks about the desert, the mountains, and the tramway. In only four minutes, tramway riders step off the gondola onto the upper terminal platform, 946 feet higher than the lower terminal.

The upper terminal is built around a complex of massive television-broadcasting towers and equipment perched on the 5632-foot summit of Ranger Peak. While the view east from the parking lot is good, the view from

El Paso and Juarez from Ranger Peak

the mountaintop can take a visitor's breath away. To the east sprawls a much higher view of the city of El Paso; to the west lies the western side of the city, plus the Rio Grande and the endless southern desert of New Mexico. Downtown El Paso and the hazy city of Juarez, Mexico, stretch many miles south from the mountains' southern foot. To the north, the view follows the rocky spine of the Franklin Mountains as it rises, reaching even higher summits than Ranger Peak. Franklin Mountains State Park, one of the state's largest parks, contains much of the range north of the tramway.

The ride to the top of Ranger Peak is spectacular any time of day, but the best time to ride is an hour before sunset. From the top, watch the last rays of the sun paint the mountain slopes gold as it sinks toward the horizon. Remain on the summit as the light dims and dusk begins. An endless sea of city lights comes to life as darkness settles in for the night.

VISITOR INFORMATION

196 acres. Hot in summer in midday. Wind can make it quite cold in winter. Open Thursday through Monday, with longer hours on weekends. Overall hours shorter in winter because days are shorter. Call ahead for details. High winds and lightning storms can temporarily close the tramway. Day use only. Scenic tramway. Full visitor services in El Paso. For information: Wyler Aerial Tramway, 1700 McKinley Ave., El Paso, TX 79930, (915) 566-6622.

TOP
View of mountains in last light from Ranger Peak
MIDDLE
View of El Paso at dusk from Ranger Peak
BOTTOM
Gondola above Franklin Mountains

Gulf Coast

The Texas Gulf Coast stretches for several hundred miles, from the Rio Grande delta on the Mexican border to the mouth of the Sabine River on the Louisiana border. State parks along the coast offer miles of beaches, important salt marshes, and historic lighthouses, battlefields, and plantations.

The Texas coast and inland coastal plain is a very flat, low-lying strip of land 50 to 100 miles wide and more than 300 miles long that adjoins the Gulf of Mexico. Few rocks are found along the coast; thick layers of sediment blanket the region, deposited over millions of years by Texas rivers after being eroded from higher terrain to the north and west. The organic matter buried with these sediments later formed plentiful deposits of oil and gas.

Rises and falls in sea level greatly affect the coast. As ice ages have come and gone, the sea level has changed considerably. When glaciers and icecaps lock up large quantities of water during an ice age, the sea level falls and the coast moves many miles offshore from where it is now. Conversely, when the ice melts, sea level rises and floods many miles inland. About 18,000 years ago, during the peak of the last ice age, the shoreline moved many miles out into the Gulf, and rivers cut deeper valleys as their gradient changed. When the ice age ended and sea levels rose, water flooded the valleys, creating large bays such as Galveston and Corpus Christi.

Long, narrow barrier islands protect most of the coast and bays from storms. They formed by the action of wind and waves on river-deposited sand as the sea level approached its current state. Padre Island, 113 miles long and the longest such island in the United States, stretches from near the southern tip of Texas to Corpus Christi. Behind the islands lie shallow, protected bays that are fertile homes and nurseries for fish, shellfish, shorebirds, and other creatures.

A number of Texas's most popular parks lie on the barrier islands and similarly formed peninsulas. Mustang Island, Galveston Island, and Sea Rim state parks all offer miles of broad, sandy beaches and developed facilities. Matagorda Island is one of just two major islands on the Texas coast that is accessible only by boat. It not only offers

38 miles of undeveloped beach, it harbors a historic lighthouse and endangered whooping cranes.

Several parks and historic sites lie on the protected bays behind the barrier islands or a short distance inland. Goose Island offers salt marshes, live-oak woodland, and a lengthy fishing pier. Many anglers visit nearby Copano Bay State Fishing Pier, a former highway causeway across the mouth of Copano Bay. At San Jacinto Battleground, marked by a 570-foot-tall limestone tower called the San Jacinto Monument, Texas rebels routed General Santa Anna's superior forces during the war for independence. The restored Battleship *Texas* floats gently in a slip adjoining the battleground, adding another attraction. Other parks preserve historic mansions, plantations, and battlefields.

Parks such as Lake Corpus Christi and Lake Texana offer traditional water recreation, including sailing, waterskiing, fishing, and swimming. Miles of bicycle trails, an astronomical observatory, and plentiful alligators make Brazos Bend particularly unique. Most Gulf Coast parks offer campgrounds and picnic areas to go with their other many attractions.

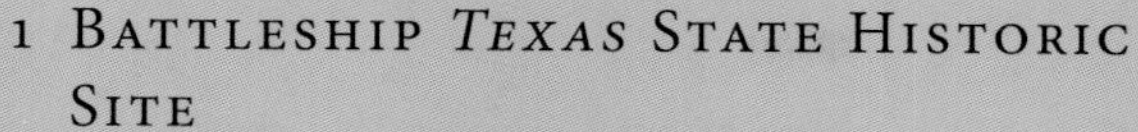

1 Battleship *Texas* State Historic Site

2 Brazos Bend State Park

3 Copano Bay State Fishing Pier

4 Fulton Mansion State Historic Site

5 Galveston Island State Park

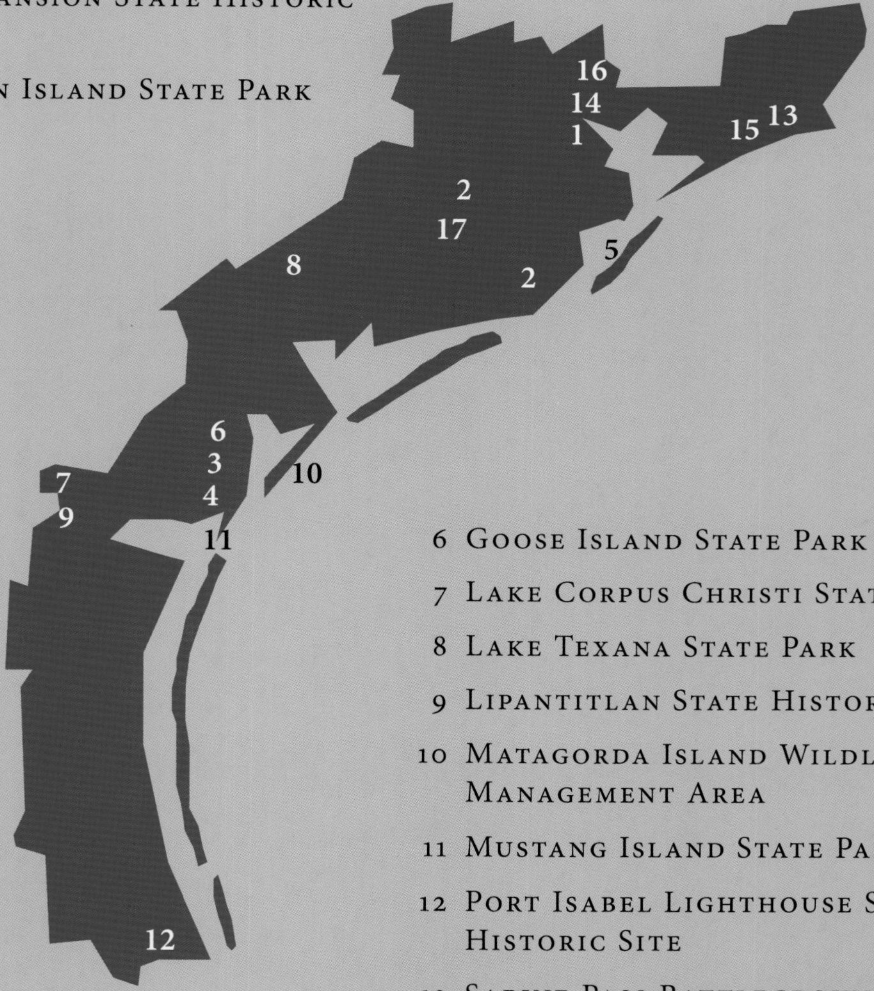

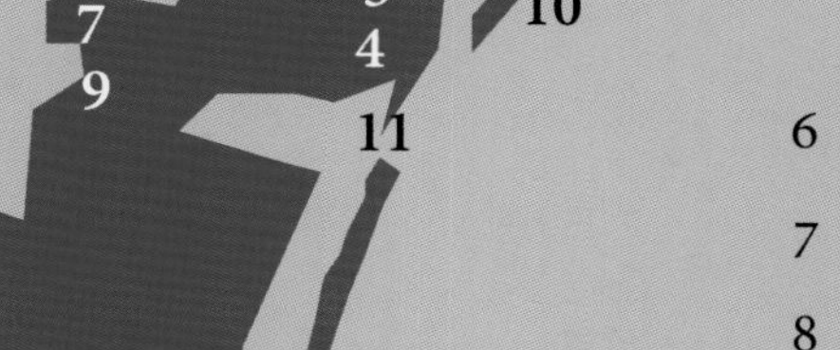

6 Goose Island State Park

7 Lake Corpus Christi State Park

8 Lake Texana State Park

9 Lipantitlan State Historic Site

10 Matagorda Island Wildlife Management Area

11 Mustang Island State Park

12 Port Isabel Lighthouse State Historic Site

13 Sabine Pass Battleground State Park and Historic Site

14 San Jacinto Battleground State Historic Site

15 Sea Rim State Park

16 Sheldon Lake State Park and Environmental Learning Center

17 Varner-Hogg Plantation State Historic Site

Battleship *Texas* State Historic Site

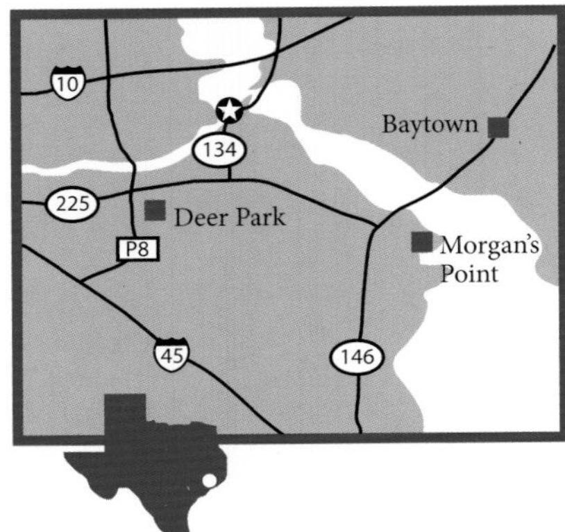

In a berth on Buffalo Bayou, adjoining San Jacinto Battleground State Historic Site, lies the mighty Battleship *Texas*. Today it floats quietly at its mooring, in stark contrast to the bitter battles in which it fought during World Wars I and II.

The *Texas* was commissioned in 1914, at which time it was the most powerful ship in the world. It first saw service in Mexico that year, and then in Europe in 1918 during World War I. Between the two world wars, the *Texas* was continually modernized, the improvements including being converted from coal to fuel oil. When the Japanese attacked Pearl Harbor in 1941, the *Texas* was docked in Portland, Maine, and escaped the destruction inflicted on many of its sister battleships. During the war in Europe, it saw action in several battles, including D-Day, the invasion of Europe on the Normandy coast, at which it was the flagship. Its massive 14-inch guns pounded salvo after salvo into German artillery positions at Omaha Beach to help landing troops gain a beachhead. After the war ended in Europe, the *Texas* steamed into the Pacific and fought in the battles at Iwo Jima and Okinawa.

In 1948, the *Texas* was decommissioned and presented to the State of Texas. It was berthed at the San Jacinto Monument until 1988, when it was removed to Galveston for a major overhaul and renovation. After 40 years, rust and corrosion had taken their toll on the massive ship. In 1990, the 573-foot *Texas*, on the way to being restored to its 1945 condition, was reopened to the public. Tours wind through the main deck and the maze-like compartments of the lower decks of the *Texas*, once one of the most fearsome weapons on earth. Today the *Texas* is the only surviving Navy ship to have served in both world wars.

Visitor Information

1200 acres (includes adjoining San Jacinto Battleground State Historic Site). The battleship is open daily all year, except Thanksgiving, Christmas Eve, and Christmas Day. Call to verify times. Hot and humid in summer. Day use only. Historical ship. All visitor services available in Houston and suburbs. For information: Battleship *Texas* State Historic Site, 3523 Highway 134, La Porte, TX 77571, (281) 479-2431.

Battleship Texas

Brazos Bend State Park

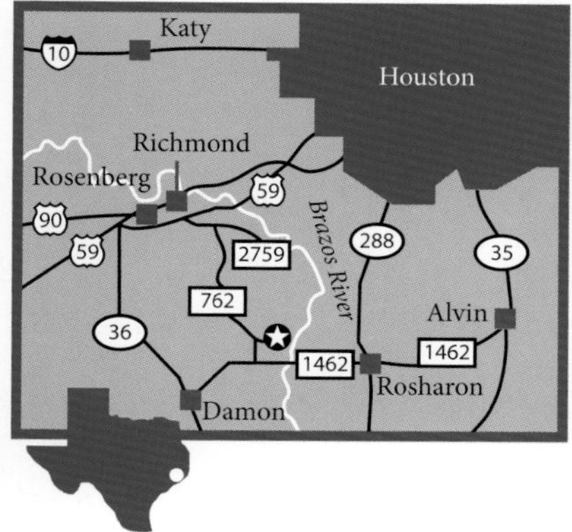

Massive live oaks arch over grassy Gulf Coast prairies. Primeval-looking alligators float motionless in sloughs and bayous, only their eyes and nostrils visible in the dark waters. White-tailed deer browse shrubs at dusk and dawn. At night, raccoons and bobcats slip through the woods, stalking their prey. The edge of the bustling city of Houston lies only 20 miles away, but is little noticed in the Brazos River bottomland of Brazos Bend State Park.

The park occupies a small portion of the flat, vast coastal plain lining the Gulf of Mexico. The mighty Brazos River, one of the largest rivers in Texas, sweeps by the park, forming its eastern boundary. Most of the park lies in its floodplain, but there are areas of dryer uplands. Big Creek meanders through the park, joining the river in the park's southeast corner. Over time the creek has created several oxbow lakes, formed when a curving meander

TOP RIGHT
Water plants on lake
BOTTOM RIGHT
Creekfield Lake, alligator
BELOW
Turtles

TOP
Forty Acres Lake, sunset
ABOVE
Hikers

OPPOSITE PAGE
Copano Bay State Fishing Pier

is cut off from the main creek flow by erosion. Marshes and several small, shallow, man-made lakes add more watery areas to the park. The shallow, slow-moving waters and warm climate favor the park's most famous resident, the American alligator. Large numbers of the reptiles live in the park, feeding on plentiful birds, fish, and other small animals.

More than 200 species of birds have been sighted at Brazos Bend. In addition to songbirds, the wetlands attract large numbers of migratory waterfowl, shorebirds, and wading birds.

Although the park is home to many species of wildlife, it is very recreation-oriented. Thirty-four miles of hiking, equestrian, and mountain-biking trails wind through the lush bottomlands. The scenic Red Buckeye Loop Trail in the southeast corner of the park circles a peninsula of land between Big Creek and the Brazos River. Dense woods of sycamore, water oak, cottonwood, and many other trees arch over the narrow hiking trail. In March, the shrubby buckeyes bloom, forming a beautiful scarlet understory. The River View Trail follows the Brazos River. Other trails, more broad and open, follow the edges of the many lakes, bayous, and marshes. An observation tower and several platforms provide viewpoints for wildlife viewing, and fishing opportunities abound.

One of the most unique features of the Texas state-park system lies within Brazos Bend: the three domes of the George Observatory nestling deep in the park woods. The largest telescope, with its substantial 36-inch diameter mirror, is used frequently for public viewing, unlike most similar telescopes at other observatories. Although the low elevation and proximity to Houston do not provide ideal conditions for an observatory, it is much more accessible than remote mountaintop sites. The rounded white dome peers deep into the heavens while alligators swim through bayous below, forming an interesting contrast at one of Texas's most popular state parks.

VISITOR INFORMATION

4975 acres. Open all year. Summers are hot and humid. Mosquito repellant is recommended in spring and summer. Campgrounds have partial hookups, along with screened shelters and showers. Primitive equestrian camping. Picnicking, hiking, cycling, fishing, wildlife viewing. Handicapped-accessible trail with signage for the blind. Nature center, gift shop, and bookstore. Because of the alligators, swimming is not allowed. Do not feed, annoy, or approach these large reptiles. Watch pets and children closely. Weather permitting, the observatory is open to visitors most Saturday evenings. All visitor services are available in Richmond, Rosenberg, and other nearby towns and cities. For information: Brazos Bend State Park, 21901 FM 762, Needville, TX 77461, (979) 553-5101.

Copano Bay State Fishing Pier

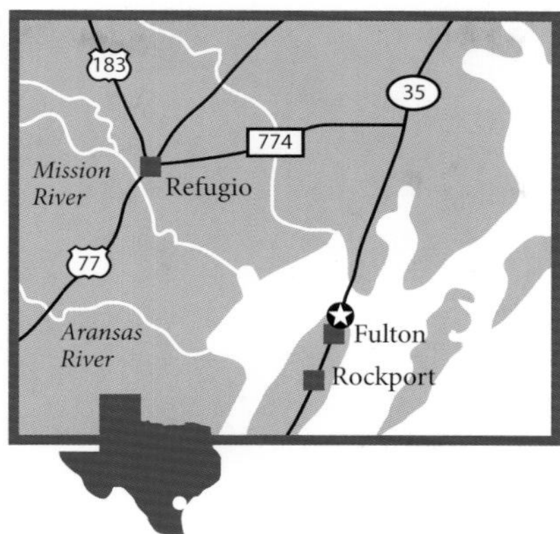

Anglers wanting some elbow room can find it at the Copano Bay State Fishing Pier. Originally, the fishing pier was a long bridge, or causeway, that spanned the mouth of Copano Bay and saved highway traffic traveling up or down the coast from having to make a long detour around the bay. When a new highway causeway was constructed that was wider and stronger to handle heavier vehicles, the old one was closed to vehicles and was converted into a fishing pier. Because the new causeway had a high section in the middle to allow taller boats to pass underneath, part of the old low causeway was removed. Today the two sections of causeway stretch 6190 feet from the north side and 2500 feet from the south, plenty of room for a lot of fishermen.

Copano Bay is a bay off of a bay, rather than being directly connected to the Gulf of Mexico. It opens off the back side of Aransas Bay, which is separated from the Gulf by San José Island, a barrier island. Like most Texas bays, Copano Bay was a river valley when sea levels were lower during the last ice age. As the ice melted, sea levels rose and flooded the old river mouths and valleys. Texas Highway 35 and the fishing pier segments span the mouth of the bay, connecting the Lamar and Live Oak peninsulas.

The shallow bays and their associated marshes are vital for the production of fish and shellfish in the Gulf of Mexico. Most of these creatures spend at least a portion of their life in the bays and marshes of the Texas coast. Fishermen using the pier take advantage of the fertile bay waters and catch redfish, flounder, speckled trout, drum, sheepshead, and many other species at the Copano Bay State Fishing Pier.

VISITOR INFORMATION

6 acres. Open all year. Operated as a Partnership Park. Fishing piers, partly lighted. Boat ramp, fish-cleaning tables, concession building, restrooms. All visitor services available in Rockport and Fulton. For information: Copano Bay State Fishing Pier, P.O. Box 39, Fulton, TX 78358, (512) 729-8633.

Fulton Mansion State Historic Site

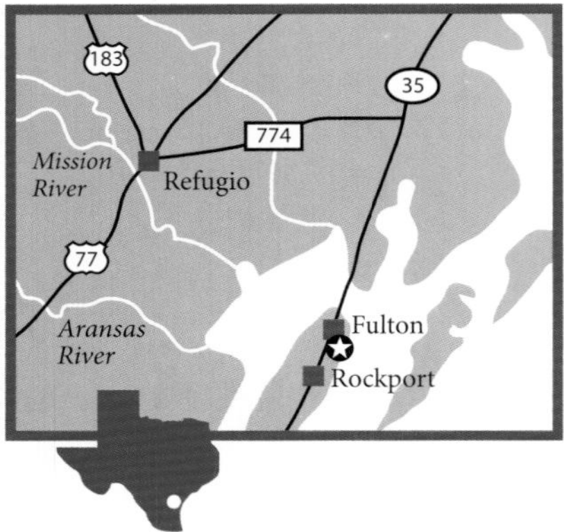

Prominent Fulton Mansion presides over sparkling Aransas Bay in stark contrast to the smaller beach homes and businesses that line the shore in Rockport and Fulton. When it was built in the 1870s, the ornate building must have dominated the area. The builder, George Fulton, came to Texas in 1837 to fight in the war for Texas independence, but arrived too late to participate. During the following years, he worked as a land developer, machinist, engineer, newspaper reporter, teacher, draftsman, railroad superintendent, and bridge builder in Texas and other states. In 1868 he and his family moved back to Texas permanently to oversee his wife's inheritance when her father died.

With his wife's inherited South Texas land, Fulton and several partners established an extensive cattle-ranching business. In 1874 the Fultons began construction of their home on the shores of Aransas Bay. They chose the French Second Empire style of architecture, with its characteristic mansard roof, for their 6200-square-foot home. Most materials and construction equipment were shipped in from New Orleans and the East Coast at considerable expense. Fulton's previous engineering experience is evident in its construction. He built it to withstand hurricanes by using concrete and concrete blocks for the basement walls and 1 x 5 pine planks spiked together on top of each other to create solid upper walls. The floors were constructed in a similar manner and were a solid five inches thick.

Fulton installed all available modern conveniences inside the house, including running water, flush toilets, central heat, and a gas lighting system. He even built a water-cooling system to preserve perishable food, and a simple clothes dryer. Finishing trim included walnut and cypress woodwork, chandeliers, fine rugs, and ornate furniture.

George Fulton died in 1893, and his wife Harriet eventually was unable to maintain the home on her own. She sold it in 1907, the first of several ownership changes that the house would undergo. Over time, the historic mansion was neglected and deteriorated physically. Finally, it was purchased by the Texas Parks and Wildlife Department in 1976 and restored to its former grandeur, an architectural monument on the Texas coast.

VISITOR INFORMATION

2.3 acres. Open all year for guided tours Wednesday through Sunday. Wear flat, soft-soled shoes to protect the floors and rugs. Historic building, picnicking. All visitor services available in surrounding Rockport and Fulton. For information: Fulton Mansion State Historic Site, P.O. Box 1859, Fulton, TX 78358, (361) 729-0386.

Fulton Mansion

Galveston Island State Park

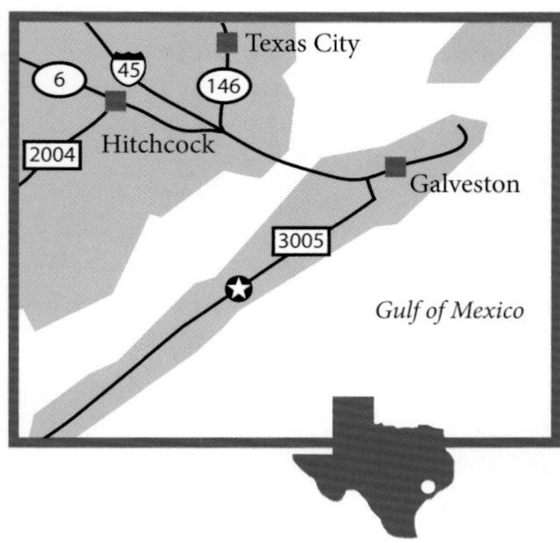

Thousands of people visit Galveston Island State Park every year, drawn primarily by the 1.6 miles of beach fronting on the Gulf of Mexico. Galveston Island is a barrier island, formed by wave action and longshore currents in the shallow waters lining the Gulf. The island is not very old geologically; the rises and falls in sea level that accompany the passing ice ages destroy and re-create barrier islands relatively quickly.

Behind the broad beach of the state park, winds have built dunes that are mostly anchored by vegetation. Behind the dunes lies a strip of coastal prairie covered with grasses and other plants. Salt marshes border the bay on the back side of the island and provide an excellent habitat for fish, crustaceans, and wading birds. The park includes the entire width of the island, from the beach to the salt marsh.

When the Europeans first arrived on the Gulf Coast, nomadic Karankawa Indians lived on the island and in other coastal areas. Alvar Núñez Cabeza de Vaca was shipwrecked here in 1528 and held prisoner by the Karankawas for six years before making his way back to Mexico City. The Spaniards returned for a short time in the mid-1700s and set up a presidio named for the Spanish governor of Louisiana, Bernardo de Galvez. They soon left, and the French gained control for a time. In 1817, Jean Lafitte and his band of pirates established a base called Campeche on the island. For several years they preyed on Spanish ships, but were finally run off after attacking an American ship.

The community that Lafitte left behind grew into a thriving port named Galveston, an Anglicized version of the earlier presidio's Spanish name. During the Civil War, Galveston changed hands more than once during battles between the Union and the Confederacy. After the war, the port prospered, becoming the largest in Texas and the third largest in the nation. Unfortunately, the city was built on a low-lying barrier island, and as such was built on sand. In 1900, disaster struck when a hurricane blasted the island with 20-foot-high storm tides driven by 100-mile-per-hour winds. More than 6000 people died, and most of the island's buildings were leveled in the greatest natural disaster in American history. Since that time, however, the city has been rebuilt as a port and major tourist destination.

Many people who visit the island come to enjoy the sand and surf offered by Galveston Island State Park. Not only does the park offer swimming, sunbathing, and fishing, the quiet bayside marshes provide opportunities for hiking and birding. On summer evenings, outdoor musicals such as *Oklahoma* and Paul Green's *The Lone Star* play at the Mary Moody Northern Amphitheater in the park. Although hurricanes strike the island occasionally, most of the time the park offers a quiet outdoor escape from the busy city of Galveston and inland cities such as Houston.

VISITOR INFORMATION

2013 acres. Open all year. Hot and humid in summer. Mosquitoes can be thick behind the dunes in warm weather. Very popular, especially in summer. Large number of campsites with partial hookups and showers. Screened shelters. Swimming, fishing, picnicking; mountain-biking, hiking, and nature trails. Outdoor musicals on summer evenings, except Sunday. All visitor services available in Galveston. For information: Galveston Island State Park, 14901 FM 3005, Galveston, TX 77554, (409) 737-1222.

Beach at sunrise

Goose Island State Park

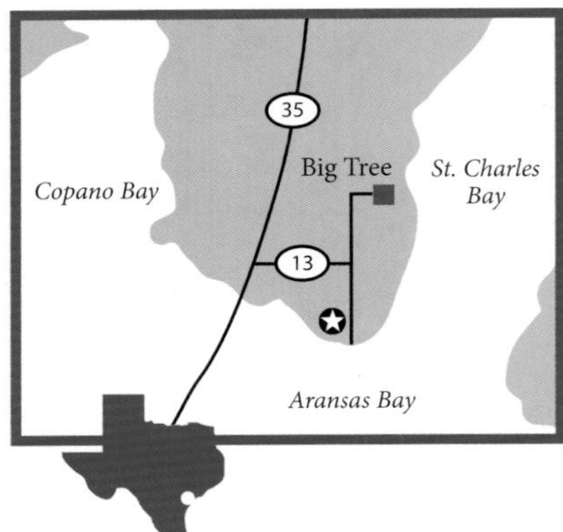

Goose Island State Park lies at the southern tip of the Lamar Peninsula, at the conjunction of Aransas, St. Charles, and Copano bays. Unlike most coastal areas in Texas, much of the coast around the state park is heavily wooded with live oaks and redbays. The outlying barrier islands, Matagorda and San José, probably offer some protection to this coastal area, making it easier for trees to survive on the salty, storm-prone coast. The sandy strip of land upon which the state park lies was once a barrier island itself when sea levels were higher during the Pleistocene era.

Goose Island State Park provides an interesting mix of habitats considering its small size. Goose Island itself, a small island barely separated by water from the mainland part of the park, is only about 140 acres, but contains a mix of salt marshes, tidal flats, and a small grassland area on the highest ground. In contrast, most of the mainland park area is a dense forest of wind-sculpted live oaks and redbays. Small patches of coastal prairie cover openings in the woods.

Two diverse types of creatures draw many people to Goose Island—birds and fish. A boat ramp and a 1620-foot fishing pier make water access easy for fishermen. The pier, lighted at night, stretches far into the bay to several islets and oyster banks. Popular fish include redfish, flounder, speckled trout, drum, and sheepshead.

The coastal area around Rockport is nationally famous for its birds; more than 400 species have been recorded here. With a mix of marshes, tidal flats, beaches, and open water, the coast attracts multitudes of wading and shore birds. Thickets of live-oak woodland and open coastal prairies provide different habitats for other species. Spring and fall migrations bring many songbirds and other migrants through every year. Probably the most famous bird in the area is the whooping crane. When standing, the large white bird is the tallest bird found in the United States. It is endangered and possibly the rarest bird in the United States; only about 200 remain. The cranes summer in western Canada, but return every winter to Aransas National Wildlife Refuge and the surrounding bay areas. The wildlife refuge is just across the narrow mouth of St. Charles Bay from Goose Island.

In addition to birds and fish, the state park offers swimming, picnicking, and boating. A short nature trail winds through the thick live-oak woods surrounding the mainland campground. The Goose Island Oak is one of the most impressive sights on the coast. The enormous tree, estimated to be 1000 years old, grows in a separate unit of the park about two miles northeast of park headquarters. The live oak, second largest in Texas, is 44 feet tall, has a trunk 35 feet in circumference, and has a crown spread of 90 feet. It has survived prairie fires, Civil War battles, and hurricanes too numerous to count. The tree is a fine symbol of the lasting appeal of the Texas coast at Goose Island State Park.

VISITOR INFORMATION

321 acres. Open all year. Hot and humid in summer. Mosquitoes can be fierce away from the shore in warm weather. Large number of campsites split between woods and shore locations; partial hookups and showers. Swimming, boating, fishing, lighted fishing pier. Short hiking/nature trail, birding, picnicking. All visitor services available in Rockport and Fulton. For information: Goose Island State Park, 202 S. Palmetto Street, Rockport, TX 78382, (361) 729-2858.

Lake Corpus Christi State Park

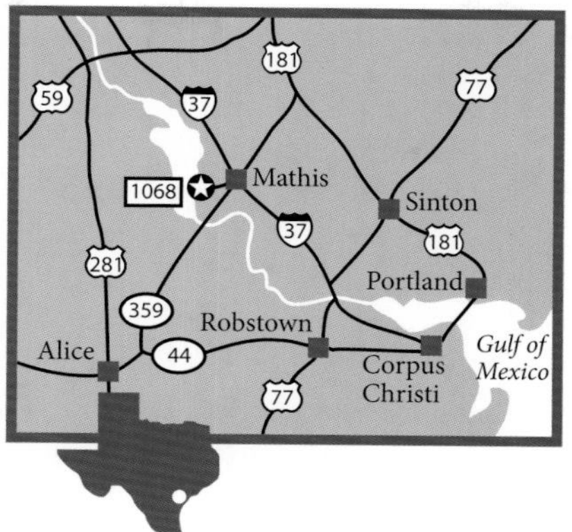

Lake Corpus Christi State Park has long been a stalwart of the Texas state-park system. The park had its beginnings with area population growth in the early part of this century. Increased demand for water led to an earth-fill dam being built across the Nueces River in 1929. Unfortunately, the dam failed only ten months later. The dam was rebuilt in 1935, and the large but shallow new reservoir was named Lake Corpus Christi. Parkland was leased from the City of Corpus Christi and opened with little development.

The Civilian Conservation Corps worked to improve the park during the Depression of the 1930s. The Corps's most notable accomplishment was the construction of the pavilion and interpretive center on a high bluff overlooking the lake. The skillfully built limestone building is still attractive today, with stone arches framing views of the lake.

During the park's early days, a herd of longhorns was established in the park to help maintain the animals' bloodlines in Texas. The cattle flourished and came into frequent conflict with park visitors. Finally the animals were rounded up and sent to Fort Griffin State Park and Historic Site.

Over the years, the Nueces River not only fed a constant supply of water to the lake, it also added copious amounts of silt and clay. The sediment gradually filled the reservoir, reducing its water storage capability while the population of Corpus Christi continued to swell. In 1958, a new dam was completed that raised the water level and greatly increased the reservoir's capacity.

Long before European settlers arrived in the Corpus Christi area, various Indian groups lived along the lush Nueces River bottomland. At that time, most of the South Texas area was flat grassland interspersed with wooded riparian areas along streams and rivers. After Spanish and Anglo

OPPOSITE PAGE, TOP
Live oaks
OPPOSITE PAGE, BOTTOM
Fishing pier at dawn
RIGHT
CCC pavilion at Lake Corpus Christi

settlers arrived, fires were suppressed, so brush began to invade the grasslands. Imported cattle accelerated the process by favoring grasses for grazing and ignoring brush, and by bringing in seeds of plant species from other areas. Today a thick brushland of mesquite, acacia, huisache, yucca, and other plants dominates most of the park and much of South Texas.

Many types of mammals are found in the park, including javelina, armadillos, jackrabbits, skunks, and raccoons. Some of the most popular animal species are birds, of which more than 300 species have been recorded at Lake Corpus Christi. The park gets an interesting mix of South Texas and Mexican species, songbirds, waterfowl, and wading birds. Its location on a major migration route increases the variety of species found.

The park not only provides a water supply and haven for wildlife, it offers excellent recreational opportunities. Swimmers and boaters who tire of the rougher salt water of the nearby coast come to the state park. Water skiers and sailboarders zip across the smooth lake waters, while fishermen troll the depths, trying for black bass, striped bass, crappie, and catfish. Lake Corpus Christi State Park has been established for many years, but is still one of the top draws among Texas state parks.

VISITOR INFORMATION

288 acres. Open all year. Hot and humid in summer. Large number of campsites with partial and full hookups and showers. Screened shelters. Fishing piers, boat ramps, swimming, waterskiing, picnicking. All visitor services available in Mathis and Corpus Christi. For information: Lake Corpus Christi State Park, P.O. Box 1167, Mathis, TX 78368, (361) 547-2635.

LEFT
CCC pavilion
OPPOSITE PAGE
Sunset over Lake Texana

Lake Texana State Park

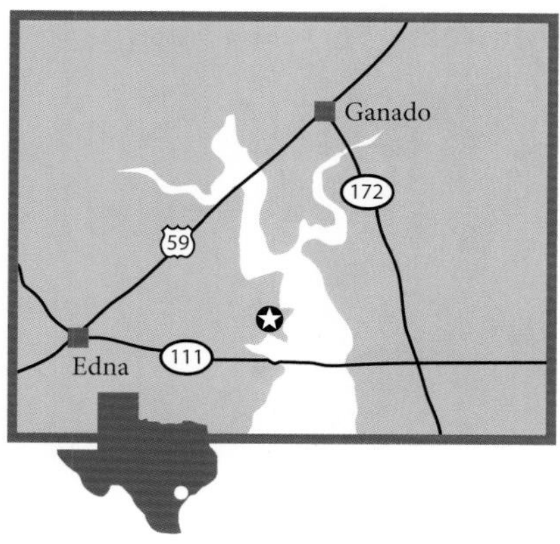

Lake Texana State Park lies off the shores of Lake Texana, an 11,000-acre reservoir filled by the waters of the Navidad River and smaller creeks. For its size, the lake is relatively shallow. It lies on the flat coastal plain, so there was not enough topographic relief along the Navidad River to create a deep body of water. Palmetto Bend Dam, a rolled earth-filled structure, was completed in 1979. To create a large lake on the flat terrain, the dam had to be built almost eight miles long with a maximum crest elevation of 55 feet. The dam backs up water for 18 miles, creating a 125-mile shoreline that winds around many tributaries, both large and small.

The lake was named for the town of Texana, founded in 1832 along the Navidad River a few miles downstream from the dam. For years the town was a prosperous inland port, but in 1883 it was bypassed by the New York, Texas and Mexican Railroad. Today little remains of Texana but a historical marker.

Most of the land surrounding the park is prairie; some is used for grazing, and some has been plowed under for crops such as rice. Most of the park, however, lies within the old river valley on the edge of the lake and is wooded with live oaks, post oaks, pecans, water oaks, cedar elms, and other trees. Yaupon, American beautyberry, palmettos, and mustang grapes form the woodland understory.

The lake is relatively new, so dead, flooded timber still stands in some areas of the lake, providing excellent fish habitat. Anglers pursue largemouth bass, crappie, and catfish in all corners of the lake. The park offers excellent facilities to fishermen, including three fishing piers, two of which are lighted, and a boat ramp.

Birding and wildlife watching are two other quiet activities enjoyed at Lake Texana. More than 225 bird species have been recorded here. Flooded rice fields and mudflats along the lakeshore attract shorebirds from the nearby coast. Spring and fall migrations can bring everything from waterfowl and songbirds to huge kettles, or groups, of migrating hawks. The most prominent mammals are the white-tailed deer that wander through campsites and picnic areas almost oblivious to people. Other common, but less seen, animals include armadillos, raccoons, opossums, squirrels, and the occasional bobcat.

For more active recreation, the lake offers plenty of room for water skiers, jet-skiers, and sailboats. Swimmers can take advantage of multiple water-access points throughout the park. Lake Texana is a popular but quiet escape from urban life, drawing people year after year.

VISITOR INFORMATION

575 acres. Open all year. Hot and humid in summer. Large number of campsites with partial hookups and showers, split into two areas. Boating, waterskiing, boat ramp, fishing piers, picnicking, birding. Canoe, kayak, and hydrobike rentals. Six miles of hike and bike trails. All visitor services available in Edna and Victoria. For information: Lake Texana State Park, 46 Park Road 1, Edna, TX 77957, (361) 782-5718.

Lipantitlan State Historic Site

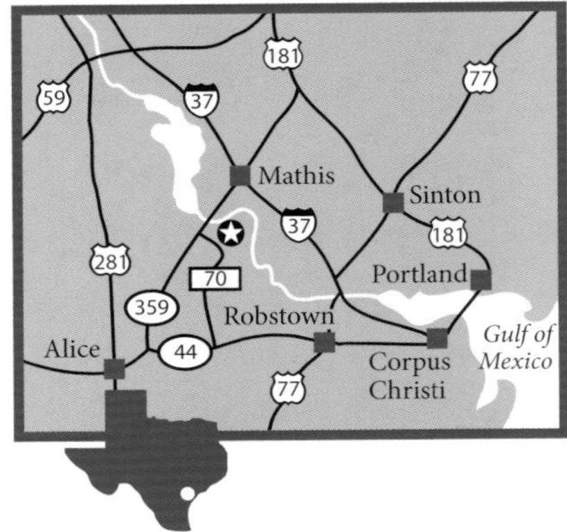

Lipantitlan State Historic Site is a small, little-developed park located near the Nueces River southeast of Lake Corpus Christi. The park is close to the site of Fort Lipantitlan, a post first built by the Spaniards in 1728 near a Lipan Apache village of the same name. The fort was abandoned after many Indians died in the Battle of Medina on August 18, 1813.

Reactivated by Mexican troops in 1831 to deter further Anglo-American colonization, the fort was little more than an earthen embankment surrounding unfinished barracks. In October 1835, Captain Philip Dimitt, commander of Texas forces at Goliad, sent a company led by Ira Westover to take the fort. His troops seized the fort on November 3 and stopped a Mexican counterattack the next day.

On June 7, 1842, volunteers under General James Davis successfully defended Fort Lipantitlan against an assault by General Antonio Canales and his "Republic of the Rio Grande" forces. The fort was abandoned after that battle and crumbled into ruin.

Today the small park bearing the old fort's name consists of several picnic tables resting in the shade of old, gnarled mesquite trees. Other than a historical marker, little remains of the once hotly contested military post.

VISITOR INFORMATION

5 acres. Open all year. Hot and humid in summer. Historical marker, picnicking. No water or other facilities. Difficult to find; obtain directions at nearby Lake Corpus Christi State Park. All visitor services available in Mathis and Corpus Christi. For information: Lipantitlan State Historic Site, c/o Lake Corpus Christi State Park, Box 1167, Mathis, TX 78368, (361) 547-2635.

Mesquite at Lipantitlan

Matagorda Island Wildlife Management Area

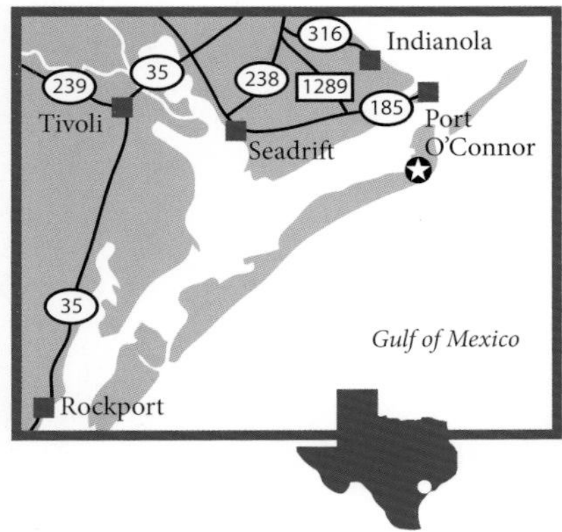

People who make the effort to visit Matagorda Island are rewarded with one of the emptiest, most isolated sections of the Texas coast. Matagorda is one of only two major coastal islands in Texas not connected to the mainland by bridges or ferries. To reach the island, it is necessary to take a boat, either your own or a chartered one.

Like the more famous Padre and Galveston islands, Matagorda is long and narrow, 0.75 to 4.5 miles wide and 38 miles long. The low-lying island is a barrier island, created from sand by longshore currents and wave action in the shallow waters at the edge of the Gulf of Mexico. Barrier islands are fragile and short-lived; changes in sea level and hurricanes can destroy the islands and rebuild them elsewhere. Even though the islands are not especially durable, they provide an important buffer for the mainland from hurricanes and tropical storms.

Unlike most coastal areas of Texas, the island is virtually undeveloped. A crumbling World War II air base and historic 1852 lighthouse lie on the northeastern end of the island; the rest of Matagorda's 56,668 acres have only a scattered ranch building or two and some dirt roads. Except for official vehicles, no motorized transportation is allowed on the island, which is jointly managed by the state and federal governments as a state wildlife management area and national wildlife refuge.

Beach dunes and sea oats

Wildlife thrives on the empty, undeveloped island. Nineteen state or federally endangered or threatened species are found there, including the famous whooping crane. More than 300 species of birds use Matagorda as either a permanent home, winter refuge, or migratory stopover point. Habitat exists for wading birds, shorebirds, waterfowl, raptors, and songbirds. Whooping cranes spill over onto the island from Aransas National Wildlife Refuge, just across San Antonio Bay.

Mammals found on the island include white-tailed deer, coyotes, raccoons, and jackrabbits. Alligators lurk in freshwater marshes, preying on unwary animals that come too close. Western diamondback rattlesnakes and other reptiles are common in the grasslands behind the beach dunes.

Rare sea turtles such as the Kemp's ridley use the island on occasion.

Fertile salt marshes behind the central grasslands provide nursery areas for crabs and many species of shrimp. Fishermen commonly catch redfish, spotted trout, flounder, mackerel, and many other species in the waters surrounding the island.

Visitors come to the island by crossing Espíritu Santo Bay from Port O'Connor with a boat. The island docks are on the bay side of the island across from the town. The beach lies on the Gulf side of the island about 1.5 miles away from the dock via a sandy road. Mountain bikes are an excellent way to get around the island. Matagorda Island may take some effort to reach, but miles of empty Gulf beaches and salt marshes are the reward.

VISITOR INFORMATION

7325 acres. Open all year. Hot and humid in summer. Boat required for access. Primitive camping is permitted in the bay-side dock area and on two miles of Gulf beach. Facilities include a limited number of picnic tables with shade shelters, pit toilets, and an outdoor cold-water rinse-off shower near the docks. No electricity, drinking water, concession, or telephones on the island; bring plenty of food, water, and sunscreen. Fishing, swimming, surfing, sunbathing, picnicking, and birding. Eighty miles of beach, dirt roads, and mowed paths provide extensive hiking and mountain-biking opportunities. Limited visitor services available in Port O'Connor and Seadrift; full services available in Port Lavaca. For information: Matagorda Island Wildlife Management Area, 1700 7th Street, Bay City, TX 77414, (979) 244-6804.

TOP
Sunrise over beach driftwood and Gulf of Mexico
BOTTOM
Matagorda Island Lighthouse and boardwalk

Mustang Island State Park

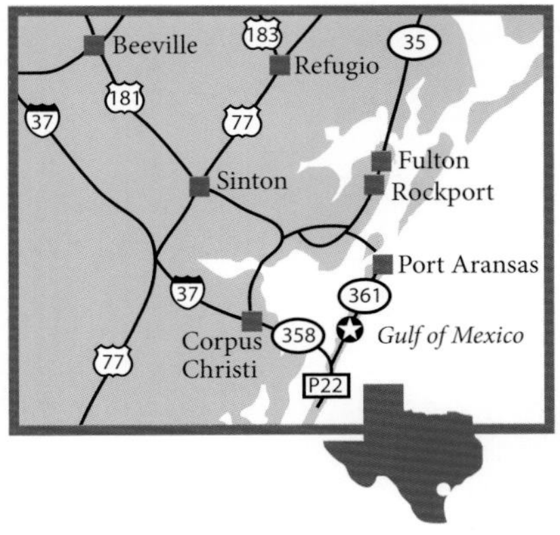

The surf washes ashore ceaselessly on the Gulf of Mexico beaches of Mustang Island, sometimes with small, quiet rollers, other times with towering waves driven by hurricanes. The endless movement of the ocean seems to draw people to the island year after year. Mustang Island State Park, one of the state's most popular parks, occupies about five miles of beachfront and the adjoining marsh on the long, narrow island.

Mustang Island is a barrier island, one of many along the Texas coast, including Padre, Matagorda, and Galveston islands. Barrier islands form when sand is deposited along the shore by wave action and longshore currents and then built into dunes by steady coastal winds. The islands form important buffers for the bays and mainland behind them, dulling the impact of violent Gulf storms and tidal surges.

The low, sandy islands change constantly as dunes move and beaches erode. Hurricanes and storms striking the barrier islands can radically change them, opening new channels, or passes, between the Gulf and the bays, or closing old ones. Fish Pass, within the state park, was a small channel connecting Corpus Christi Bay and the Gulf, but has now been sanded in and closed. Large granite jetties that mark

TOP
Mustang Island jetty
BOTTOM
Dunes and beach

the mouth of the old channel now provide a favorite fishing site and surf break for surfers. Likewise, the channel that once separated Mustang and Padre islands, to the south of the state park, has also closed.

Behind the dunes of Mustang Island lie grasslands carpeted with salt-tolerant plants. Low areas in the grasslands fill with rainwater and become freshwater marshes vegetated with bulrushes and cattails. Close to the bay, fingers of salt water reach up into the island, creating salt marshes and mudflats, depending on the level of the tides. The marsh areas are a prime habitat for wading birds and small fish.

The varied habitats of the island provide homes for many creatures, large and small. Mammals range from small herbivores such as gophers and cottontails to predators like the coyote. Birdlife is abundant and attracts many park visitors. Water and shore birds, such as herons, gulls, pelicans, and terns, are commonly seen all year. In spring and fall, large numbers of migrants pass through the park.

Before Europeans arrived, the Karankawa Indians lived on Mustang Island and in other coastal areas. The Spanish explorer Alonso Alvarez de Piñeda first sailed this part of the Texas coast in 1519. Later, part of a Spanish treasure fleet was washed ashore on Padre Island in 1553, but the area was little visited until the 1700s, when the Spanish missionary effort was in full swing. Until several cattle ranches were established on the island in the 1850s, no settlements were built. Except for the small shipping town of Port Aransas at the north end of Mustang Island, it remained quiet and relatively undeveloped until a causeway was built to Padre Island in 1954. In 1972 the parkland was purchased, and damage done by vehicles driving on the dunes was repaired. Today, many thousands of people visit Mustang Island State Park every year, to swim in the surf, fish from the jetties, sunbathe, surf, or just relax to the soothing sound of waves rolling onto the wide, sandy beach.

VISITOR INFORMATION

3954 acres. Open all year. Hot and humid in summer. Very busy in summer, especially on weekends. Moderate-sized campground with partial hookups and showers behind dunes, large primitive beach camping area with no hookups. Swimming area with bathhouse, rinsing showers. Swimming, fishing, picnicking, hiking, mountain biking. No glass containers allowed on beach. Breeze usually keeps mosquitoes off beach, but they can be fierce behind the dunes, especially on warm-weather evenings. Avoid jellyfish and stingrays on beach and in water. Some visitor services available on north end of Padre Island at junction of Park Road 22 and Texas Highway 361. Full services available in nearby Corpus Christi and Port Aransas. For information: Mustang Island State Park, P.O. Box 326, Port Aransas, TX 78373, (361) 749-5246.

OPPOSITE PAGE
Beach sunrise
BELOW
Port Isabel Lighthouse

Port Isabel Lighthouse State Historic Site

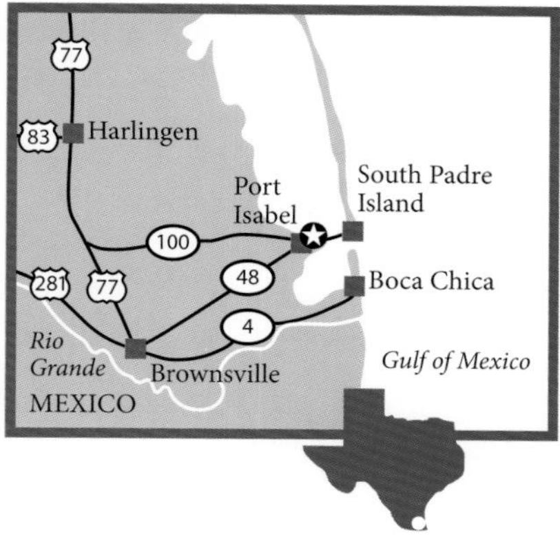

The Port Isabel Lighthouse was built in 1852 to guide shipping through Brazos Santiago Pass to Point Isabel. Prior to construction of the lighthouse, General Zachary Taylor used the site as a supply depot during the Mexican-American War. Fighting returned to the area during the Civil War, and the light was darkened for its duration.

Confederate troops held the site until 1863, when federal forces sent to strengthen the blockade on Southern shipping gained control. Both sides used the lighthouse as a lookout during the war. Confederate troops captured 113 Union soldiers at a battle at nearby Palmito Ranch on May 13, 1865—ironically, more than a month after General Robert E. Lee had surrendered at Appomattox. The clash is believed to have been the last of the Civil War.

After the war, the light was repaired and guided ships until 1905, when traffic declined. During this period, its use was interrupted from 1888 to 1894 owing to a squabble over ownership of the land under the lighthouse. In 1950, the lighthouse was acquired by the State Parks Board from private owners; it was dedicated as a state park in 1952, the centennial of its construction. The tower was repaired and renovated before its opening as a park, and today looks out on a resort community. In 1996 a visitor center was built that replicates the original lighthouse-keeper's quarters. In 2000, the lighthouse was restored again. Of the 16 lighthouses that have been constructed along the Texas coast, only the Port Isabel Lighthouse is open to visitation.

VISITOR INFORMATION

0.88 acre. Open daily all year except Christmas Day, 10 AM to 6 PM Sunday through Thursday and 11 AM to 8 PM Friday and Saturday in summer, and 9 AM to 5 PM the rest of the year. Historic building, visitor center, picnicking. Park operated by the city of Port Isabel. All visitor services available in Port Isabel and South Padre Island. For information: Port Isabel Lighthouse State Historic Site, 421 E. Queen Isabella Blvd., Port Isabel, TX 78578, (956) 943-2262, (800) 527-6102.

Sabine Pass Battleground State Historic Site

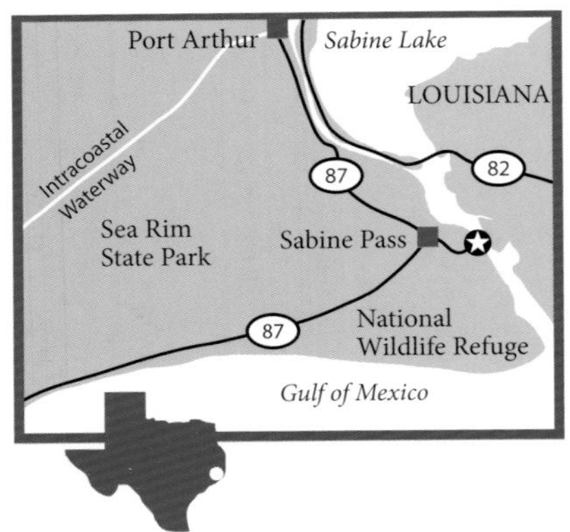

Sabine Pass is a channel of water that connects the Gulf of Mexico with Sabine Lake and separates Texas and Louisiana. Today the waterway is calm, the quiet interrupted only by occasional ocean-going ships, shrimp boats, and pleasure craft, but during the Civil War the pass was the site of an important battle.

A bronze statue of Lt. Richard W. "Dick" Dowling overlooks the site of the conflict. During the Civil War, Texas was a major source of supplies for Confederate forces, although few battles took place on Texas soil. In an attempt to limit Texas's ability to supply the South, Union forces established a naval blockade of the Gulf Coast. To circumvent the blockade, an industry of "blockade runners" developed in Sabine City (now called Sabine Pass), a small town on the Texas shore, and in many other Confederate ports. In 1862, the Union limited the blockade running at Sabine City by stationing ships outside the mouth of the pass and by entering the pass and destroying Fort Sabine. They soon left because the town was under quarantine with a yellow-fever epidemic.

On July 3, 1863, Confederate forces surrendered at Vicksburg and lost control of the Mississippi River, freeing thousands of Union troops for service elsewhere. Plans were made to invade Texas, starting by taking Beaumont to sever the railroad link between Texas and Louisiana. An amphibious assault on Sabine Pass would be followed by the landing of 15,000 troops who would take the Beaumont region.

Meanwhile, Texas defenses at Sabine Pass were in pitiful condition. Texas District commander General John Magruder ordered a new shore battery named Fort Griffin to be built at the pass to replace Fort Sabine. Defense of the pass was left to two small gunboats and several small companies of the Texas Infantry. In July, second-in-command Dick Dowling, a native of Ireland, occupied Fort Griffin along with his company of rough Irish dockhands.

By the first week in September, the Union fleet with 4000 troops and supplies was approaching the pass, but no more than 300 Confederate troops were within 50 miles of the area. The bulk of Magruder's troops had been sent to northwestern Louisiana. Magruder, hearing of the imminent invasion of Sabine Pass, ordered the few remaining troops to retreat. Dowling and his band of 47 mutinous Irishmen ignored the order and adopted the motto "Victory or death!"

Before dawn on September 8, following delays and mistakes on the part of the Union forces, the invasion began. Sandbars in the channel made travel difficult for the Union ships. The gunboat *Clifton* made the first entry, but remained out of range of Fort Griffin's guns. A second entry into the pass was led by the *Sachem*, one of the four Union gunboats. The *Arizona* then got stuck on a sandbar.

The *Sachem* moved into range of Fort Griffin's guns. Dowling's men finally opened fire, striking the gunboat at will while a strong current drove it aground on the Louisiana shore. The *Clifton* forged ahead, but was struck by a shot that cut its wheel rope. Currents pushed it aground on the Texas shore in close range of the fort's guns. In less than an hour, Dowling's men had captured two gunboats and 350 men. The remainder of the Union fleet retreated to New Orleans, not to return to Sabine Pass until after the end of the war. Not a single one of Dowling's men was injured in the battle.

Dick Dowling memorial

After recent losses at Vicksburg and Gettysburg, the Confederacy was heartened by the victory at Sabine Pass. Fort Griffin was not abandoned until a month after the war ended. Its flag was the next to the last to be lowered in the entire Confederacy. Although the Battle of Sabine Pass did not stop the ultimate defeat of the South, it did prevent a Union invasion of Texas and the resulting devastation suffered by many other Southern states. After the war Dick Dowling became a successful businessman, but sadly, he died of yellow fever only a short time later, on September 28, 1867.

VISITOR INFORMATION

58 acres. Open all year. Hot and humid in summer. Small number of campsites with partial hookups. (The park was damaged by Hurricane Rita. Call before visiting.) No showers. Replica of Fort Sabine, historic markers, picnicking, fishing, boat ramp. All visitor services available in Port Arthur. For information: Sabine Pass Battleground State Park and Historic Site, c/o Sea Rim State Park, P.O. Box 1066, Sabine Pass, TX 77655, (409) 971-2559.

San Jacinto Battleground State Historic Site

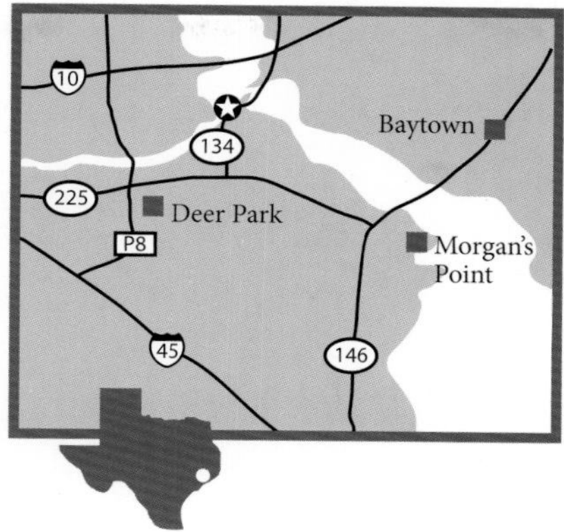

In March of 1836, the war for Texas's independence was not going well for General Sam Houston and his Texan troops. On March 11, Houston abandoned Gonzales and retreated eastward in advance of the numerically superior forces of General Antonio de Lopez de Santa Anna, the President of Mexico. Houston's poorly trained troops were restless, eager for revenge after the Goliad massacre and the fall of the Alamo. Houston realized, however, that the Texans had little chance of winning over Santa Anna's much larger army without some sort of advantage.

On April 18, Houston arrived at Buffalo Bayou and found that Santa Anna had already sacked the small town of Harrisburg. Through a captured Mexican courier, he learned that Santa Anna had isolated himself from the bulk of his troops and had a force of about 750 men, only slightly smaller than Houston's 820 men. Houston realized that his chance had come. On April 19, Houston and his men crossed to the south bank of Buffalo Bayou, marched east, and set up camp near Lynch's Ferry on April 20. An advance guard of the Texans captured a boatload of the Mexican Army's provisions at the ferry, providing food to the famished Texan soldiers.

A small party of Texans was dispatched to New Washington on Galveston Bay to learn Santa Anna's position. After a brief skirmish with the Mexican Army, the Texans retreated back to Houston's position near Lynch's Ferry, the Mexican forces not far behind. Upon his arrival at nearby San Jacinto, Santa Anna tried to draw the Texans into battle. Skirmishes continued into the late afternoon, when Santa Anna established a camp about three-quarters of a mile east of Houston's position.

In a brief skirmish at sunset, a detail of Texan cavalry almost met disaster, stoking Houston's fears about his poorly trained, individualistic troops. As darkness fell, both armies settled into camp for the night. Houston ordered his men to eat and rest, while he stayed up all night worrying. Santa Anna, realizing that Houston's force was slightly larger, built fortifications using saddles, baggage, and anything else available and hoped that reinforcements would soon arrive. Even though his men were exhausted, he kept them up all night on alert, believing that the Texans would attack at first light.

On April 21, dawn came with no attack and Santa Anna relaxed. At about 9 AM, about 500 more Mexican troops arrived, to the chagrin of Houston and his men. Houston sent a small detail to destroy Vince's Bridge to delay additional Mexican reinforcements. At noon, he held a council of war in which no decision was reached.

That afternoon, Houston assembled his troops and laid out a plan of battle. The main force advanced quietly in a frontal assault, hoping for the advantage of surprise. Two other groups circled around to the left and right flanks of the Mexican camp. The Mexican troops had relaxed with their numerical superiority, and many were eating and sleeping.

The Texans had advanced to within 200 to 300 yards of the Mexican position before they were discovered and the alarm sounded. The main group of Texans charged the camp, screaming, "Remember Goliad! Remember the Alamo!" A pitched battle quickly ensued, much of it hand to hand at the Mexican fortifications. The two other

groups of Texans attacked the flanks, quickly overwhelming the Mexican camp. Houston was wounded, but fought on with his men. In less than 20 minutes, organized resistance ended and many Mexicans fled toward the San Jacinto River, hoping to swim to safety. Even though Houston and his officers tried to stop the slaughter, many Mexicans were killed by revenge-driven Texans even as they tried to surrender. As the sun set to the west, the battle ended, the marshes stained scarlet with blood. Nine Texans and 630 Mexicans lay dead or mortally wounded, a tremendous defeat for the Mexican Army.

Those with medical training did their best with minimal supplies to treat the Texan and Mexican wounded. The 700 uninjured Mexican troops were disarmed and placed under guard. A small number, including Santa Anna, escaped from the battle and headed westward to the several thousand troops waiting west of the Brazos River. Houston knew that if Santa Anna was able to reunite with the main body of his army, the war would continue, so he sent out scouts to search for the escapees the next day. By noon, Houston's men had captured Santa Anna disguised as a private. Santa Anna ordered his troops to withdraw from Texas, securing independence for the Republic of Texas.

To commemorate the pivotal battle, the 570-foot-tall San Jacinto Monument was built, along with the San Jacinto Museum of History at the base. An elevator in the massive concrete and limestone tower takes visitors to an observation level near the top, under the crowning limestone star. On a clear day, the view encompasses the historic battleground, the nearby Battleship *Texas*, and many square miles of Gulf Coast country east of Houston.

VISITOR INFORMATION

1200 acres. The park is open daily all year except Thanksgiving, Christmas Eve, and Christmas Day. Call to verify times. Hot and humid in summer. Day use only. Historical structures, museums, theater presentation, interpretive markers, nature trail, picnicking, fishing. All visitor services available in Houston and suburbs. For information: San Jacinto Battleground State Historic Site, 3523 Battleground Road, La Porte, TX 77571, (281) 479-2431; San Jacinto Museum of History, One Monument Circle, La Porte, TX 77571, (281) 479-2421.

Sea Rim State Park

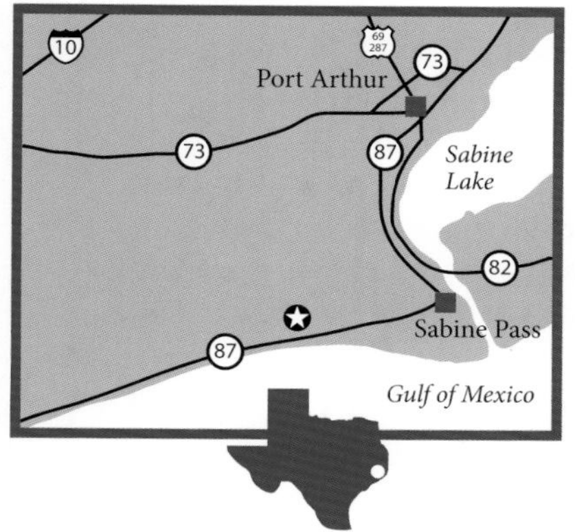

Sandy beaches line the vast majority of the Texas Gulf Coast, but at Sea Rim State Park, marshes extend into the surf along part of the shore. These "sea rim" marshes give the park its name. Mud and silt swept westward along the coast from the Sabine River by longshore currents are deposited along the shore at Sea Rim. Salt marshes grow in the layers of mud and silt. Farther west in the park, the typical sandy beach and dunes reappear along the shore.

Most park visitors favor the beach, where they can swim, surf, fish, and sunbathe. A low ridge of dunes, mostly anchored by vegetation, backs the broad beach. Behind the dunes lies a vast area of lightly visited marshlands. A short boardwalk nature trail behind the dunes introduces the marsh area to visitors. Ponds form in the low-lying terrain through a combination of storms and alligators digging holes during dry spells. Water in the ponds and wet areas has varying degrees of salinity, from almost fresh to as salty as seawater. Evaporation and storm tides carrying in salt water raise salinity, while rains lower salinity. Plants and animals in the marshes adapt to the salt water through a high tolerance to salt or by moving to fresher water.

Salt-tolerant grasses are the principal plant component of the marshlands. Reptiles and amphibians thrive in the shallow waters of ponds and sloughs in the marsh. Alligators, snakes, and turtles bask on the banks, but slide into the water at the approach of humans. Frogs leap into the water with a splash and disappear from sight.

Alligators were once endangered, but have made a remarkable comeback. Only a few are usually seen along the boardwalk trail, but many live in the marshlands unit behind Highway 87. The large sprawl of the marshlands unit makes up the largest part of the park, but is relatively undiscovered. A boat ramp leads into a system of channels, ponds, lakes, and sloughs ideal for a canoe or shallow-draft boat with a small motor. The park has built a number of wooden platforms in the marsh for camping and wildlife observation.

Birds love the marshes at Sea Rim. Wading birds, such as herons, egrets, and rails, stalk the shallow waters, hunting for crustaceans, fish, frogs, and other prey. Songbirds perch in the tall grasses, feeding on plentiful insects.

At dusk, the mammals come out to eat. Small rodents scurry through the tall grasses, foraging for seeds and tender shoots. Nutria and muskrats feed upon the marsh grasses and build their dens. Raccoons roam the marsh, feeding on anything they can catch. Even a few rarely seen river otters and minks make their home in the marsh.

People have learned that the fertile waters of the marsh wetlands are very important to Gulf of Mexico fisheries. The shallow, nutrient-rich waters act as a nursery for many fish and crustacean species, including redfish and shrimp. In addition, the marshes provide a habitat for large numbers of wintering waterfowl. The importance of the marsh habitat is emphasized by the nearby location of McFaddin, Texas Point, and Anahuac national wildlife refuges. The beach at Sea Rim State Park is very attractive, but the marshes make an interesting alternative destination.

VISITOR INFORMATION

The park was heavily damaged by Hurricane Rita. Call before visiting to check on status of facilities. 4141 acres. Open all year. Hot and humid in summer. Insect repellent a necessity in the marshes. Do not approach, feed, or touch alligators. Modest number of developed campsites with partial hookups and showers. Primitive camping on designated beach area and marsh platforms. Interpretive exhibits and nature trail. Swimming, picnicking, fishing, sunbathing, surfing, boat ramp, canoeing, boating, and birding. All visitor services available in Port Arthur. For information: Sea Rim State Park, P.O. Box 356, Sabine Pass, TX 77655, (409) 971-2559.

OPPOSITE PAGE
San Jacinto monument
RIGHT
Gulf Coast beach

Sheldon Lake State Park and Environmental Learning Center

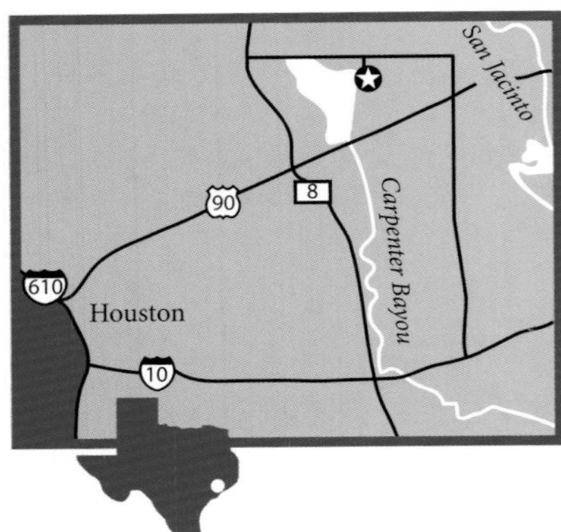

Sheldon Lake State Park lies only about 13 miles northeast of downtown Houston. It consists of a 1200-acre lake and surrounding land. Sheldon Reservoir was built in 1941 by damming the waters of Carpenters Bayou, a tributary of Buffalo Bayou. It was used as a water supply by World War II industries located on Buffalo Bayou. After the war, the federal government designated it as surplus and transferred it to the City of Houston. The city, in turn, conveyed the lake to a predecessor agency of the Texas Parks and Wildlife Department.

The lake was converted into a waterfowl refuge and fishing lake. Florida bass, crappie, sunfish, and catfish were stocked, and surrounding land was farmed to provide grain for wintering geese and ducks.

About 800 acres of the lake are permanently inundated with water; another 400 acres are marsh. Because the terrain is very flat, the lake's levees have created a very shallow body of water. Much of the lake's surface has been covered by water plants, and bald cypresses and other water-loving trees have taken root. Because the lake is small and shallow with numerous navigation hazards, boat motors are limited to 10 HP. From November 1 to February 28, boats are not allowed on the lake, to protect waterfowl.

Primary activities are fishing, boating, and wildlife observation. Waterfowl viewing is best between late November and early March. Alligators are frequently seen in addition to waterfowl. Several heron and egret rookeries thrive on several small islands in the lake in the spring. The Environmental Learning Center has a nature trail, fishing ponds, and a native plant garden. The center offers interpretive programs of all kinds, particularly ones aimed at children.

VISITOR INFORMATION

2800 acres. Park open all year, Environmental Learning Center closed on Monday and Tuesday. Hot and humid in summer. No camping. Boating, fishing piers, hiking, birding. All visitor services available in Houston. For information: Sheldon Lake State Park and Environmental Learning Center, 15315 Beaumont Highway, Houston, TX 77049, (281) 456-2800.

Lush water plants on Sheldon Lake

Varner-Hogg Plantation State Historic Site

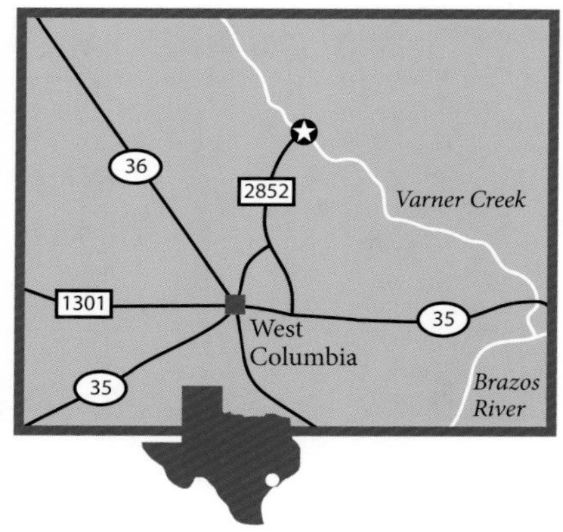

Martin Varner, a member of one of Stephen F. Austin's first colonizing families in Texas, known as the "Old Three Hundred," started the Varner-Hogg plantation in 1824. Varner's land grant of 4605 acres on the Brazos River was the nineteenth of 300 issued under Austin's first contract with the Mexican government. He built a small home on the site, planted corn and sugarcane, and raised livestock. He is believed to have produced the first rum in Texas.

In 1834, Varner sold the property to Columbus Patton and his parents. With the labor of black slaves, the property became a large and prosperous sugar plantation with slave quarters and a sugar-processing building. The two-story main house was built using a regional variant of Greek Revival architecture. Brick made by slaves from Brazos River clay was used in its construction. To lessen the risk of fire, the kitchen was built in a separate building, as was common at the time. Patton kept one slave, Rachel, as his mistress. She lived openly with him, had her own slaves, and exercised freedoms unheard of at the time for a black woman.

Patton was declared insane in 1854, possibly because of a brain tumor, and died two years later. After Patton's stewardship, the plantation began to decline because of low sugar prices, the Civil War, and unfavorable weather. The property underwent a series of ownership changes in the latter half of the nineteenth century. Sugar and cotton continued to be produced, but the plantation never recovered its earlier levels of prosperity.

In 1901, former Texas governor James S. Hogg purchased the property, initially as an investment, though he ended up using it as a second home and vacation retreat. Hogg believed that oil lay under the land and drilled several unsuccessful wells trying to find it before his death in 1906. His belief was vindicated when the West Columbia Oil Field was discovered in 1920, adding greatly to the family's wealth.

In 1920, Governor Hogg's children undertook a major remodeling of the property. The eldest son, William Hogg, planned an agricultural experiment station and planted tree orchards boasting 39 varieties of pecans. The architectural style was changed to Colonial Revival, and the house was reoriented so that the front faced west instead of east. The kitchen building was enlarged, and cement stucco replaced plaster on the exterior. The home remained in the Hogg family until 1958, when daughter Ima Hogg presented the furnished home and surrounding historical structures to the state for a park. The furnishings include many Hogg family heirlooms, period furniture, and other historical items and documents. Today, tall magnolias and pecans shade the historic home, an excellent example of an antebellum plantation house.

VISITOR INFORMATION

66 acres. Day use only. Open for tours Wednesday through Sunday all year; call for hours. Historic structures and exhibits, picnicking, interpretive trail. All visitor services available in West Columbia and Lake Jackson. For information: Varner-Hogg Plantation State Historic Site, P.O. Box 696, West Columbia, TX 77486, (979) 345-4656.

Varner-Hogg home

Hill Country

Many of Texas's favorite state parks lie in the hilly, rocky terrain of the Hill Country in the center of the state. Although most of the parks share a similar ecosystem and geologic underpinning, considerable variety marks many of the sites. Several parks, such as Garner, Guadalupe River, and Pedernales Falls, contain sections of clear, cool Hill Country rivers; Kickapoo Cavern and Longhorn Cavern offer tours deep into the limestone heart of the land; the ruins of Fort McKavett stand watch over the western edge of the Hill Country, once the Texas frontier; some of the best fall color in the state is hidden in the rugged canyons of Lost Maples State Natural Area; and other parks offer everything from lake recreation to a living-history farm.

Most of the Hill Country shares a similar geologic history. About 100 million years ago, thick layers of limestone and other sedimentary rocks were deposited in horizontal layers on the bottom of a Cretaceous sea. About ten to twenty million years ago, a large area of Central Texas was uplifted about 2000 feet along the Balcones Escarpment, a long, curving fault that stretches from north of Austin southwest to San Antonio and west to the Del Rio Area. The rock layers were raised upward with little deformation and formed a relatively high, flat-surfaced area called the Edwards Plateau. During the many millennia since the uplift, erosion has carved the plateau into hilly terrain, especially along the eastern and southern margins.

The thick limestone layers were conducive to cave formation, and hundreds of known caves lie hidden under the surface. Many are large and beautiful, and a number have been opened to the public both in state parks and in private sites. The sedimentary rocks of the Hill Country are also known for fossils and dinosaur tracks.

Although Cretaceous limestones underlie most of the Hill Country, a unique group of rocks lies in the center of the region. In an area centered around Llano, pink granite domes and twisted masses of schist and gneiss lie in sharp contrast to the surrounding whitish limestones. The overlying Cretaceous layers have been eroded away, exposing rocks more than a billion years old, the oldest in Texas, to the surface. The gneiss and schist are the remains of ancient mountain ranges that were eroded into sediment that was heated and pressured to such an extent that it formed metamorphic rocks visible today at Inks Lake State Park and other sites.

Masses of molten rock, or magma, rose within these rock layers and slowly cooled and solidified into large masses of granite. This high-quality stone is quarried at several Hill Country sites for use in buildings, monuments, jetties, and other construction projects. Not only does the durable stone provide a good building material, its sheer faces attract rock climbers to the massive granite domes at Enchanted Rock State Natural Area.

The Hill Country has a distinct ecosystem, shaped by its soils, slopes, elevation, and climate. Thick woodlands of live oaks, red oaks, Ashe junipers, and cedar elms are interspersed with open grasslands. Along permanent streams and rivers, lush riparian woodlands of bald cypresses, sycamores, and pecans thrive. The broad floodplain at South Llano River State Park is noted for its large, mature pecan bottomland forest. In areas such as Lost Maples State Natural Area, deep canyons provide shelter from sun and wind and allow trees such as the colorful bigtooth maple and black cherry to grow.

A number of Hill Country parks are notable for their wildlife. Most have good populations of white-tailed deer, armadillos, raccoons, opossums, and other mammals. A number of parks host endangered species, such as the black-capped vireo and the golden-cheeked warbler. A large flock of wild turkeys roosts in the pecans at South Llano River in winter. A number of Hill Country caves harbor large colonies of Mexican free-tailed bats, including caves at Kickapoo Cavern State Park and Devil's Sinkhole State Natural Area.

Last but not least, the parks of the Hill Country offer a broad range of recreational opportunities, from water sports at Inks Lake and Guadalupe River to rock climbing at Enchanted Rock. Horse owners like the miles of trails at Hill Country State Natural Area, while mountain bikers can pedal through the backcountry at Pedernales Falls. At Colorado Bend, visitors can tour a wild cave and walk to a waterfall tumbling over a fern-and-moss-covered cliff. Some of the Hill Country parks are among the most popular in the state.

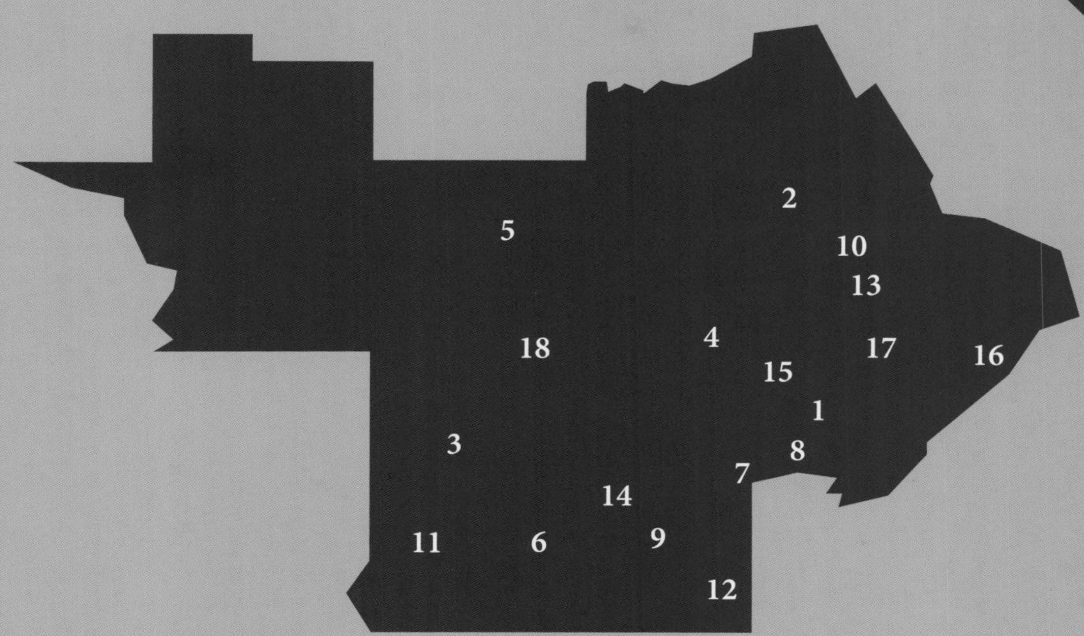

1 Blanco State Park

2 Colorado Bend State Park

3 Devil's Sinkhole State Natural Area

4 Enchanted Rock State Natural Area

5 Fort McKavett State Historic Site

6 Garner State Park

7 Government Canyon State Natural Area

8 Guadalupe River State Park • Honey Creek State Natural Area

9 Hill Country State Natural Area

10 Inks Lake State Park

11 Kickapoo Cavern State Park

12 Landmark Inn State Historic Site and Bed & Breakfast

13 Longhorn Cavern State Park

14 Lost Maples State Natural Area

15 Lyndon B. Johnson State Park and Historic Site

16 McKinney Falls State Park

17 Pedernales Falls State Park

18 South Llano River State Park

Blanco State Park

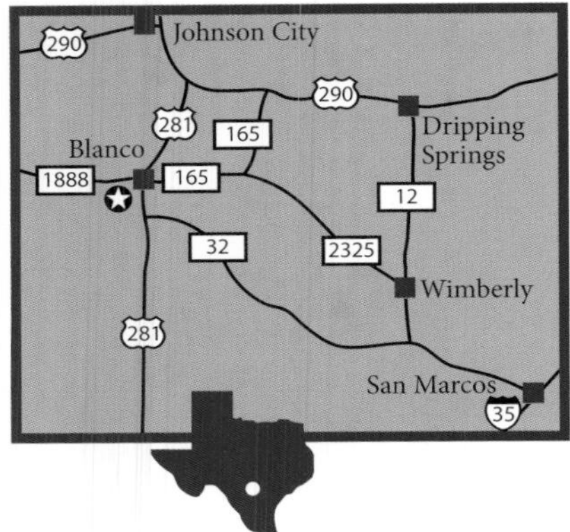

Blanco State Park may be small, but it provides a quiet, accessible Hill Country retreat from the nearby cities of Austin and San Antonio. The park contains about a mile of the sparkling Blanco River on the south side of the small town of Blanco. The river is fed by springs and seeps in the limestone hills to the west.

Within the park, the river flows over Glen Rose limestone. It dates from the Cretaceous period of about 100 to 120 million years ago, when shallow seas covered much of central Texas. The rock has alternating layers of soft marl and hard limestone that erode at uneven rates and create a stair-step topography in the surrounding hills.

Dinosaurs roamed on the shores and mudflats lining the ancient seas and left their tracks to harden into stone. Although there are no tracks exposed within the park, there are many in central Texas, including some areas of private land around Blanco. The best display in the state is located in Dinosaur Valley State Park, near the town of Glen Rose.

The Blanco River flows through typical Hill Country terrain, with rolling rocky hills dotted with live oak, Spanish oak, Ashe juniper, and various shrubs. Trees that need more moisture, such as bald cypresses, sycamores, and pecans, thrive along permanent streams and rivers like the Blanco. Commonly seen wildlife include white-tailed deer, armadillos, squirrels, raccoons, and rabbits.

Blanco River

Like many Texas state parks, Blanco was originally developed by the Civilian Conservation Corps in the 1930s. Among other facilities, they built two small low-water dams in the river that create a popular swimming area. While kids play in the cool water, fishermen can pursue crappie, bass, catfish, perch, and even stocked rainbow trout in winter.

The small town of Blanco lies just outside the state park boundary. It was founded in about 1853, but hostilities between settlers and Indians slowed development for about 20 years. The Blanco County seat was first located in Blanco, but moved to Johnson City in 1891 after a bitter battle between the two towns. After more than 100 years, the striking stone courthouse still dominates the center of town, although it is no longer used as such.

Visitor Information

105 acres. Open all year. Hot in summer. Small campground with partial and full hookups and showers. Swimming, fishing, picnicking, seasonal paddleboat rental, nature trail, limited canoeing. All visitor services available in Blanco. For information: Blanco State Park, P.O. Box 493, Blanco, TX 78606, (830) 833-4333.

Colorado Bend State Park

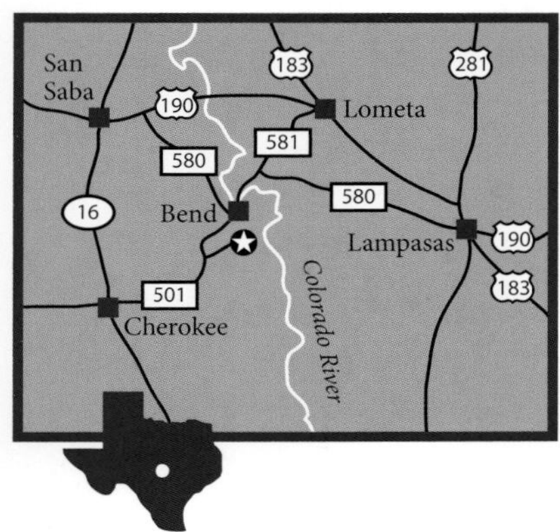

Hidden away in the far reaches of the Texas Hill Country, the Colorado River still flows freely at Colorado Bend State Park. For many miles upstream from Austin, the river has been harnessed and tamed by a series of dams, with the upper end of each resultant lake reaching almost to the next dam. Colorado Bend lies at the very upstream end of Lake Buchanan, the last of the chain of Highland Lakes. Here the Colorado River appears as it once did throughout its length. It flows through a deep canyon rimmed with limestone bluffs not flooded by lake waters. Large oaks, pecans, willows, and elms tower over the narrow canyon bottom floodplain, thriving in the deep, moist soil. Spring-fed creeks tumble down waterfalls and cascades to the river, depositing travertine. Wildlife is undisturbed; even bald eagles winter at the park.

Above the river lies typical Hill Country terrain—rolling country dotted with live oaks, Ashe junipers, and other trees and shrubs. Since the end of livestock grazing in the park, grasses have recovered well and now blanket open areas of the uplands.

The weathered, grayish rock shaping the hills is limestone laid down in ancient seas. Within the limestone lie many caves, forming one of the park's less obvious assets. The largest and best-known cave, Gorman Cave, tunnels 3000 feet into Ellenburger Limestone. The park offers guided tours of the undeveloped cave on weekends. Although most of the trip is in an easy walking passage, a small stream and pools of water in the long tunnel mean wet feet for visitors. The park also offers tours of other park caves that require crawling and other strenuous activities. Because the caves are both fragile and dangerous, entry is allowed only by tour and special permit. Hidden dangers in some of the caves include pits and bad air.

Gorman Falls is a small Hill Country paradise within the park. A spring-fed stream creates the large waterfall when it tumbles over a cliff lining the Colorado River canyon. The calcium-carbonate-rich water has deposited travertine in the form of many small dams and other formations at the falls. Moss and maidenhair ferns cover the travertine, sprayed constantly by the falling water. Tall elms and other trees shade the cool, moist environment at the base of the falls. Because the falls were damaged by heavy trampling in the past, the park allows access only with guided tours on Saturdays and Sundays.

Birders will especially enjoy the park. The rare golden-cheeked warbler builds its nests in thick stands of Ashe juniper in the hills above the river, and the black-capped vireo inhabits patches of brush containing a variety of plant species. In winter, bald eagles migrate south from northern states to fish in the river.

The park is still relatively primitive, with a gravel entry road subject to flooding. The undeveloped campground along the river has several water taps, picnic tables, fire rings, and composting toilets, but no other facilities. A boat ramp at the south end of the park allows access to the upper end of Lake Buchanan. Canoeists often

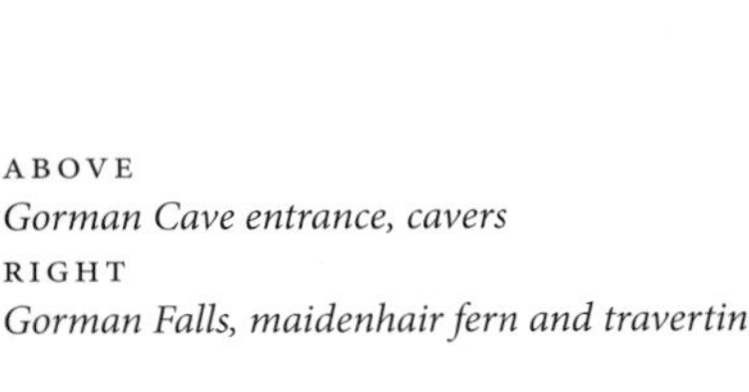

ABOVE
Gorman Cave entrance, cavers
RIGHT
Gorman Falls, maidenhair fern and travertine

put in at the town of Bend, and float downstream to take out in the park.

The white bass run attracts fishermen to Colorado Bend between February and April. The fish swim upriver from Lake Buchanan in large numbers to spawn every spring. Other fish that draw anglers include striped bass, crappie, and catfish.

Hikers enjoy trails along the river and Spicewood Creek and in the rolling uplands with a total length of 16 miles. About 14 miles of trails are open to fat-tired mountain bikes. Bicycling or hiking, caving or fishing, Colorado Bend State Park offers a wealth of activities.

VISITOR INFORMATION

5328 acres. Open all year, except during public hunts. Hot and humid in summer. Busiest during spring white bass run. Relatively undeveloped with gravel roads and composting toilets. Campground area is undeveloped with designated sites, and operated on a reservation basis. Tables, fire rings, water taps, composting toilets, fish-cleaning station only. Boating, boat ramp, picnicking, mountain-biking and hiking trails, fishing, swimming. Guided tours of caves, Gorman Falls; call ahead for dates and times. Some food available in Bend. Full visitor services available in Lampasas, Llano, and San Saba. For information: Colorado Bend State Park, P.O. Box 118, Bend, TX 76824, (325) 628-3240.

Devil's Sinkhole State Natural Area

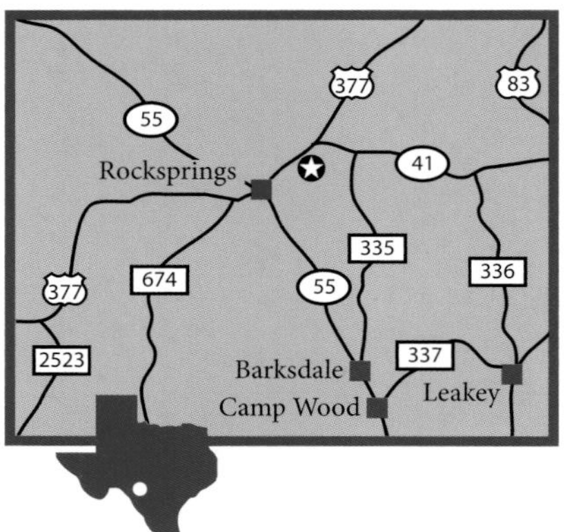

There is little to warn first-time visitors of the awesome, gaping pit of Devil's Sinkhole as they enter the park in the rolling Hill Country terrain near Rocksprings. Live oaks and junipers dot the rocky limestone hills as in most of the Hill Country, although this part of the Hill Country is drier than the eastern areas closer to Austin and San Antonio. A few pinyon pines grow here, unique to this part of the Hill Country.

The entrance to the sinkhole comes as a surprise. It lies on a relatively flat upland section of the natural area. The entrance drops precipitously into a massive cavern from an oval entrance of about 40 by 60 feet. The opening quickly bells outward into a large chamber, meaning that the lip of the sinkhole is only a thin ledge overhanging the deep pit.

The sinkhole formed when underground water made acidic with atmospheric carbon dioxide slowly dissolved out a huge underground cavern. Eventually, as the chamber enlarged and the ground surface above eroded away, the ceiling became too weak to support itself and collapsed, creating an opening to the outside world. The collapsing ceiling formed a large, cone-shaped pile of rubble in the chamber. From the surface to the

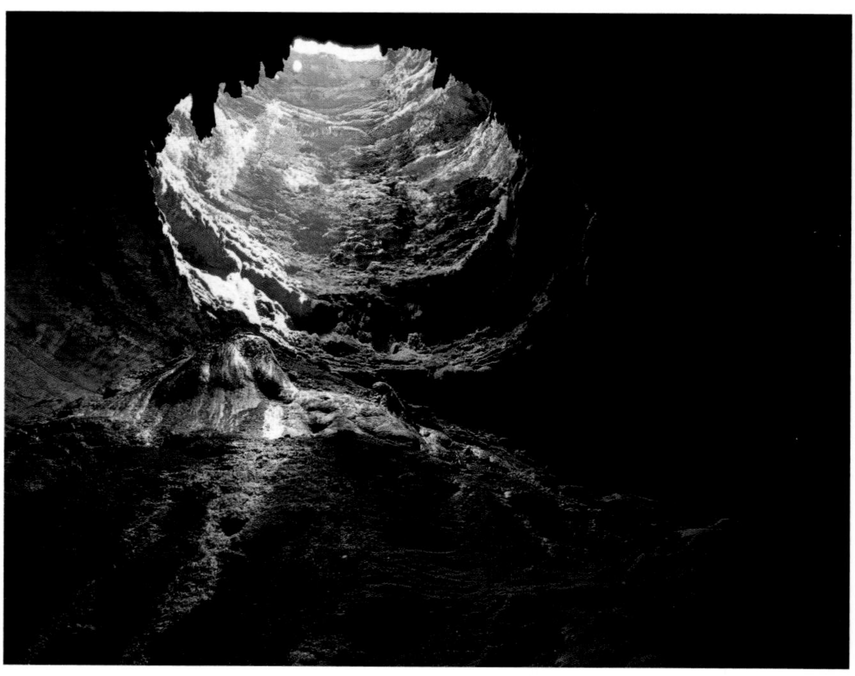

TOP
Cavers
RIGHT
Devil's Sinkhole

top of the rubble pile is a free fall of about 150 feet. The deepest parts of the sinkhole lie 350 feet below the surface around the base of the rubble pile.

The sinkhole supports an important colony of up to three million Mexican, or Brazilian, free-tailed bats. In spring, the bats migrate north from Mexico to the sinkhole and other Hill Country caves to live and raise young until cold weather in fall again sends them south. Because these large bat colonies eat huge quantities of insects, they are very important ecologically. Although individual members of this species are small, they eat roughly half their weight in insects every night. A large colony of bats, such as at the sinkhole, eats as much as seven million pounds of insects annually.

Devil's Sinkhole State Natural Area is open only to scheduled guided tours by reservation. Most tours are in the evening to watch the impressive flight of the bats as they emerge in the evening to begin their nightly hunt. Before the bat flight starts, be sure to walk out onto the edge of the viewing platform hanging over the sinkhole and peer down into the vertigo-inducing abyss.

VISITOR INFORMATION

1860 acres. Open by guided tour only from May through mid-October, Wednesday through Sunday. Reservations required; call the Devil's Sinkhole Society at (830) 683-2287 for reservations and information. Tours meet at the Devil's Sinkhole visitor center at 101 N. Sweeten Street in Rocksprings. Wildlife observation—bat colony. All visitor services available in Rocksprings. For information: Devil's Sinkhole State Natural Area, P.O. Box 678, Rocksprings, TX 78880, (830) 683-3762.

Enchanted Rock State Natural Area

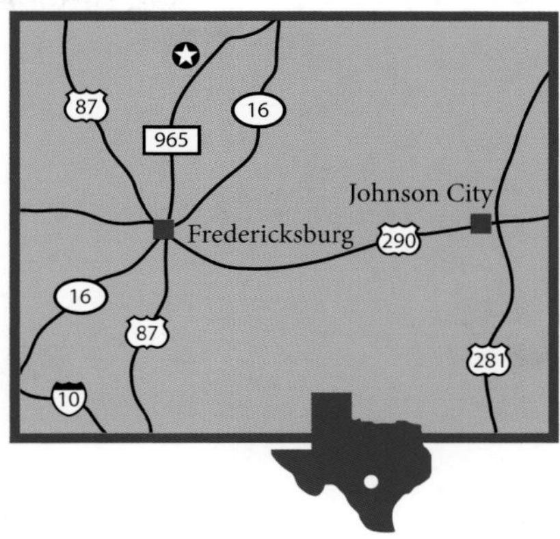

Legends surround Enchanted Rock, the massive granite dome that lies in the center of the Texas Hill Country. Early settlers, including Stephen F. Austin, told of Indian ceremonies being held at Enchanted Rock because it was considered sacred. Many Indians feared the rock, believing it to be haunted, and would not climb to its summit. Tales were even told of human sacrifices made by the Comanches, and pioneers reported odd noises emanating from the rock and strange fires on its summit. The many stories swirling around the dome led to it being named Enchanted Rock early in the 1800s.

In 1978, the site came under Texas Parks and Wildlife Department stewardship. Since pioneers moved into the Hill Country, the rock has been an important landmark and tourist attraction. As a state natural area, it continues to increase in popularity. The natural area contains Enchanted Rock, an enormous curving dome of pinkish granite that towers 400 feet above Sandy Creek. Several smaller peaks and domes surround the main rock within the natural area, including Little Rock, Turkey Peak, Freshman Mountain, and Buzzard's Roost.

The domes within the natural area are but a small part of the Enchanted Rock batholith that is exposed to the surface in an area of more than 60 square miles. The batholith formed when molten rock, or magma, intruded into rock layers below the surface. It cooled slowly and crystallized into granite. Over time, the area was uplifted and erosion removed the concealing layers of rock, exposing the batholith to the surface. The granite is ancient, approximately a billion years old, and has been buried by new rock layers and re-exposed more than once as seas have come and gone in past geologic ages.

Once the batholith was exposed

Vernal pool on granite dome

to the surface, erosion shaped it into its present form. Geologists call Enchanted Rock an exfoliation dome because of the way plates of rock break off the dome, or exfoliate, in thin curving layers, similar to the layers of an onion. Freezing and thawing water helps split the rocks of the dome. The strange noises reported at Enchanted Rock may be nothing more than creaks made as the rock heats and cools with changes between day and night.

Other granite domes in the area have been heavily quarried for the beautiful granite of the Enchanted Rock batholith. Fortunately, Enchanted Rock, the largest granite dome in Texas and second largest in the United States, escaped such a fate. Buildings, monuments, and other structures throughout the country have used the durable, attractive stone. Prominent uses in Texas include the state capitol building in Austin and jetties along the Gulf Coast.

From a distance, much of the rock appears bare and devoid of life. Closer inspection reveals plant communities thriving in pockets of soil eroded from the dome. Colorful lichens grow on the rock itself, while mosses, grasses, ferns, and flowers blanket smaller pockets of soil. In deeper soils, prickly pear cacti and even oak trees find a toehold. Some of the moist, shady crevices hold rare plants, such as the rock quillwort, basin bellflower, and even a tropical fern. Around the base, cedar elms, mesquites, pecans, hickories, and oaks grow in deep soils.

The strong, well-consolidated granite of Enchanted Rock draws rock climbers from all over Texas. Only Hueco Tanks State Historic Site in far West Texas offers such an excellent climbing area. On a pleasant spring or fall weekend, climbers tackle everything from boulders at the base of the rock to the high cliffs on the northwest side of the main dome. A trail system circles Enchanted Rock and some of the smaller domes, and leads to several primitive backpacking campsites. A cave near the summit is also a popular site with park visitors. It was formed when boulders roofed over a deep crack in the dome.

Most people visit simply to make the irresistible climb to the summit, a short but steep walk. Lie back on the smooth granite and enjoy the view, one of the best in the Hill Country. Gentle breezes cool you as they blow unobstructed across the bare summit. Vultures circle high overhead, attracted by rising thermals and good roosting sites. As the sun sets to the west and darkness descends, listen for sounds of the rock and imagine the ancient Indian ceremonies once held there.

TOP
Granite dome
MIDDLE
Sunset view from top of Enchanted Rock
BOTTOM
Rock climber at Enchanted Rock

VISITOR INFORMATION

1644 acres. Open all year. Entry is limited by available parking; the park often fills to capacity by noon on weekends, so arrive early. Hot and humid in summer. The developed campground is small with walk-in tent sites only; no RVs. Showers. Primitive backpacking sites require hiking to reach. Reserve campsites well ahead on spring and fall weekends. Picnic area. Watch children closely near cliffs. Climbers must register at park headquarters. No bolts, pitons, or other rock-damaging equipment allowed. Lights and hardhats are recommended when visiting the cave near the summit. All visitor services are available in nearby Fredericksburg and Llano. For information: Enchanted Rock State Natural Area, 16710 Ranch Road 965, Fredericksburg, TX 78624, (325) 247-3903.

Fort McKavett State Historic Site

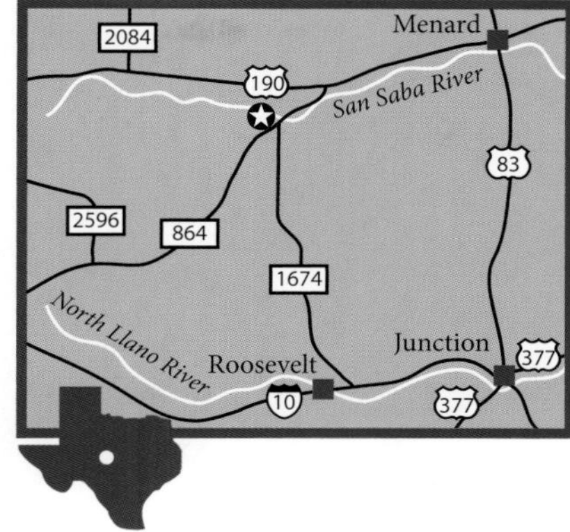

Fort McKavett was established in 1852 to protect settlers on the western frontier and travelers on their way farther west. A Comanche war trail passed near the fort, and both Comanches and Lipan Apaches were common in the area. The fort was built on a hill above the San Saba River and was initially named Camp San Saba. The following year, it was renamed in honor of Captain Henry McKavett, a hero of the Battle of Monterrey in the Mexican-American War. The fort was built with native limestone, oak, and pecan, along with finished lumber freighted in from San Antonio. After solving some initial problems, the post was well maintained and stocked and received good reviews from inspecting officers.

The fort was abandoned in 1859 when problems with the Indians decreased in the area and moved farther north. Settlers moved into the buildings during the following years. By the end of the Civil War, Indian raids had become more frequent again,

Fort McKavett ruins

and the post was reactivated in 1868. The facilities had fallen into ruin and were rebuilt under the leadership of Colonel Ranald S. Mackenzie. Much of the work was done by black "buffalo soldiers" stationed at the fort. Construction was frequently interrupted by military actions and scouting expeditions, but official inspectors and civilian visitors alike were impressed with Fort McKavett. It was "the prettiest post in Texas," said General William Tecumseh Sherman after an inspection in 1871.

As the years passed, the frontier moved farther west and the need for Fort McKavett once again declined. The main body of troops was reassigned in the fall of 1882, and by June 30, 1883, the remaining soldiers had completed their official duties. The flag was taken down, and Company D of the 16th Infantry marched away for the last time.

Local settlers again moved into some of the post's buildings, and the military installation became the town of Fort McKavett. In 1968, the fort was acquired by the state and managed as a historic site. Today visitors see a mix of restored fort buildings and ruins. The visitor center, located in the former post hospital, contains displays and exhibits detailing the fort's history. Reenactments, with men and women dressed in authentic clothing, periodically bring Fort McKavett to life again as a busy post on the western frontier.

VISITOR INFORMATION

80 acres. Open 8 AM to 5 PM, Friday through Monday. Picnicking, museum in visitor center, interpretive trail. Full visitor services available in Menard, Junction, and Sonora. For information: Fort McKavett State Historic Site, P.O. Box 68, Fort McKavett, TX 76841, (325) 396-2358.

Garner State Park

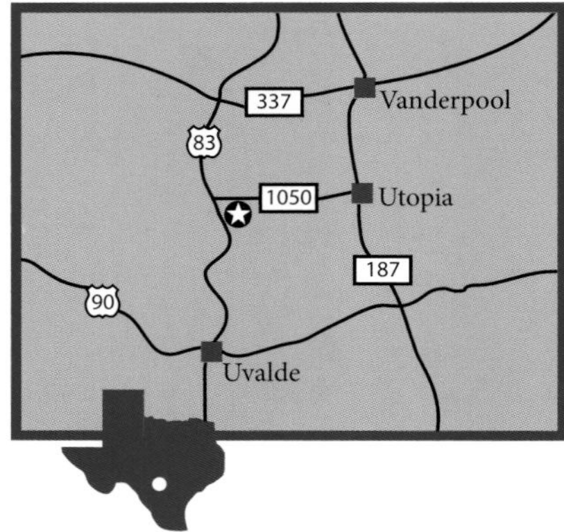

Garner State Park is one of the classic state parks of Texas, demonstrated by its enduring popularity. The clear, cold Frio River tumbles over cascades and boulders as it flows past the park's wooded slopes. It swirls and eddies as it washes over smooth, polished limestone bedrock. Tall bald cypresses line the banks below rocky bluffs covered with live oaks, cedar elms, and Ashe junipers.

The park lies on the southwestern edge of the Hill Country, north of Uvalde. Millions of years ago, the Edwards Plateau was uplifted along a curving fault that stretched from north of Austin southwest to San Antonio and westward, to north of Uvalde. The plateau was uplifted approximately 2000 feet and has been eroding ever since. Rivers and streams, such as the Frio, have cut the once-flat plateau into a particularly rugged land of hills and canyons along the southwestern side of the Hill Country in the Garner area.

Garner State Park was named after John Nance Garner, vice president under Franklin Roosevelt and former resident of nearby Uvalde. The park was developed during the 1930s to preserve a section of the Hill Country for public use and to put unemployed young men to work during the Depression. In 1935, the Civilian Conservation Corps (CCC) set up camp at the park site and began construction. The CCC workers used native materials, such as cypress, oak, and limestone, to build many park facilities that are still in use today. Among these is the large, central concession building, with its adjoining open-air pavilion, that is the park's premier building. Using excellent craftsmanship, the CCC built it in the French-Alsatian style with stone walls and massive exposed wooden beams. The Corps also built cabins, roads, and trails in the park.

Garner State Park officially opened in 1941 and has been welcoming increasing numbers of visitors ever

RIGHT
Garner State Park from above
OPPOSITE PAGE
Frio River with sunset reflections

since. The state park is the most popular camping park in the state-park system, evidenced by its enormous campgrounds. Many people return year after year, drawn by the rugged hills and sparkling Frio River. Water-oriented activities are most popular, with swimmers, tubers, and kayakers filling the river in summer. Cyclists pedal along park roads, while hikers climb the heights of Mount Baldy for spectacular views.

Saturday night dances were started by the CCC men in the 1930s and have grown in popularity since then. On summer evenings, as many as several hundred people congregate at the outdoor pavilion by the concession building to dance to jukebox music or live bands. The dances attract a mix of young and old, both newcomers to Garner and people who have been returning for years to one of the most popular destinations in Texas.

VISITOR INFORMATION

1420 acres. Open all year. Very busy park, especially in summer and on spring and fall weekends. Park sometimes reaches day-use capacity on summer weekends by late morning and temporarily closes; arrive early to ensure entry. Large campgrounds with partial hookups; reservations recommended, especially in summer and on holidays. Cabins, screened shelters; reservations always recommended. Swimming, tubing, kayaking, fishing, picnicking, hiking, bicycling, nature trails. Seasonal park store, paddleboat and kayak rental, miniature-golf course. Limited visitor services available in Leakey, Utopia, and Concan. Full services available in Uvalde. For information: Garner State Park, 234 RR 1050, Concan, TX 78838, (830) 232-6132.

Government Canyon State Natural Area

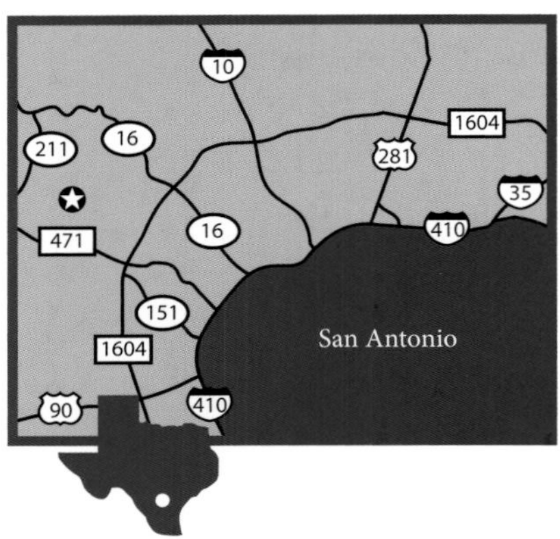

Government Canyon is a new state natural area that is still under development. The large natural area is located on the northwest side of San Antonio on the transition point between the Hill Country of the Edwards Plateau and the South Texas Plains. The rectangular park is oriented north-south, with dimensions of roughly 5.5 x 4.5 miles.

The Edwards Plateau was uplifted by the long Balcones Fault that stretches northeast from San Antonio through Austin and curves west through the northern part of San Antonio toward Uvalde and Del Rio. Government Canyon State Natural Area straddles the fault, with the northern 90 percent of the property on the Edwards Plateau and the southern 10 percent in the South Texas Plains. The fault line is quite distinctive in the park. To the north, the terrain becomes hilly and is wooded with typical Hill Country vegetation, such as live oaks, Ashe junipers, and cedar elms. To the south, the terrain flattens out and mesquite becomes much more common.

Not only did the fault create the Hill Country by lifting up a large piece of the earth's crust, it also allowed the important Edwards Aquifer to develop. Some of the rain that falls on this part of the plateau seeps downward through cracks and fissures into buried layers of limestone in what is called a recharge zone. This water later resurfaces in springs or is tapped by wells. The water is extremely important to area farmers, ranchers, and cities. San Antonio is primarily dependent on Edwards Aquifer water. The 90 percent of the state natural area that lies north of the fault is part of the recharge zone. To protect this area's ability to direct water into the aquifer, most future park development will be concentrated in the southern 10 percent of the park.

The new natural area was named for Government Canyon, a large, normally dry creek that runs through the property. A rough, unimproved dirt road follows the canyon upstream, approximately following the old western travel route from San Antonio to Fredericksburg and El Paso. Within the park lies the old homestead known as the Zizelmann House. Christian and Emilie Zizelmann constructed the house of locally quarried limestone in 1882.

The natural area has opened more than 40 miles of hiking and mountain-biking trails, with equestrian trails planned for the future. Although the natural area is open only for day use now, walk-in tent campsites and primitive backpacking sites are planned for the future. A visitor center was completed in 2005, with exhibits, a store, and a covered picnic pavilion.

VISITOR INFORMATION

8622 acres. Open Friday through Monday, 8 AM to 6 PM. Day use only. Extensive hiking and mountain-biking trails. Trails sometimes close in bad weather or when too muddy. Visitor center, picnicking. All visitor services available in San Antonio. For information: Government Canyon State Natural Area, 12861 Galm Road, San Antonio, TX 78254, (210) 688-9055.

Guadalupe River State Park • Honey Creek State Natural Area

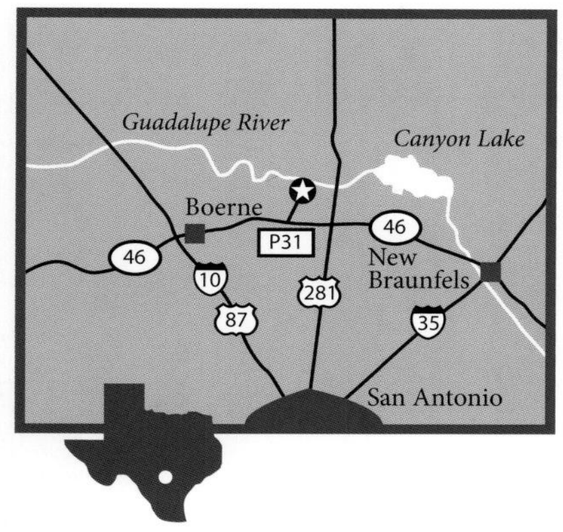

OPPOSITE PAGE
Hiker at Government Canyon
BELOW
Guadalupe River with stormy sunset

The cool, sparkling waters of the Guadalupe River drain from a large area of the central Texas Hill Country. The river has cut deeply into the limestone hills, carving narrow canyons and broad valleys. Tall bald cypresses thrive in the wet soils of the river's banks and grow into massive trees that line the waterway. Guadalupe River State Park provides access to an upper section of what may be the quintessential Hill Country river.

The Guadalupe River rises in the hills west of Kerrville, fed by a series of springs. The river flows eastward through the Hill Country, slowly gaining volume. Well before it reaches the state park, it usually has enough volume to attract canoeists, kayakers, and tubers. Occasional rapids punctuate long calm stretches of the river in and near the state park. Because most land along the river is privately owned, the state park has become a popular site to put in and take out canoes and other small watercraft. Fortunately, however, this section of the river does not have the crowds—and their attendant problems—of the lower section of the river below Canyon Lake.

Guadalupe River State Park lies on the Edwards Plateau, a large area of central Texas that was uplifted about 2000 feet roughly ten million years ago. The plateau was raised up along a long series of faults, known as the Balcones Fault, that starts north of Austin, continues southwest to San Antonio,

and curves west toward Del Rio. Cretaceous limestones, formed in ancient seas that once covered much of Texas, make up most of the surface rocks of the Edwards Plateau. Because the limestones were formed in the ocean, in large part from the skeletons of marine creatures, fossils are common in the Hill Country limestones. Some of the limestones are quite hard and durable and form large cliffs, such as those found along the river within the park. Rivers, such as the Guadalupe, have slowly carved downward into the plateau, creating the canyons, valleys, and hills of the Hill Country.

Vegetation typical of the Hill Country blankets the state park. Upland areas are covered by a mix of grasslands and extensive groves of Ashe juniper and live oak. Plants that favor more moisture, such as cypresses, sycamores, pecans, and other trees, thrive along creeks and on the river bottomland.

The cool waters of the Guadalupe attract most of the park visitors. Canoeists, tubers, swimmers, and waders all flock to the park during the heat of summer. Although the river is usually calm and quiet, occasional floods sweep down the Guadalupe with surprising ferocity. A tremendous flood in 1978 crested at 63 feet above normal levels, uprooting trees and washing out riverbanks. The flow volume was at least 240,000 cubic feet per second (cfs), far more than the typical 150–200 cfs usually found at the park. Fortunately, adequate upstream warnings of impending floods usually prevent any danger to people within the park. Such floods are rare in any case, and are unlikely to interfere with visits to Guadalupe River State Park, one of the Hill Country's jewels.

In the dry, rocky Hill Country adjoining Guadalupe River State Park lies one of the hidden gems of the state-park system. The sparkling spring waters of Honey Creek tumble down a narrow canyon lined with tall bald cypresses and sycamores to the Guadalupe River. The clear stream bubbles over small cascades and calms in long, deep pools dotted with spadderdock, a

and adjoining state park. Of particular interest are rare species like the golden-cheeked warbler and Honey Creek Cave salamander. The creek contains several species of fish, including the native Guadalupe bass.

Because the creek environment is very fragile, access is limited to guided tours offered by park personnel and volunteers. The guides are knowledgeable and offer an excellent opportunity to see a beautiful, undisturbed Hill Country stream.

VISITOR INFORMATION

Guadalupe River State Park: 1939 acres. Open all year. Hot in summer. Large number of campsites, from walk-in tent sites to partial hookup sites, with showers. Canoeing, tubing, swimming, fishing, hiking, 5.3-mile equestrian/ mountain-biking trail, picnicking.

Honey Creek State Natural Area: 2294 acres. Open by guided tour only. Tours are offered on most Saturdays throughout the year. Call ahead for specific dates and times. Day use only.

All services available in Boerne. For information: Guadalupe River State Park/Honey Creek State Natural Area, 3350 Park Road 31, Spring Branch, TX 78070, (830) 438-2656.

pond lily. With Spanish moss draping the trees and palmettos dotting the banks, the creek seems almost more typical of East Texas than of the Hill Country. The stream and the surrounding uplands form Honey Creek State Natural Area.

Various Indian tribes used the land until the mid-1800s, when the area was settled by German immigrants. The land was used as a ranch by a succession of owners until it was purchased by the Texas Nature Conservancy in 1980 and later conveyed to the Texas Parks and Wildlife Department. Since that time, efforts have been made to return the land to its original live-oak grassland.

Like Guadalupe River State Park, Honey Creek lies on the Edwards Plateau. Three major sedimentary rock formations of the Cretaceous period make up the hills of the natural area. The most important is the Glen Rose Limestone, a rock well known for its many caves. Honey Creek Cave is the longest known cave in Texas. One particularly notable geological feature is an igneous dike formed when molten rock squeezed into vertical cracks in the Glen Rose Limestone. It hardened into a hard, black basalt of uncommon composition.

White-tailed deer, armadillos, wild turkeys, raccoons, and opossums are common within the natural area

OPPOSITE PAGE, TOP
Guadalupe River canoeist
OPPOSITE PAGE, MIDDLE
Hiker on Honey Creek
OPPOSITE PAGE, BOTTOM
Bald cypresses on Guadalupe River
ABOVE
Honey Creek

Hill Country State Natural Area

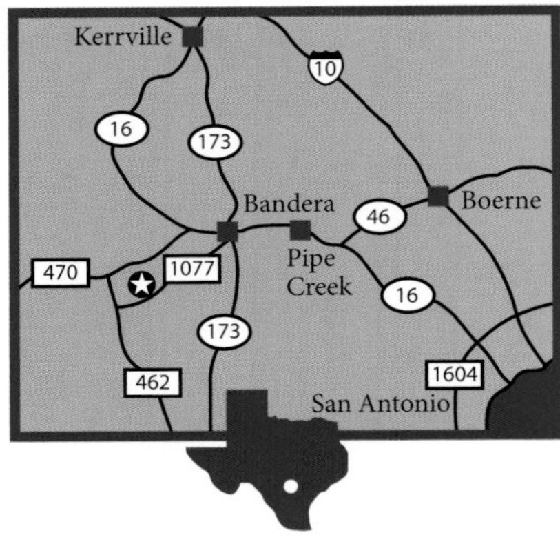

Tucked away in the rugged terrain southwest of Bandera is Hill Country State Natural Area, a secluded retreat little known outside the equestrian community. Horse lovers have discovered its 40 miles of dirt roads and primitive trails that wind up grassy valleys, cross spring-fed streams, and climb steep limestone hills.

The Merrick Bar-O Ranch that became the natural area was originally part of a Spanish land grant. It was registered during the republic period in 1840, but the State of Texas first deeded the land to William Davenport in 1877. He and his family worked the ranch until 1925, when it was sold to the next in a succession of owners. In 1945, the land was purchased by S. E. Lindsey, who conveyed the property to his daughter, Louise Lindsey Merrick, the following year. She and her husband operated the ranch for the next 29 years. During its years of operation, the ranch was known for its productivity.

After Merrick's husband died, she decided to donate the 4753-acre property to the state. As an avid horsewoman who enjoyed riding across her property, she wanted Texans to have a public place where they could ride their horses across a large tract of undeveloped land. Her deed stated that the ranch was "to be kept far removed and untouched by modern civilization, where everything is preserved intact, yet put to a useful purpose." The state took over full ownership in 1982, purchased an adjoining tract of land, and opened the site as a natural area in 1984.

The Parks and Wildlife Department has left the ranch undeveloped. The natural area lies on the Edwards Plateau, a large uplifted area of land in central Texas. Over the course of millennia, erosion has carved steep hills and broad valleys out of the limestone plateau. A mix of grasslands and scrubby woods of live oak, Ashe juniper, and red oak covers the hills. Along West Verde Creek and other watercourses, large sycamores, cedar elms, and oaks arch over clear pools.

An extensive complex of old dirt roads and trails creates miles of paths for equestrians, hikers, and mountain bikers. Novice riders, hikers, and cyclists may want to stay on the easier, main routes in the valley bottoms. Several backcountry camp areas offer primitive campsites to backpackers and equestrians. Facilities are primitive and require that food, water, and camping gear be carried in.

Hill Country State Natural Area is a quiet, undeveloped site with few amenities in one of the most rugged parts of the Hill Country. To challenge visitors even more, it lies on an unpaved county road not even shown on many maps. The extra effort leaves the crowds behind and makes the scenic Hill Country park even more appealing.

VISITOR INFORMATION

5370 acres. Open daily February through November. Open from noon Friday to Sunday evening in December and January, except for Christmas week when it is open daily. Call ahead before visiting to verify. Hot and humid in summer. Primitive camp area near headquarters has an equestrian area and ten walk-in tent sites near swimming holes with tables, fire rings, and chemical toilets. Portable stalls and nearby water for horses. Several primitive campsites for backpackers and equestrians in backcountry. Bring drinking water; there is no potable water in the park. Extensive hiking, mountain-biking, and horse trails. To get there, take Texas Highway 173 south of Bandera less than a mile, turn right on FM 1077, and follow it about eight miles until the pavement ends. Continue on the county gravel road to the natural area. All visitor services available in Bandera. For information: Hill Country State Natural Area, 10600 Bandera Creek Road, Bandera, TX 78003, (830) 796-4413.

OPPOSITE PAGE, TOP
Dead juniper trunks and sotol plants
OPPOSITE PAGE, BOTTOM
Hiker on Twin Peaks
ABOVE
Morning mist on Inks Lake
RIGHT
Wildflowers on arm of Inks Lake

Inks Lake State Park

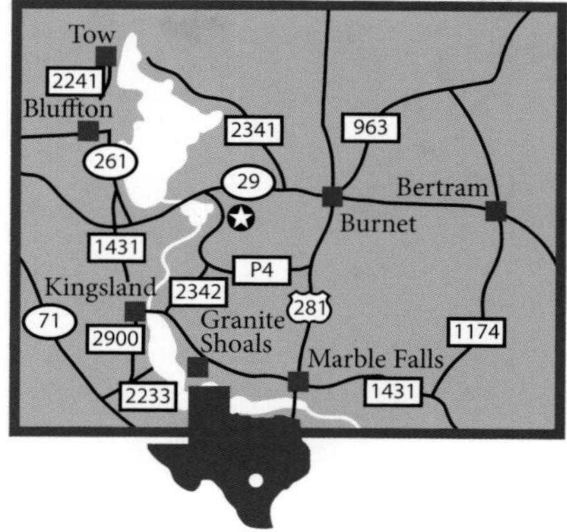

In the 1930s, periodic flooding by the Colorado River led to widespread calls for damming of the river. Llano businessman and mayor Roy Inks worked hard promoting the project, but it took a calamitous flood in 1935 to finally spur the federal government to approve it. Ultimately a series of six dams were constructed from upstream of Inks Lake to Austin; the reservoirs created became known as the Highland Lakes. Unfortunately, Roy Inks did not live to see the projects built; a ruptured appendix plus a bout of pneumonia ended his life in August 1935. The Lower Colorado River Authority named the second dam and its reservoir in his honor.

Inks Lake State Park lines much of the eastern shore of Inks Lake on a solid bed of pinkish Valley Spring gneiss. The hard metamorphic rock resembles the pink granite of nearby Marble Falls and Enchanted Rock. The gneiss formed when volcanic rocks were recrystallized by heat and pressure. The rock is more than a billion years old and possibly the oldest in Texas. Outcrops of it are common throughout the area.

Vegetation cloaks the rocky hills of the state park. Ashe juniper, live oak, and mesquite are common on the rocky slopes; cedar elm, pecan, and hickory prefer the deeper, moister soils along creek bottoms. In spring, arrays of bluebonnets, Indian paintbrushes,

and Indian blankets splash color across open fields and hills.

Wildlife thrives at Inks Lake, and in fact, some animals are almost tame. White-tailed deer roam the campgrounds, searching for deer corn and other handouts. At night, raccoons brazenly raid food carelessly left out by campers. Wild turkeys, armadillos, opossums, and other animals also frequent the area.

Fishing piers and a boat ramp make access easy for anglers wanting to pursue striped bass, white bass, catfish, and other species. Inks Lake even hosts a rarity in the Texas state-park system—a nine-hole golf course. The course borders the lakeshore, providing a large water hazard for golfers who have not refined their strokes. More than seven miles of trails wind through hills of gneiss to overlooks and a primitive camping area. Although the lake is relatively small, it welcomes water skiers and sailboats. The extensive recreational opportunities draw many thousands of people to Inks Lake State Park every year, making it one of the state's most popular parks.

VISITOR INFORMATION

1201 acres. Open all year. Very popular in spring and summer, especially on weekends. Hot and humid in summer. Large campgrounds in several areas, with partial hookups and showers. Screened shelters. Limited-use cabins with air conditioning but no plumbing. Primitive camp area for backpackers. Fishing piers, boating, waterskiing, swimming, hiking, picnicking. Park store with canoe and paddleboat rental. Full visitor services available in Burnet, Marble Falls, and Llano. For information: Inks Lake State Park, 3630 Park Road 4 West, Burnet, TX 78611, (512) 793-2223.

Kickapoo Cavern State Park

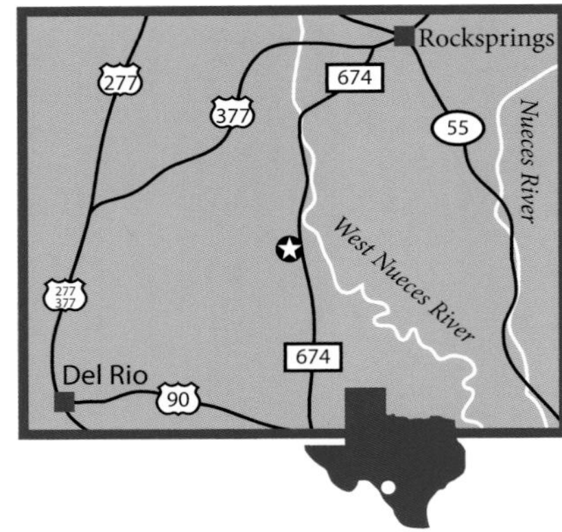

Kickapoo Cavern State Park lies in the far southwestern part of the Hill Country. Steep rocky hills rise above dry, boulder-strewn washes in the former ranch. Because of the park's far western location, it is relatively dry. However, although vegetation is more sparse than in areas to the east, much of the plant life is typical of the Hill Country. Live oaks and Ashe junipers are common, along with papershell pinyon pines, which are small, hardy pines found in the southwestern part of the Hill Country that are related to other species of pinyon found in the mountains of West Texas, Mexico, and the southwestern United States.

The rocky hills of the park conceal the namesake attraction, Kickapoo Cavern. The 1400-foot-long cave is known for its sizable chambers and large calcite formations, including several massive floor-to-ceiling columns. Another cave, Stuart Bat Cave, hosts a colony of approximately a million Mexican, or Brazilian, free-tailed bats from spring through fall. Except during stormy weather, the bats make a dramatic exit flight from the cave every evening to forage for insects.

Stuart Bat Cave, Kickapoo Cavern, and other smaller caves are common in the Devils River limestone of the park. The limestone of the Hill Country was deposited in ancient seas. Later, the Balcones Fault raised up a large section of central Texas known as the Edwards Plateau, exposing it to erosion. Over the course of millions of years, water eroded the relatively flat plateau into rolling hilly terrain.

Water carrying small amounts of carbon dioxide from the atmosphere becomes slightly acidic, giving it the ability to dissolve limestone and create caves. The slow-dissolving action of the water formed the caves at Kickapoo and many other Hill Country areas. Later, dripping water deposited some of the dissolved limestone, or calcium carbonate, on cavern surfaces, creating stalactites, stalagmites, and other formations.

Although the two large caves are the main attractions of the park,

RIGHT
Stuart Bat Cave bat flight
OPPOSITE PAGE, LEFT
Kickapoo Cavern
OPPOSITE PAGE, RIGHT
Landmark Inn

other features draw visitors. Kickapoo harbors one of the state's largest nesting populations of the endangered black-capped vireo. Other bird species of interest include the Montezuma quail and varied bunting. The pinyon pine thrives here, but does not grow in the wetter, more heavily visited eastern areas of the Hill Country. In fall the tree produces a large, tasty nut popular with both wildlife and local residents.

Although the park has changed considerably from its original appearance because of brush clearing and heavy livestock grazing, it is slowly recovering its original character. The natural area offers reserved guided tours of Kickapoo Cavern and the Stuart Bat Cave bat flight. Access for other activities, such as birding, hiking, and mountain biking, also requires advance arrangements.

VISITOR INFORMATION

6368 acres. Open all year by reservation only. Hot in summer. Primitive camping with no water or bathrooms. Cave tours, bat-flight observation, birding, hiking, mountain biking. All visitor services available in Brackettville and Rocksprings. For information: Kickapoo Cavern State Park, P.O. Box 705, Brackettville, TX 78832, (830) 563-2342.

Landmark Inn State Historic Site and Bed & Breakfast

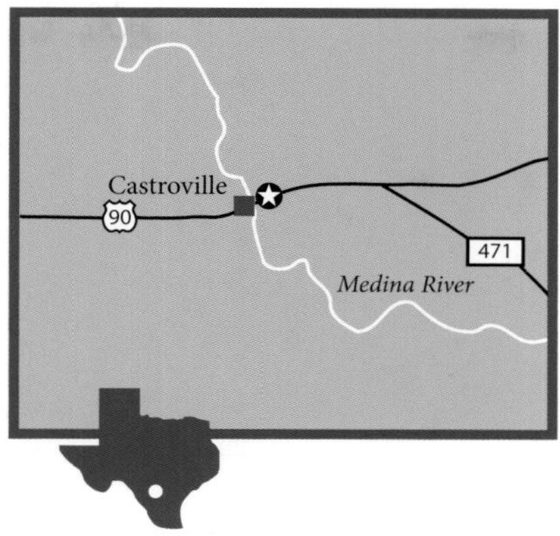

The history of Landmark Inn began shortly after Texas gained independence from Mexico, when the government authorized large land grants to colonists willing to settle in Texas. In 1842, Henri Castro, a French entrepreneur, obtained a colonization contract; his first settlement near his colony was Castroville, founded in 1842. Most of his colonists came from the French-German provinces of Alsace and Lorraine. Some elements of Alsatian architectural influence can still be found in some historic Castroville buildings.

In about 1849, Cesar Monod bought two lots along the Medina River in Castroville and constructed a plastered-stone building that he used as a general store and residence. In 1853, John Vance purchased the property, and through the years he added a store wing and second story, along with broad first- and second-floor galleries. Castroville was located on the busy road from San Antonio to El Paso, inspiring Vance to rent rooms to travelers and to outfit them with supplies. The property became known as the Vance Hotel. The hotel prospered, and Vance continued to add to the property. He built a bathhouse and a separate residence for his family to increase the available room in the inn.

In 1854, Vance sold the riverfront part of his property to George Haass and Laurent Quintle. By constructing a small dam on the Medina River, they were able to build a water-powered grist mill that allowed area farmers to mill their grain in Castroville, rather than shipping it to San Antonio for processing. Joseph Courand purchased the mill in 1876 and adapted it to also mill lumber and gin cotton. In 1899 his son purchased the hotel.

Jordan Lawler purchased the entire property in 1925 and converted the mill to a small hydroelectric plant that provided Castroville's first electricity. With his sister, Ruth Curry Lawler, he reopened the hotel as the Landmark

Inn. In 1974, it was donated to the Texas Parks and Wildlife Department.

Today the inn still provides overnight guests with attractive whitewashed rooms decorated with antiques, and serves a continental breakfast in the morning. In keeping with the historic nature of the property, no phones or televisions are in the rooms; however, the inn has installed unobtrusive air-conditioning units in rooms in deference to the warm Texas climate. Day visitors may tour the inn and landscaped grounds, including the partially restored mill.

VISITOR INFORMATION

4.7 acres. Ten guest rooms are available all year. Group rentals available. To protect historic furnishings, pets and smoking are not allowed. The grounds are open to day-use visitors during the daytime. Historic structures with exhibits, interpretive trail, picnicking, fishing. All visitor services available in Castroville. For information: Landmark Inn State Historic Site, 402 E. Florence Street, Castroville, TX 78009, (830) 931-2133.

BELOW LEFT
CCC administrative building
BELOW RIGHT
"Dog" formation at Longhorn Cavern

Longhorn Cavern State Park

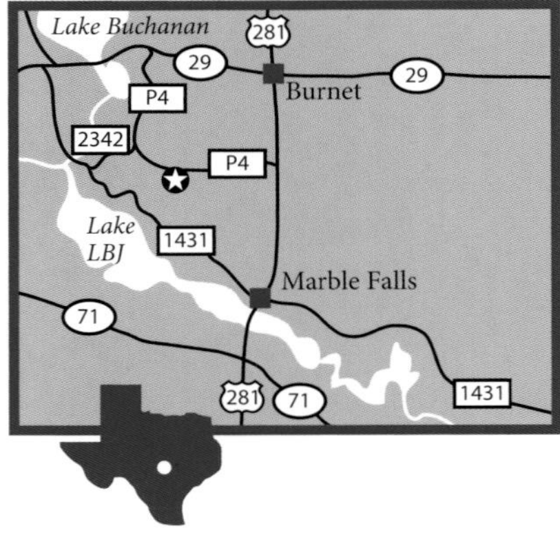

For many millennia, rainwater has been carving Longhorn Cavern from thick beds of Ellenburger Limestone. The cave lies on top of Backbone Ridge, a wedge of sedimentary rocks surrounded by billion-year-old igneous and metamorphic rocks. The limestone was laid down almost 500 million years ago in ancient seas that once covered central Texas. In West Texas, the deeply buried Ellenburger is an important natural gas and oil reservoir rock.

Rain picks up small amounts of carbon dioxide as it falls and becomes slightly acidic. As it percolated through cracks and faults in the limestone of this area, it slowly dissolved chambers and passages. Later, flowing underground streams enlarged the passages, eroding them with suspended sand and silt. The water table fell, and eventually the cave dried out. Unlike many caves, conditions were not right for large quantities of stalactites, stalagmites, and other dripstone decorations to form. However, large masses of sparkling calcite crystallized in some areas of the cave, and the erosive action of the water left smoothly sculptured, marble-like walls as it receded.

Fossil evidence indicates that the Hill Country cave was used by animals that preyed on extinct creatures such as prehistoric camels, giant bison, and mammoths. Later, after humans appeared, early Indian hunting cultures used the cave as a shelter. More recently, Comanches camped in the cave and even, stories tell, battled with Texas Rangers in one of its chambers. During the Civil War, Confederate soldiers manufactured black powder in Longhorn Cavern. Later, it was rumored to be a hideout for outlaws, including the notorious Sam Bass, who, legend has it, hid a fortune in gold somewhere in the cave or nearby.

By the turn of the century, the Comanches had been defeated and the outlaws routed. A local rancher constructed a wooden dance floor and created a popular area gathering place. At times the cave served as a dance hall, church, nightclub, and restaurant.

The State of Texas acquired the

cavern and dedicated it as a state park in 1932. During the Depression, the Civilian Conservation Corps (CCC) made many improvements to the new park. With great workmanship, they used native limestone and timber to construct buildings, retaining walls, and an observation tower. The corps excavated 2.5 million cubic yards of sediment from cavern passages and chambers, built trails, and installed an electric lighting system. The CCC projects were built well, and most are still in use today. Interpretive exhibits, housed in the Corps's old administrative building, describe the work.

VISITOR INFORMATION

646 acres. Open all year by guided tour, except Christmas Eve and Christmas Day. Hours are longer on weekends and in summer; call for tour times. Cave is a constant 68 degrees F, so a sweater may be desired on tours. Wear comfortable, low-heeled, rubber-soled walking shoes. Interpretive exhibits, picnicking, hiking, nature trail. All visitor services available in Burnet and Marble Falls. For information: Longhorn Cavern State Park, P.O. Box 732, Burnet, TX 78611, (830) 598-2283 or (877) 441-2283.

Lost Maples State Natural Area

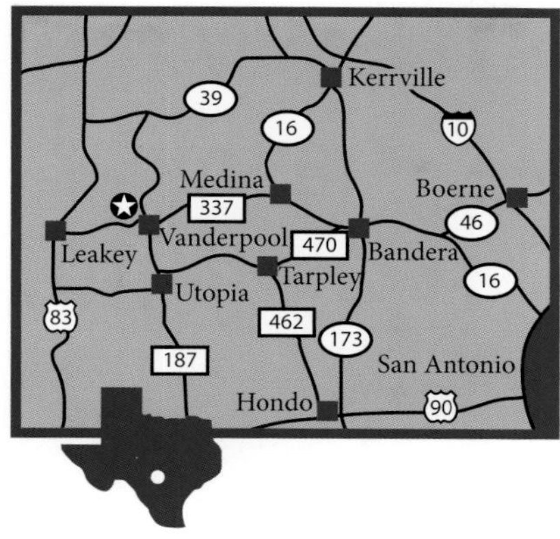

Some people believe that fall color in Texas is a contradiction in terms. However, hidden deep in an area of remote Hill Country canyons lies a fall color display that rivals any found in New England. Lost Maples State Natural Area contains some of the most scenic of these canyons.

Some of the most rugged terrain of the Texas Hill Country lies along the southern margin of the Edwards Plateau, a large piece of the earth's crust uplifted along the ancient Balcones Fault. Rivers, such as the Sabinal, Frio, Medina, and their tributaries, have cut deep canyons into the southern edge of the plateau near the towns of Leakey, Vanderpool, and Medina. Because these canyons are deeper and more steep-walled than in most other areas of the Hill Country, they provide more shelter from the sun and drying winds. Within this moist environment grows a unique community of plants, the most famous being the bigtooth maple.

Bigtooth maples grow in the Rocky Mountains, from Idaho through West Texas and into northern Mexico. Biologists believe that the trees at Lost Maples are relicts left from the last ice age. During this cooler and wetter time, the trees migrated eastward across Texas. When the climate became hotter and drier, the trees retreated west, surviving only in isolated pockets, such as the canyons of the natural area, where they receive extra shade and moisture. Small numbers of the maples also survive in two other central U.S. sites, Fort Hood and the Wichita Mountains of Oklahoma.

The fall color at Lost Maples is dependent on weather conditions during the preceding months. A combination of sunny days, cool fall nights, and adequate rainfall will spark a blazing display of gold, scarlet, and orange

Fall bigtooth maples in Hale Hollow

foliage from mid-October to mid-November. Two other trees that favor the deep moist canyons of Lost Maples, the black cherry and red oak, add their share of color during good years.

Other rare and interesting plants found at Lost Maples include the American smoketree, sycamore-leaf snowbell, common witchhazel, and canyon mockorange. One particularly interesting tree, the Texas madrone, thrives here. It boasts a distinctive smooth, thin, peeling bark that ranges in color from cream to maroon, complemented by bright red berries and evergreen leaves.

Other more common trees grow with the maples in the canyon bottoms, including sycamores, pecans, oaks, and hackberries. Dense woodlands of Ashe juniper, red oak, and Lacey oak cloak the upper slopes, mixed with a sprinkling of Texas ash, black cherry, and other trees and shrubs. Grassland blankets most of the more exposed upland areas, along with scattered mottes of live oak, juniper, and other trees. One shrub, the mountain laurel, thrives here, blooming with fragrant purple flowers every year. Because the evergreen shrub is hardy and attractive, it has become a popular native landscaping plant in Texas.

Wildlife thrives in the rugged, undeveloped terrain. White-tailed deer are abundant, along with other mammals, such as the armadillo, raccoon, opossum, fox squirrel, and striped skunk. The bobcat, gray fox, and ringtail are common but rarely seen. The bear and wolf are very rare or extinct in the area, but mountain lions are occasionally seen. Many bird species flourish at Lost Maples, including the endangered black-capped vireo and golden-cheeked warbler.

Early peoples lived in the area possibly as much as 12,000 years ago. These early groups were nomadic and lived by hunting and gathering. In the 1700s, Apaches and Comanches moved into the area from the north and west. In 1762, the Spaniards established two short-lived, unsuccessful missions west of the natural area near Camp Wood. The first Anglo settlers arrived in the mid-1800s to cut cypresses for shingles, grow crops in the flat river bottoms, and raise livestock in the rugged hills. Like visitors to the natural area today, the Indians and early pioneers probably enjoyed the brilliant fall color of the bigtooth maples.

VISITOR INFORMATION

2174 acres. Open all year. Small developed campground with partial hookups and showers, along with primitive campsites for backpackers. Small museum and store at headquarters. Picnic area, nature trail, ten miles of hiking trails allow extensive backcountry exploration. Fall color usually occurs between mid-October and mid-November, but quality varies from year to year. To avoid crowds during fall, go on weekdays if possible. Arrive early and reserve campsites well ahead of time. Limited food, lodging, and gas are available in Vanderpool, Leakey, and Utopia. More extensive services can be found in Kerrville, Bandera, and Uvalde. For information: Lost Maples State Natural Area, 37221 FM 187, Vanderpool, TX 78885, (830) 966-3413.

OPPOSITE PAGE, TOP
Fall color
OPPOSITE PAGE, BOTTOM LEFT
Pond on Can Creek with fall maples
OPPOSITE PAGE, BOTTOM RIGHT
Backlit red oak
ABOVE
Maples and cherries along Sabinal River

Lyndon B. Johnson State Park and Historic Site

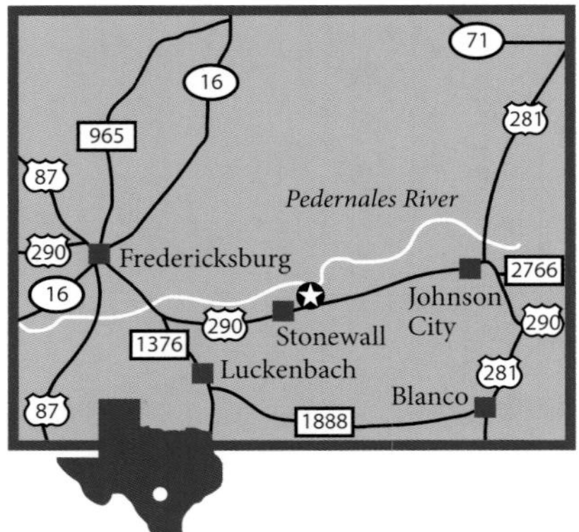

Lyndon B. Johnson State Park had its beginnings when friends of President Johnson raised money to buy the land across the Pedernales River from his ranch. The Texas Parks and Wildlife Commission accepted the land in 1965 and created the park to honor President Johnson as a "national and world leader."

Johnson, the 36th President of the United States, presided over a turbulent period of American history, marked by bitter disputes over the Vietnam War, civil rights, and expansion of government power. Exhibits in the visitor center describe the president's life in the Hill Country and display presidential mementos and items given to Johnson by heads of state and others during his period in office. A restored two-room dogtrot cabin built in the 1870s by Johannes Behrens is attached to the visitor center.

Another cabin in the park was built in the mid-1800s by Casper Danz, among the first of many German immigrants to settle in the Hill Country. The rustic wood and stone dogtrot cabin faces U.S. Highway 290 just west of the park entrance. In spring, fields of bluebonnets, Indian paintbrushes, and phlox surround the cabin, making it a popular subject with photographers.

The Sauer-Beckmann Farmstead, a working historical farm, is probably the most interesting feature of the park. Park employees recreate Hill Country farm life of about 1915 by wearing period clothes and operating the farm as it was at that time. They raise livestock, till a garden, can fruit, milk cows, butcher animals, make soap, smoke meat, and do the many other chores necessary to sustain a farm in those years. The farm was originally built by Johan Sauer and his family in the late 1800s, and was added to after the turn of the century by Herman Beckmann and his sons.

The park also offers a number of recreational opportunities, including a swimming pool, tennis courts, and a baseball field. Fishing is permitted in the Pedernales River, which borders the back side of the park along Ranch Road 1. Fenced pastures contain bison, longhorns, and white-tailed deer.

The state park lies in the heart of the Hill Country, between Johnson City and Fredericksburg. The Hill Country was created when a large piece of the earth's crust, called the Edwards Plateau, was uplifted about

2000 feet. Erosion of this plateau by creeks and rivers such as the Pedernales created a land of rolling limestone hills, broad valleys, and clear-running streams. A scrub forest dominated by live oak, Ashe juniper, Spanish oak, and cedar elm covers the slopes. The moist, deep soils along watercourses nourish bald cypresses, sycamores, pecans, and other trees. A nature trail connecting the visitor center and the Sauer-Beckmann Farm identifies and describes many Hill Country plants and animals.

Lyndon B. Johnson National Historical Park lies across the river from the state park and is operated by the National Park Service. The national historical park contains the LBJ ranch and house, the Junction schoolhouse (where Johnson first attended school), the former president's reconstructed birthplace, and the Johnson family cemetery. Tour buses that visit these sites start at the state park's visitor center. The National Park Service manages another unit of the park in nearby Johnson City.

VISITOR INFORMATION

733 acres. Open all year. No camping. Historic structures and exhibits, living-history farm. Bookstore in visitor center with wide array of LBJ, Hill Country, and Texas topics. Nature trails, picnicking, swimming pool, fishing, tennis courts, baseball field. Limited visitor services available in Stonewall, all services available in Johnson City and Fredericksburg. For information: LBJ State Park, P.O. Box 238, Stonewall, TX 78671, (830) 644-2252.

OPPOSITE PAGE, TOP
Sideboard and pitcher wth produce on porch
OPPOSITE PAGE, BOTTOM LEFT
Separating milk at Sauer-Beckmann Farm
OPPOSITE PAGE, BOTTOM MIDDLE
Canned goods
OPPOSITE PAGE, BOTTOM RIGHT
Lantern lighting
ABOVE
Bluebonnets and paintbrush by Casper Danz cabin

McKinney Falls State Park

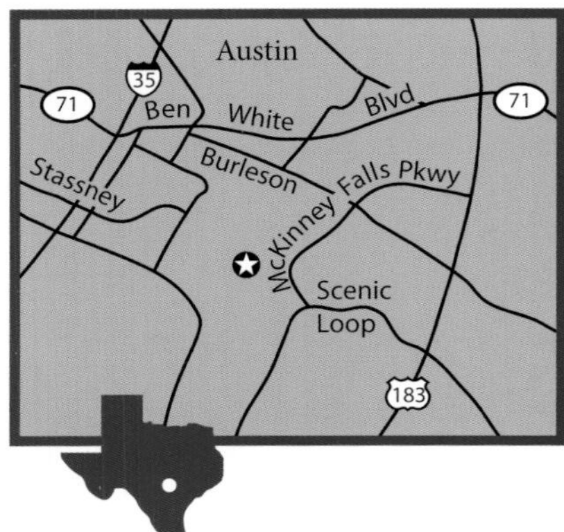

Two small waterfalls pour off limestone ledges and tumble into deep pools in Onion Creek not far from the center of Austin. McKinney Falls State Park provides a quiet, natural retreat from the noisy, busy city just beyond the park boundary. The highlights of the park, the upper and lower falls, were created when hard layers of limestone resisted erosion by the creek's water better than adjoining softer rocks. Eventually, the softer rocks eroded away, leaving higher ledges from which the water pours in cascades and falls.

Although the landscape around McKinney Falls is quiet today, at one time it was quite violent. The limestone layers exposed by Onion Creek were deposited in a shallow Cretaceous sea about 80 million years ago. When fractures broke the earth's crust along the Balcones Fault, hot molten rock, or magma, worked its way to the surface through these cracks. When the lava hit wet sediments and seawater, massive steam explosions erupted, forming craters around the vents and eventually islands in the shallow sea. Pilot Knob, the hill just to the south of the park, was one of these volcanoes. After the volcano became dormant, reefs built up around its edges. Wave action ground up shells and crumbled the rock. Later sediments buried the debris and compressed it into reef-beach rock that can be seen today at the falls.

Today, Onion Creek and its tributary Williamson Creek wind peacefully through the countryside, supporting a lush riparian woodland of bald cypresses, sycamores, pecans, and oaks. On the drier uplands away from the water, live oaks, Ashe junipers, prickly pears, and mesquites thrive. In spring, open areas often boast patches of wildflowers such as bluebonnets, Indian blanket, Indian paintbrush, and many other species.

In several places, the flowing waters of the creek have carved out large shelter caves from the limestone. Archaeologists have found extensive remains of prehistoric peoples in the shelters, which, apparently, were favored camping sites for many years.

In 1832, Santiago del Valle bought a large area around McKinney Falls from the Mexican state of Coahuila y Texas and became the site's first landowner. Later, in 1839, Thomas McKinney, one of Stephen F. Austin's original 300 colonists, bought part of the land from Michel Menard. McKinney was a prominent man who aided Texas during the war of independence, co-founded Galveston, and helped start the Texas Navy. He loved horses and retired to the McKinney Falls land to raise them. The ruins of his homestead, horse trainer's cabin, and grist mill lie within the park. Sadly, the Civil War and poor investments destroyed his wealth, and his widow sold the land after he died to pay creditors.

Ultimately the land was acquired by the Parks and Wildlife Department and opened as a state park in 1976. The rushing waters of Onion Creek are still the main attraction as they rush through channels of sculptured limestone and pour over the two small waterfalls. Swimming and fishing engage many park visitors, while others take the interpretive trail through one of the prehistoric rock shelters. Road cyclists enjoy the paved trail that winds through the campground and upland areas. Volcanoes may be part of McKinney Falls' past, but today the park allows a tranquil escape from the hustle and bustle of the city of Austin.

VISITOR INFORMATION

744 acres. Open all year. Hot and humid in summer. Relatively large campground with partial hookups and showers. Interpretive center, hiking, road biking, mountain biking, swimming, fishing, picnicking, nature trail. All visitor services available in Austin. For information: McKinney Falls State Park, 5808 McKinney Falls Parkway, Austin, TX 78744, (512) 243-1643.

Pedernales Falls State Park

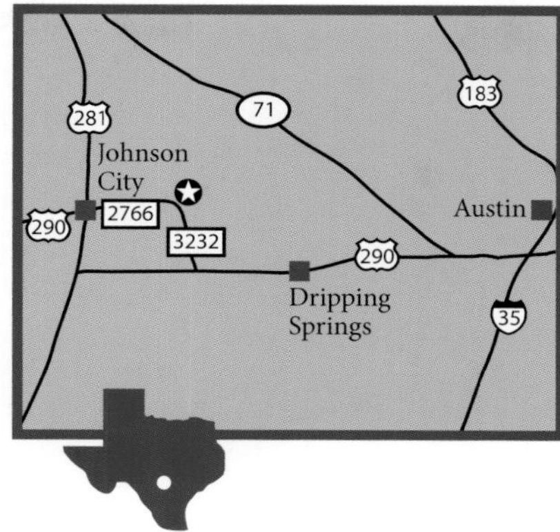

Crystal-clear water rushes over rocks and into deep pools, bubbling and foaming. It races through polished limestone chutes and cascades over ledges, drawn toward the sea by the relentless pull of gravity. Within the heart of the Texas Hill Country, the Pedernales River drops rapidly through a series of waterfalls and cascades in Pedernales Falls State Park.

The Pedernales River originates in the rolling hills west of Fredericksburg, but owes its fame to the section where it flows through the ranch of former President Lyndon B. Johnson. He often said that few places compared with the beauty of the Pedernales River and his beloved Hill Country. Some miles downstream from the LBJ ranch, the Pedernales flows into the state park. It enters a rocky canyon and runs into tilted beds of durable Marble Falls limestone. The Pennsylvanian period limestone was laid down about 300 million years ago and then was tilted in the succeeding time of Ouachita Mountain building. Overlying rocks

OPPOSITE PAGE
Lower McKinney Falls
RIGHT
Pedernales Falls

of the later Cretaceous period lie flat on top of the tilted Pennsylvanian rocks. Erosion of the Cretaceous rocks exposed the tilted Pennsylvanian rock layers. The falls and cascades of the river are formed as the water tumbles down over the tilted ledges.

Below the falls, the river calms and continues flowing downstream at a slower pace. Bald cypresses line the banks, although most are relatively small or stunted because of past floods. The Pedernales River is notorious for sudden, violent floods, making it difficult for streamside vegetation to become well-established. One of its most famous floods occurred in September 1952, when as much as 26 inches of rain fell on the watershed in three days. Massive flooding ensued, uprooting trees and washing out river-banks. A highway bridge upstream in Johnson City trapped debris, temporarily damming the river. When it broke, the resulting torrent did serious damage downstream in the park and elsewhere. Large sand deposits below the falls and the broken-off tops of cypress trees still serve as reminders of that flood. Since then, the park has installed sirens along the river to warn people of impending floods. If the sirens sound or if the river begins to rise, all visitors should immediately leave the river area and climb to higher ground.

The park lies in typical Hill Country terrain, a hilly landscape wooded with a scrub forest of live oaks, red oaks, and Ashe junipers. Dryland plants, such as the prickly pear and mesquite, are also common. Before the area was heavily grazed and natural fires suppressed, the Hill Country was grassier than it is today, and trees were less dominant. The Ashe juniper in particular has spread widely; it now blankets entire hillsides of the park. Juniper bark is a crucial nest-building material for the endangered golden-cheeked warbler. Areas with mixed shrubs, such as the mountain laurel, agarita, shin oak, and Mexican persimmon, are favored by another rare bird, the black-capped vireo.

The canyons of the river and its tributaries support plant life that is more lush. Pecans, sycamores, American elms, and bald cypresses thrive in the deeper, moister soils of the canyon bottoms. These areas are more protected from the sun and dry wind than are upland areas. The short Pedernales Hill Country Nature Trail introduces many of the plants and animals of the park. The highlight of the trail is an observation platform that overlooks the confluence of Bee and Regal creeks, two small tributaries of the river. Tiny cascades tumble into a fern-lined pool in the canyon bottom, shaded by towering bald cypresses unaffected by the 1952 flood. Because the site was heavily damaged by trampling in the past, entry is no longer allowed into this area. Enjoy the view from above.

The park offers plenty of recreational pursuits, including swimming and tubing in a designated area 2.5 miles below the falls. When the river is high, schools of shad sometimes make their way upstream to the falls. Fishing is allowed with a single pole or rod and reel.

Hikers and backpackers will enjoy the developed 8-mile Wolf Mountain Trail. It leads to a primitive backcountry camping area, viewpoints, historic sites, and the river. Mountain bikers can also enjoy the broad, relatively easy route. More adventurous hikers and mountain bikers may want to try the miles of trail in the primitive trail system across the river. Horseback riders can enjoy trails set aside for their use.

VISITOR INFORMATION

5212 acres. Open all year. Hot in summer, but river is cool and pleasant. Busy on spring, summer, and fall weekends. Moderate-sized campground with partial hookups and showers. Primitive campground for backpackers. Swimming and tubing allowed beginning 2.5 miles below the falls. Fishing, picnicking, hiking, mountain biking, horseback riding. All visitor services available in Johnson City. For information: Pedernales Falls State Park, 2585 Park Road 6026, Johnson City, TX 78636, (830) 868-7304.

ABOVE
Mountain biker
OPPOSITE PAGE
South Llano River

South Llano River State Park

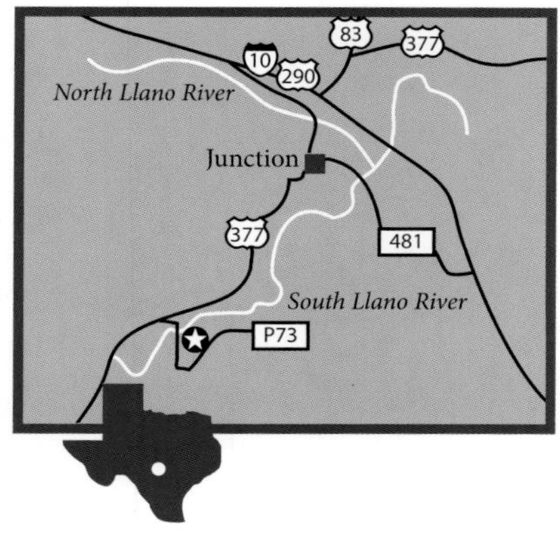

The clear, cool waters of the South Llano River wind through a broad valley a few miles upstream from the confluence with the North Llano River at the town of Junction. For a mile and a half in this broad valley, the South Llano River forms the north boundary of South Llano River State Park. Most of the park lies in the broad floodplain, a lush, shady area thickly wooded with large, majestic pecan trees and lesser numbers of cedar elms, live oaks, American elms, and chinkapin oaks.

The pecan bottomland of the park and adjoining properties is one of the largest and oldest winter roosting sites of the Rio Grande turkey in central Texas. Although the wild turkeys frequent the park all year, in winter as many as five hundred or more turkeys congregate in the floodplain. Because of the roost's importance, most of the bottomland is closed to visitors from October 1 through the end of March to prevent disturbance of the turkeys. However, the campground and other facilities are still open, including a blind that allows observation of the large, impressive birds. During the rest of the year, easy trails allow hikers and mountain bikers to travel through the open woodland, along the riverbank, and by two small oxbow lakes where fishermen can try their luck.

The headwaters of the South Llano River rise some miles to the southwest in Edwards County. Water levels fluctuate depending on rainfall, but springs ensure that the river always flows. In the warm months, the cool water attracts canoeists and tubers. Various access points allow trips of differing lengths, both within the park and on adjoining sections of river. In shallow areas, where the water flows over gravel bars, canoes may scrape bottom, but overall, the river offers easy, enjoyable float trips.

Additional recreational opportunities exist in the adjoining Walter Buck Wildlife Management Area. In 1977, Walter Buck donated the land for the wildlife management area, along with the state-park land, to the state for wildlife protection and enjoyment by the public. The 2123-acre wildlife management area begins at the south side of the state park, at the edge of the valley bottom. Unlike the broad, relatively flat bottomland of the state park, it consists of rugged, hilly terrain typical of the Texas Hill Country. Along with a blanket of grasses, stunted Ashe junipers and live oaks dot the hills. The small ravines and canyons are more lushly vegetated with larger trees and thicker grasses. Wildlife, such as white-tailed deer, turkeys, rabbits, and armadillos, is common. The rare black-capped vireo can sometimes be seen.

Several miles of old ranch roads provide access to the wildlife management area for mountain bikers and hikers. One short, steep hike leads to a scenic overlook that gives tremendous views of the park bottomlands and river valley. At various times of the year, parts or all of the wildlife management area may be closed because of wildlife management activities or endangered species protection.

Through the generosity of Walter Buck, the combined state park and wildlife management area protect important wildlife habitat and offer a broad range of recreational activities.

VISITOR INFORMATION

524 acres. Open all year. Some parts of the park may be closed at various times, as described above. Hot in summer. Moderate number of campsites with partial hookups and showers. Small number of walk-in tent sites. Wildlife viewing, hiking, mountain biking, fishing, canoeing, tubing, picnicking. Local businesses rent canoes and tubes. All visitor services available in Junction. For information: South Llano River State Park, 1927 Park Road 73, Junction, TX 76849, (325) 446-3994.

Panhandle Plains

ALTHOUGH MUCH OF THE Panhandle and adjoining Rolling Plains to the east are flat and treeless, the region contains a number of parks that are scenic and historic jewels, including Palo Duro Canyon, arguably the best-known state park in Texas. Other Panhandle parks contain red-rock scenery, the ruins of frontier forts, and water-recreation areas.

The High Plains, also known as the Llano Estacado, cover much of the Panhandle. The very flat grassy plains are the smooth surface of a broad sheet of debris washed eastward from the slopes of the Rocky Mountains of New Mexico and southern Colorado. Eventually the Pecos River cut its way headward through eastern New Mexico and into northern New Mexico, and intercepted the mountain streams that had been depositing sediment in the Panhandle. The Pecos cut a broad valley, leaving the High Plains as a large, isolated, eastward-tilting plateau. The sediment layers have become an important water-bearing aquifer, the Ogallala.

Erosion continues to gnaw away at the edges of the High Plains. Tributaries of the Pecos River continue to cut into the western edge of the plains, while the Red, Canadian, and Brazos rivers carve their way into the eastern margin. Only the Canadian River has managed to cut its way through the High Plains into northern New Mexico, but eventually the Red River and other rivers will slice all the way across the plains.

The area east of the High Plains is commonly known as the Rolling Plains. The gently rolling terrain is not quite as flat at the High Plains, is considerably lower in elevation, and tends to be more brushy. Rainfall increases to the east across Texas, giving the eastern part of the Rolling Plains significantly more precipitation than the High Plains.

A steep escarpment creates a dramatic division between the High Plains and Rolling Plains. Deep, sheer-walled canyons, mostly tributaries of the Red River, cut westward into this escarpment, exposing colorful walls of red, ocher, and lavender sandstones and shales. The most spectacular example is the 800-foot-deep Palo Duro Canyon. Other rugged canyons lie within Caprock Canyons State Park.

Several state parks preserve important historical sites in this part of Texas. The ruins of Fort Griffin and Fort Richardson are remnants of the frontier days of Texas. Abilene, Big Spring, and many other Texas state parks still utilize the buildings and facilities constructed by the Civilian Conservation Corps during the Depression of the 1930s.

Modern-day visitors to the Panhandle Plains parks enjoy hiking, camping, picnicking, and historical museums. A unique feature at Caprock Canyons is the 64-mile-long Caprock Canyons Trailway. Hikers, mountain bikers, and equestrians enjoy the former railroad grade as it descends from the High Plains to the Rolling Plains down canyons, across high trestles, and through a long tunnel.

Fishing and water sports are popular at lake parks in the eastern part of the region. Two of the parks, Possum Kingdom and Lake Brownwood, are far enough east to take on some of the ecological characteristics of the adjoining Hill Country and Prairies and Lakes regions. Scrubby oaks, cedar elms, and Ashe junipers dot the hills of these parks, unlike in the mostly treeless areas farther west.

Panhandle Plains

1 Abilene State Park

2 Big Spring State Park

3 Caprock Canyons State Park and Trailway

4 Copper Breaks State Park

5 Fort Griffin State Park and Historic Site

6 Fort Richardson State Park, Historic Site, and Lost Creek Reservoir State Trailway

7 Lake Arrowhead State Park

8 Lake Brownwood State Park

9 Lake Colorado City State Park

10 Palo Duro Canyon State Park

11 Possum Kingdom State Park

12 San Angelo State Park

Abilene State Park

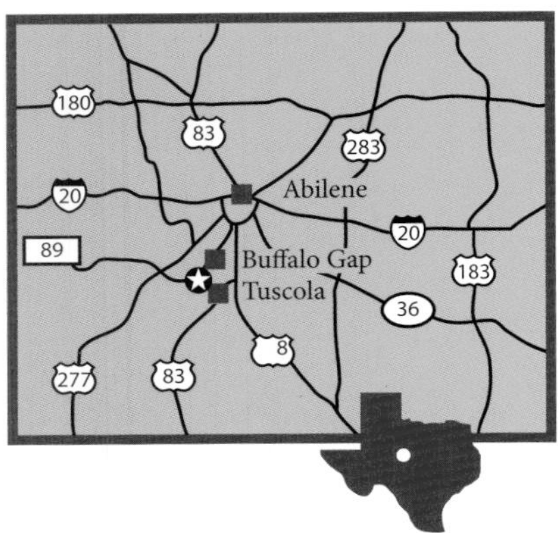

Much of the country surrounding the city of Abilene is rolling grassland dotted with mesquite that is hot and dry much of the year. First-time visitors to Abilene State Park may be surprised to find a wooded oasis on the banks of Elm Creek. The park lies in a valley surrounded by the low limestone hills of the Callahan Divide, south of the city of Abilene. The divide is an area of higher country that separates the watersheds of the Brazos and Colorado rivers. The hills are sparsely wooded with mesquite and stunted junipers, but Elm Creek waters a lush ribbon of woodland.

Pecans, live oaks, red oaks, willows, hackberries, and elms provide a thick canopy of shade in the creek's floodplain. People were attracted to the site long before it became a state park. Comanches, Tonkawas, and many other Indian groups camped in the shade of the thick woodland lining Elm Creek before the area was settled by American pioneers.

The Civilian Conservation Corps did much of the early development of the park. The organization was created in the 1930s to employ young men during the hard times of the Depression. The most prominent reminders of the men's labors are the stone water tower and swimming pool complex, still the centerpiece of the park today. The men used a rust-red sandstone quarried locally for construction material. The masonry arches and intricate stonework of the pool complex have proved both durable and attractive. A roofed observation platform on top of the concession building gives an overview of the pool and the surrounding hills.

The area surrounding the park is also important historically. From prehistoric times to the present, the woods and waters of Elm Creek have attracted people from the surrounding semiarid country. A few miles north of the park lies the small town of Buffalo Gap, the first county seat of Taylor County. It is located in a break in the hills of the Callahan Divide, also known as Buffalo Gap. The gap created an easy travel route through the hills and was used for many years by thousands of buffalo during their seasonal migrations. Indians used the travel route, and the gap was later used by cattle drives and the Butterfield Stage.

Today, kids splash in the large pool and campers relax in the shade of the bottomland forest. Lake Abilene, adjoining the park to the west, offers fishing and boating.

VISITOR INFORMATION

529 acres. Lake Abilene adds approximately 1200 additional acres. Open all year. Swimming pool open Memorial Day weekend through Labor Day. Call for exact schedule. Hot in summer. Large number of campsites with partial hookups and showers. Group trailer area. Screened shelters. Hiking, picnicking, fishing, Texas longhorn herd. All visitor services available in Abilene; limited services in Buffalo Gap. For information: Abilene State Park, 150 Park Road 32, Tuscola, TX 79562, (325) 572-3204.

ABOVE
Elm Creek
RIGHT
CCC-built swimming pool
OPPOSITE PAGE
Limestone rimrock at Big Spring State Park

Big Spring State Park

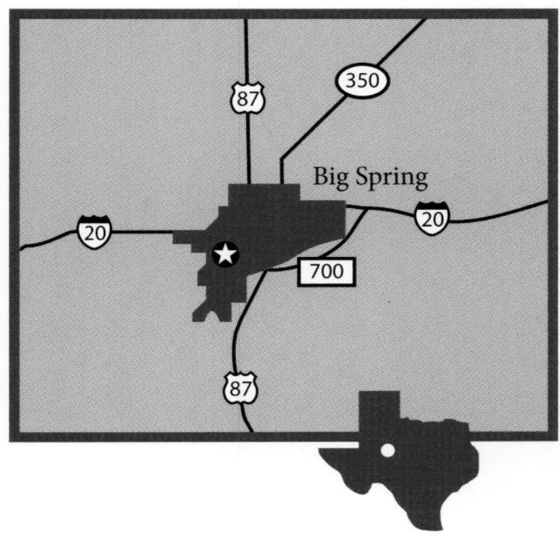

Much of west-central Texas is a relatively flat, dry region noted for its geographic monotony. At Big Spring State Park, however, the northern limit of the Edwards Plateau is reached, culminating in a series of bluffs rising 200 feet above the Rolling Plains. The Edwards Plateau is a vast, relatively flat upland area stretching as far southeast as Austin and San Antonio. Thick beds of Lower Cretaceous limestone form the plateau, deposits of an ancient sea that once covered much of Texas. The eastern and southern parts of the plateau have been cut by rivers and streams into hilly terrain known as the Hill Country.

Big Spring State Park caps one of the limestone bluffs at the northern edge of the plateau. Below the bluff, known as Scenic Mountain, sprawls the town of Big Spring, named for a large spring that once flowed nearby. As happened with many West Texas springs, excessive groundwater pumping ended its flow.

Vegetation typical for the semiarid region blankets the park. Bigger plants include mesquite, scrubby shin oak, and redberry juniper. Prickly pear and other cacti are common on the rocky slopes of the park. Wildlife, such as cottontails, jackrabbits, and roadrunners, is common, particularly early or late in the day. Even a small prairie-dog town lies in a little valley on the south side of the park.

In the past, Comanches and earlier Indian groups frequently visited the park area, probably attracted by the permanent source of spring water. Spaniards may have first visited the area as early as 1768, but the first recorded mention of the spring is from an October 3, 1849, entry in the journal of Captain R. B. Marcy.

The park was acquired by the state in 1934 and developed shortly thereafter by the Civilian Conservation Corps (CCC), an organization created during the Depression to employ young men unable to find jobs. Using limestone quarried on the site and quality workmanship, the CCC built the pavilion, headquarters, park residence, pumphouse, and restroom. Its biggest project was the three-mile drive that loops around the mountain. Retaining walls for the drive were built using large blocks of limestone—some weighing as much as two tons—and mortarless masonry techniques.

The CCC-built loop road is the highlight of the park. Most of the route follows the edge of the limestone rimrock capping the bluff. Early in the morning, before park gates open to cars, joggers, walkers, and cyclists from the city of Big Spring circle the loop, enjoying the dramatic views as they exercise. Later, others drive the loop, enjoying the same views as the early morning visitors. Today the city sprawls out across the valley below, and Interstate 20 transports high volumes of traffic east and west across Texas. Not so long ago, however, Comanches visited the spring and U.S. Cavalry troops trekked across the empty country.

VISITOR INFORMATION

382 acres. Open all year. Hot in summer. Limited number of campsites without hookups; no showers. Pavilion can be reserved for group functions. Picnicking, nature and hiking trails, Fourth of July fireworks display, interpretive center, combined scenic drive and walking route. All visitor services available in Big Spring. For information: Big Spring State Park, #1 Scenic Drive, Big Spring, TX 79720, (432) 263-4931.

Caprock Canyons State Park and Trailway

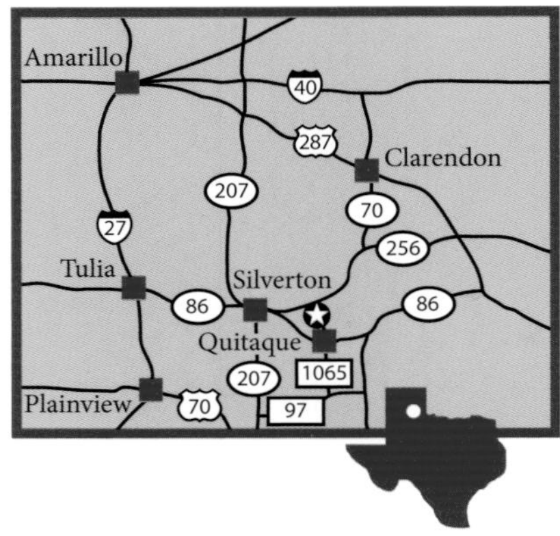

Caprock Canyons State Park and Trailway provides a startling contrast to the flat plains that make up most of the Texas Panhandle. Within the park, the flat, high plains of the Llano Estacado give way to the lower Rolling Plains in a long, serrated, red-rock escarpment as much as 1000 feet high.

A million years ago, the High Plains of the Panhandle were a smooth surface of material eroded from the southern Rocky Mountains and washed eastward along a very gentle slope. The Pecos, Canadian, and Red rivers slowly cut valleys upstream in a process called headward erosion. In time, the Pecos and Canadian rivers cut all the way through the High Plains and diverted flow from across them. The High Plains, also known as the Llano Estacado, were left as an isolated plateau.

The Red River also cut into the Llano Estacado, but was slowed by thick beds of red sandstone. Erosion by the river cut deep, narrow canyons in the durable rock rather than the broad valleys carved by the Pecos and Canadian rivers. Interestingly, the 1300-mile Red River is one of the longest rivers in North America that does not originate in mountains. It continues to erode the Llano Estacado today, the narrow fingers of its canyons and tributaries slowly cutting westward from the lower plains to the east. The most prominent canyon is Palo Duro, but Caprock Canyons State Park contains two impressive smaller canyons, the North and South Prongs of the Little Red River.

Humans arrived at least 10,000 years ago, building campsites near what is now Lake Theo, as well as in other areas. The earliest documented people, members of what is known as the Folsom culture, are identified by the distinctive design of their projectile points. Their craftsmen carefully chipped a large flake from the base of each side of the point and then

Caprock's rugged margin

mounted it on a spear that was used to kill large animals. These early people were nomadic and followed game across the High Plains, as did many later groups. Contrary to modern myth, these hunter-gatherer groups did not leave the land undisturbed. They used fire to encourage grassland growth and to help with hunting. Many archaeologists now believe that they contributed to the extinction of many Pleistocene mammals, including the mammoth, the giant bison, and a species of camel.

More recent cultures utilized pottery and the bow and arrow to improve their standard of living. Starting about a thousand years ago, some groups established permanent settlements and began cultivating crops of beans, corn, and squash. The Spaniards first appeared in 1541, with Coronado's epic journey across the High Plains. The Comanches arrived from the north in the early 1700s, establishing a nomadic culture centered around bison hunting using horses acquired from the Spaniards. In the late 1800s, Anglo settlers founded towns and vast cattle ranches across the High Plains.

The state park preserves a large area of rugged canyons on the eastern margin of the High Plains. Some of

ABOVE
Windmill and distant thunderstorm at sunset

LEFT
Clarity Tunnel with backpacker

to spectacular viewpoints on Haynes Ridge. Two backcountry campsites allow overnight backpacks along the hiking trails. A large loop trail draws equestrians to another section of Caprock Canyons. Small Lake Theo, fed by Holmes Creek on the south side of the park, offers fishing and boating opportunities. The park is home for the official Texas State Bison Herd. Caprock Canyons State Park and Trailway, one of the largest in Texas, provides a welcome change from the flat terrain of most of the Panhandle.

VISITOR INFORMATION

15,314 acres. Open all year. Hot in summer during the day, but cools off pleasantly at night. Occasional snowstorms in winter. Developed campgrounds with partial hookups and showers. Walk-in tent campgrounds in attractive setting in mouth of South Prong Canyon and at Little Red. Primitive backcountry campsites for backpackers and equestrians in North and South Prong canyons and along Trailway. Picnicking, fishing, limited boating. Limited visitor services available in nearby Quitaque. All services available in Plainview. For information: Caprock Canyons State Park and Trailway, P.O. Box 204, Quitaque, TX 79255, (806) 455-1492.

the plants tucked away in the deep canyons, such as the Rocky Mountain juniper, are at the limit of their range. Bison, wolves, and black bears no longer roam the canyon country, but mule deer, bobcats, coyotes, porcupines, jackrabbits, and many other animals are common. Aoudads, a sheep native to northern Africa, were introduced nearby in 1957 and have thrived. Although they are an interesting addition to the rugged canyon country of the Red River, they compete directly with the native mule deer for food.

The park offers one of the most unique features of any state park. A railroad line abandoned in the 1980s that passes by the park was converted to a combination hiking, biking, and equestrian trail. The 64-mile route traverses rugged Quitaque Canyon, a long railroad tunnel, and many tall trestles as it climbs its way up from the Rolling Plains onto the High Plains. With several access points, trips of many different distances can be arranged. By setting up a car shuttle, hikers, mountain bikers, and equestrians can do a one-way, mostly downhill run from the west end of the trail high on the Caprock down into Quitaque through the most scenic section of the trail.

In addition to the converted railroad trail, visitors are attracted to the many miles of trail within the park, particularly those that climb up the North and South Prong canyons

ABOVE
Eroded red rock, Quartermaster formation, sunrise
OPPOSITE PAGE
Lake Copper Breaks

Copper Breaks State Park

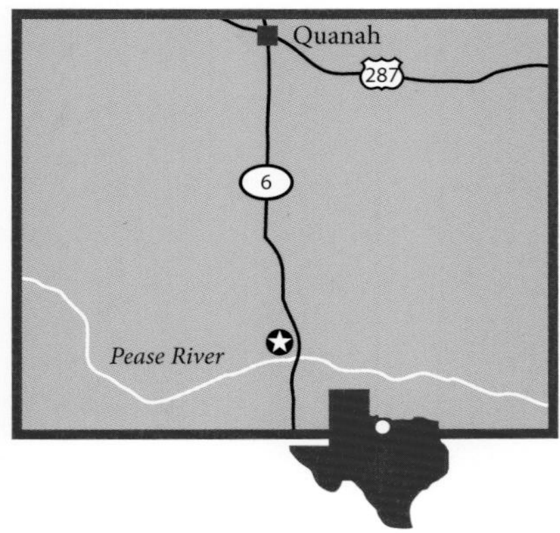

Copper Breaks State Park lies in the vast, lonely rolling plains north of Abilene, near the Red River. Grass- and mesquite-covered mesas are broken up by low, reddish cliffs and juniper-covered escarpments along the Pease River. Old copper-mining activities in the area gave the park its name.

Comanches arrived in the Copper Breaks area in the 1700s, mounted on horses obtained from the Spaniards. For more than 150 years, they followed a nomadic lifestyle of hunting bison and raiding. In 1860, some troops led by Captain Sul Ross caught a group of Comanches near the park and recaptured Cynthia Ann Parker, a young white woman captured 24 years earlier as a small child by a Comanche raiding party near Mexia. She had grown up with the tribe, and when she was reunited with her relatives, she did not adjust well to the white man's ways. She died only a few years later, supposedly of a broken heart. Her son, Quanah Parker, became the last great war chief of the Comanches.

The broken country along the Pease River consists of layers of shale, clay, and gypsum deposited more than 230 million years ago during the Permian period. In places, greenish rock and soil indicates copper mineralization. The prairie region once supported extensive grasslands, but many years of heavy livestock grazing and fire suppression have encouraged invasion by mesquite, red-berry juniper, prickly pear, and other shrubby plants. In moist areas along the river, in canyon bottoms, and around ponds, cottonwoods, western soapberries, hackberries, and willows provide welcome shade. Commonly seen wildlife includes cottontails, hawks, roadrunners, mule and white-tailed deer, jackrabbits, raccoons, and many species of songbirds. More elusive creatures, such as beavers, porcupines, bobcats, coyotes, and even rare mountain lions, live in the broken country.

The state park provides an excellent escape for area residents. The small 60-acre Lake Copper Breaks offers a sandy beach for swimming, no-wake boating, and fishing. Largemouth bass, crappie, catfish, sunfish, and even rainbow trout, stocked in winter, challenge anglers. A smaller pond within the park affords additional fishing opportunities. Hiking and nature trails give access to the backcountry and lead from shady canyon bottoms to high viewpoints. An equestrian trail and campground allow horse owners to explore a system of old ranch roads on the north side of the park. The visitor center has excellent exhibits of the human and natural history of the area, and is dominated by a large, bronze sculpture of three bison.

VISITOR INFORMATION

1899 acres. Open all year. Hot in summer. Developed campground with partial hookups and showers, in two areas. Separate developed equestrian campground, primitive camp area for backpackers. Swimming, fishing, limited boating, volleyball court; hiking, equestrian, mountain-biking, and nature trails. Longhorn herd. Evening interpretive programs on summer weekends, outdoor play in June, exhibits in visitor center. Seasonal paddleboat rental, park store. Trout stamp required for trout fishing. All services available in Quanah; limited services in Crowell. For information: Copper Breaks State Park, 777 Park Road 62, Quanah, TX 79252, (940) 839-4331.

Fort Griffin State Park and Historic Site

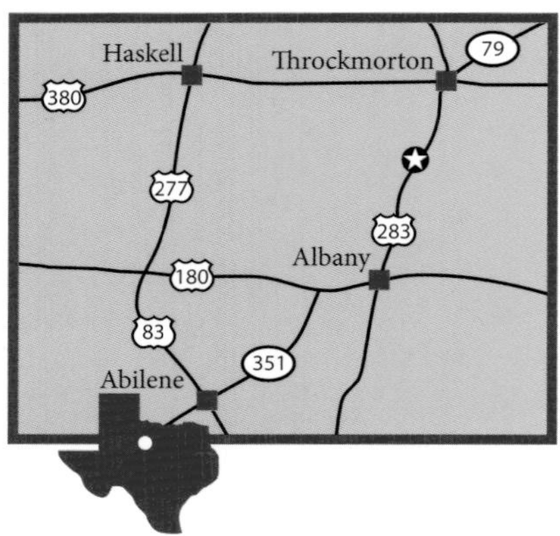

After the Civil War, the United States government re-garrisoned forts abandoned during the war and established new ones to protect travelers and settlers on the western frontier. Troops began building Camp Wilson on a high, mesquite-dotted bluff above the Clear Fork of the Brazos River in 1867 to protect buffalo hunters, settlers, travelers, and cattle herds from raids by Comanches and Kiowas. The following year the post was renamed Fort Griffin in honor of the late General Charles Griffin.

The plans called for an elaborate fort consisting of solidly built stone buildings. However, the troops were away from the fort on various campaigns too often to complete much of the original plan. Only five stone buildings were completed; the rest of the fort consisted of tents and crude huts built of rough lumber. In winter, the accommodations were drafty, cold, and miserable.

Over the years, a number of cavalry and infantry units were stationed at the fort, including units of the black buffalo soldiers. The troops provided escort duty to travelers and conducted long campaigns on the High Plains in search of raiding Indian parties.

Fort Griffin was the primary supply point for units attempting to force the Comanches onto Oklahoma reservations. Ultimately, Colonel Ranald Mackenzie drove the last of the Indians from the High Plains in the 1870s, helped by the extermination of their primary food source, the buffalo. With the defeat of the last of the Comanches, Fort Griffin's reason for existence ended, and it was abandoned in 1881.

Today, the only remaining structures are those built of stone. Of these the bakery is intact; the others are in arrested stages of decay. Little remains of the other buildings but scattered foundations. The park has reconstructed a few of the old wooden buildings.

Although the old fort is the main attraction, the park offers much more, including fishing in the Brazos River, camping, and hiking on the trails. Part of the official Texas longhorn herd grazes in park pastures.

VISITOR INFORMATION

506 acres. Open all year. Hot in summer. Small number of campsites with partial hookups and showers. Two group equestrian campsites. Historic buildings and interpretive exhibits, hiking and nature trails, picnicking, fishing, longhorn herd. All visitor services available in Albany. For information: Fort Griffin State Park and Historic Site, 1701 N. U.S. Highway 283, Albany, TX 76430, (325) 762-3592.

Fort Griffin ruins

Fort Richardson State Park, Historic Site, and Lost Creek Reservoir State Trailway

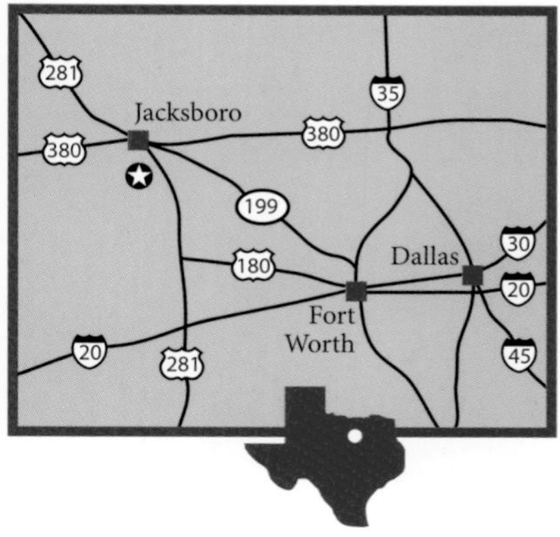

In 1867, the area around Jacksboro lay on the western edge of the frontier. Settlers and travelers were moving into the area, displacing Comanches, Kiowas, and other Indians. Violence and constant conflict resulted from the cultural clash, and had worsened in Texas during the Civil War when federal troops were withdrawn and the Confederacy was unable to effectively police the frontier. Fort Richardson was established as one of a line of outposts to protect people from the bloodshed.

With establishment of the fort, the settlement of towns, farms, and ranches increased in the area. Jacksboro grew, partly as a supplier of services for the fort. Within the fort, many buildings were constructed around the central parade ground. By 1878, the Indian problems had ended and the fort, once a thriving community, was abandoned. Many of the buildings no longer exist, but nine structures remain, including seven original buildings. Of these, the most impressive is the large two-story hospital. Original and recreated furniture, beds, cabinets, tables, supplies, and other items within the restored building show life as it was in the post hospital during the fort's active days. They show, too, how primitive medical techniques were back then, making visitors appreciative of modern medicine. Other remaining buildings of the fort include a reconstructed officers' barracks on the south side of the parade ground that today houses an interpretive center.

Although the old fort is the main attraction of the park, other features also draw many people. The fort lies in flat to rolling prairie country, blanketed with grass and scattered mesquite trees. Hidden in a narrow valley behind the fort lies Lost Creek, a permanent stream shaded with a dense woodland of live oaks, cedar elms, post oaks, hackberries, and other trees. Several springs tumble out from underneath the limestone ledges lining the creek and feed it their cold, clear waters. From a part of the campground that is tucked into the creek bottom, a short trail leads to Rumbling Spring. Another short, very well-constructed nature trail follows the creek from the campground to the picnic area, a shady walk on a hot summer day. On cooler days, a longer trail can be taken that winds through the open upland area of the park.

The creek is not the only surprise for park visitors. Behind the headquarters building, a former quarry has filled with water, providing opportunities for fishing. Anglers catch black bass, perch, and catfish from the small lake. The ten-mile-long Lost Creek Reservoir State Trailway passes through open prairie and patches of woodland near Lost Creek and along the shores of Lost Creek Reservoir and Lake Jacksboro, offering a lengthy scenic route for hikers, equestrians, and cyclists. Visitors may first visit the park to see the fort, but other lesser-known attractions encourage longer stays.

VISITOR INFORMATION

456 acres. Open all year. Hot in summer. Small number of campsites with full and partial hookups and showers. Primitive camping area. Screened shelters. Historic structures and interpretive center, hiking and nature trails, fishing, picnicking, swimming at Lost Creek Reservoir. All visitor services available in Jacksboro. For information: Fort Richardson State Park and Historic Site, 228 State Park Road 61, Jacksboro, TX 76458, (940) 567-3506.

Quarry Lake and visitors' center

Lake Arrowhead State Park

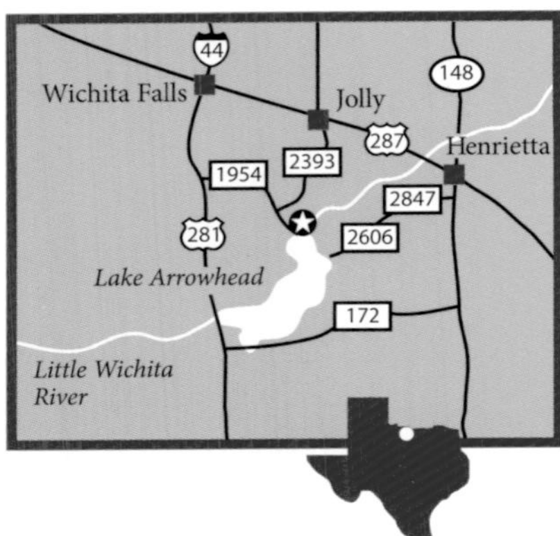

In the vast, flat prairies near Wichita Falls lies Lake Arrowhead, a magnet for area boaters and fishermen. The reservoir, which was built in 1965 by damming the Little Wichita River, provides one of Wichita Falls' water supplies. The three-mile-long earth-fill dam created a reservoir with a surface area of about 16,400 acres and a shoreline length of 106 miles. Because the terrain is relatively flat, the lake is shallow. Interestingly, a number of steel oil derricks dot parts of the lake surface, indicating petroleum reservoirs that lie deep under the lake waters.

The area is part of what is called the Rolling Plains, a vast area that stretches from the eastern part of the Texas Panhandle to east of Wichita Falls. The gently rolling terrain is open prairie, except along creeks and rivers where additional moisture allows woodlands to grow. Past grazing practices have allowed mesquite and other brushy plants to invade much of the rich grasslands. At the state park, grasses and mesquite are probably the most common plants.

Within the park, small animals, including raccoons, skunks, and prairie dogs, are the most commonly seen forms of wildlife. Waterfowl and wading birds frequent the lake, while crappie, catfish, bass, and perch swim through its waters. Fishing piers, a boat ramp, and a lengthy shoreline give anglers plenty of lake access. The waters around the oil derricks seem to favor good populations of fish and are popular fishing sites on the lake. Fishing and water sports, such as waterskiing, attract many people every year to Lake Arrowhead State Park.

VISITOR INFORMATION

524 acres. Open all year. Hot in summer. Moderate number of campsites with partial hookups and showers. Boating, swimming, waterskiing, fishing piers, boat ramps, picnicking, 18-hole disc-golf course, and hiking, nature, and equestrian trails. All visitor services available in Wichita Falls. For information: Lake Arrowhead State Park, 229 Park Road 63, Wichita Falls, TX 76310, (940) 528-2211.

Picnic area at Lake Arrowhead

Lake Brownwood State Park

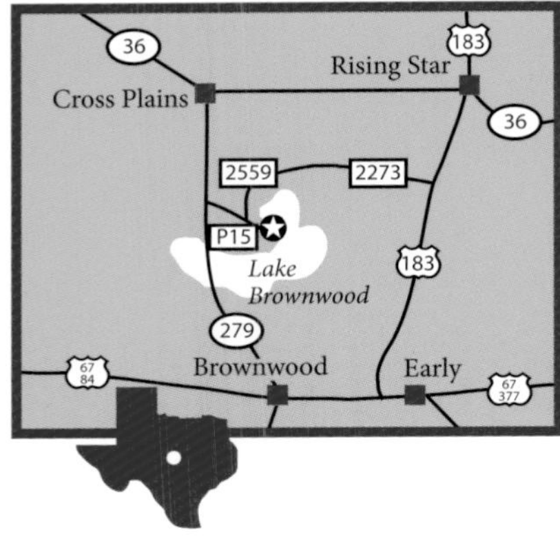

Popular Lake Brownwood State Park has drawn visitors to the North Texas area ever since it was developed in the 1930s. The park lies on the shore of Lake Brownwood, a 7300-acre lake that was created when a dam was built at the confluence of Pecan Bayou, a Colorado River tributary, and Jim Ned Creek. It was built in 1932 by the Civilian Conservation Corps (CCC), whose workers also built most of the basic facilities of the state park, including roads, cabins, and the notable recreation hall, constructed of locally quarried stone.

The park lies in an area of mixed habitats. Limestone bedrock in parts of the park encourages growth of Hill Country species such as live oak and Ashe juniper. Cedar elms and post oaks are more reminiscent of the Cross Timbers country to the northeast, while mesquite are common in the drier Rolling Plains to the northwest.

The recreation hall is situated on top of a hill in the middle of the park; its rooftop observation deck gives a good view of the park, lake, and surrounding rolling hills. Other good viewpoints lie along the park hiking trail, especially at its terminus on Council Bluff, a high ridge overlooking the lake.

The park has many attractions for visitors. A fishing pier and boat ramp provide easy lake access for boaters,

water skiers, and fishermen; the roads and trails attract hikers and cyclists; and historians are interested in the recreation hall, stone pavilions, and other buildings constructed by the CCC.

In the past, Comanches and earlier Indian groups frequented the banks of Pecan Bayou and Jim Ned Creek, drawn by water and abundant game. Settlers farmed the floodplains and ranched the hills around the lake. Today people come to Lake Brownwood State Park to relax and escape the hectic pace of modern life.

VISITOR INFORMATION

538 acres. Open all year. Hot in summer. Large number of campsites with partial or full hookups and showers. Cabins and screened shelters. Hiking and nature trails, picnicking, fishing pier, swimming, boat ramp, waterskiing. Park store. All visitor services available in Brownwood. For information: Lake Brownwood State Park, 200 Park Road 15, Brownwood, TX 76801, (325) 784-5223.

TOP
Lake Brownwood
ABOVE
Dusk, Lake Brownwood

Lake Colorado City State Park

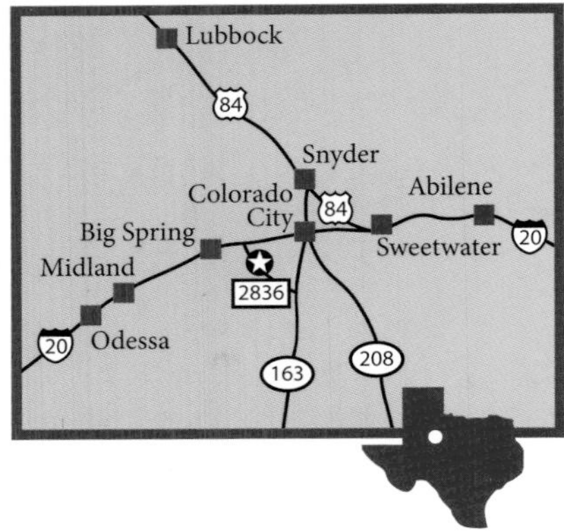

Lake Colorado City State Park lies off the southwest shore of Lake Colorado City, a small 1600-acre lake built on Morgan Creek, a tributary of the Colorado River. The dam is just upstream of the confluence of the river and Morgan Creek. The lake was created in 1949 to supply cooling water to a Texas Electric Service Company power plant. The plant, fueled with natural gas produced from area oil and gas fields, is the largest in West Texas.

The lake lies in the slightly rolling plains of west-central Texas. The climate is relatively dry, so the plains are generally treeless except along watercourses. Grasses and shrubs, particularly mesquite and juniper, cover the park uplands. Prickly pear and other cacti are also quite common.

The lake, combined with the channels of blue water that wind upstream along Morgan Creek and several smaller tributaries, provides a welcome contrast to the surrounding plains. Water skiers zip across the lake while small sailboats glide through the water, pushed by frequent West Texas breezes. Fishermen pursue bass, redfish, and catfish from the rocky shoreline, boats, and park fishing piers.

Because of the power plant, lake water stays warmer than normal for this area of the country. The warmer water extends the season for swimming and waterskiing, and provides a longer growing and feeding season for fish.

The town for which the lake is named originated as a construction camp for the Texas and Pacific Railroad in 1880, although it had been a Texas Ranger camp earlier. After the railroad was completed, the town developed as a supply and shipping center for area farms and ranches. Later, after oil and gas were discovered in the area, the petroleum industry became the most important part of the local economy. Creation of the lake not only provided water for the power plant and the town, it also created recreational opportunities still enjoyed today at Lake Colorado City State Park.

VISITOR INFORMATION

500 acres. Open all year. Hot in summer. Large number of developed campsites with partial hookups and showers. Limited-use cabins with heat, A/C, and electricity, but no plumbing. Boating, boat ramp, waterskiing, picnicking, swimming, fishing piers, nature trail. All visitor services available in Colorado City. For information: Lake Colorado City State Park, 4582 FM 2836, Colorado City, TX 79512, (325) 728-3931.

Fishermen

Palo Duro Canyon State Park

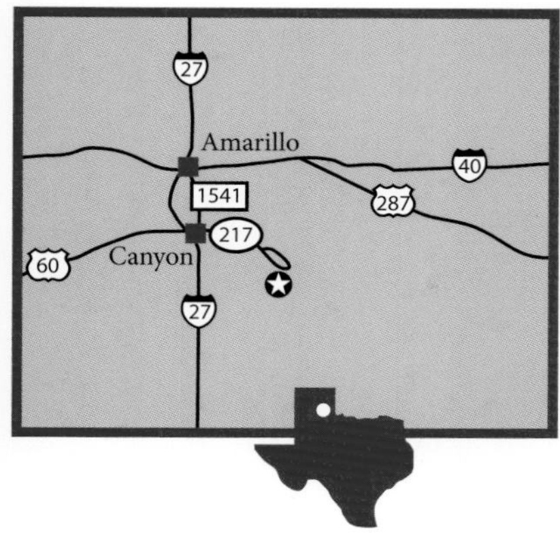

As you cross the High Plains south of Amarillo on the way to Palo Duro Canyon, the flat treeless country inspires only drowsiness. The horizon stretches to infinity, broken only by occasional windmills and ranches. Heat waves shimmer, and mirages seem to form pools of water on the pavement. Before you enter the park, a small canyon on the right side of the road might raise an eyebrow or two, but it only foreshadows what lies ahead. Boredom vanishes after you enter the park and drive to the first overlook on the rim of the canyon.

In startling contrast to the surrounding country, a massive 800-foot-deep abyss appears below, the flat plains dropping away abruptly. Cliffs of red, yellow, and purple color the scene. Scrubby forests of gnarled junipers soften the slopes and add greenery. At the bottom, a tiny creek flows downstream, its waters nourishing a narrow ribbon of lush cottonwoods.

Without a doubt, Palo Duro Canyon is one of the most spectacular sights in the Panhandle and one of the premier state parks in Texas. At one time it was even considered by the federal government for national park status. The common juniper trees gave the canyon its name; *palo duro* means "hard wood" in Spanish.

Visitors to the canyon are sometimes amazed that the tiny Prairie Dog Town Fork of the Red River could have carved the deep, 60-mile-long canyon. However, in the past the area received more rainfall, helping erosion to proceed more quickly. Anyone who has witnessed one of the canyon's notorious floods will not doubt the erosive power of the Prairie Dog Town Fork when filled with torrents of rushing water.

The colorful red rocks through which the creek has cut its canyon belong to several different geologic periods. The oldest rocks of the canyon, the bright red shales, clays, and sandstones of the Permian period, line the bottom and lower slopes of the canyon. These soft rocks, called the Quartermaster Formation, were formed about 250 million years ago in shallow waters on the edge of ancient seas. Slightly newer Triassic shales and sandstones, called the Trujillo and Tecovas, lie on top of the Permian rocks, and are distinguished by their multiple colors, often shades of yellow, pink, and lavender. The Trujillo, the top Triassic layer, is a hard sandstone that resists erosion better than the other rocks, so it forms cliffs and capstones on formations like the Lighthouse, the 75-foot-tall rock pinnacle that has become the canyon's trademark.

LEFT
Basket flowers below canyon wall
ABOVE
Fall cottonwood leaves on red sandstone

Above the Trujillo lies the Ogallala Formation, a mix of sandstone, siltstone, conglomerate, and caliche that is between two and ten million years old. The Ogallala is very porous and permeable and is an important aquifer for the Panhandle. Fossils of many different extinct species of mammals have been found in the formation. There is a gap in time of more than 200 million years between the Trujillo and the Ogallala. Either the intervening rocks eroded away, or they never existed.

The flat surface of the High Plains resulted when sediment that had eroded from the uplifted Rocky Mountains to the west was carried east and deposited in sheets across the plains. With time, the Pecos River eroded northward and "captured" mountain streams that had been flowing eastward across the plains. The Pecos ultimately cut a broad valley, and the High Plains were left as a large, flat, eastward-tilting plateau. The eastern edges of this plateau retreated westward over time as streams flowing toward the Gulf of Mexico eroded headward, leaving today's canyon-riddled escarpment. Only the Canadian River has managed to cut entirely across the High Plains in Texas, but the Prairie Dog Town Fork and other watercourses will continue to erode westward and eventually cut canyons all the way through the plains.

Palo Duro Canyon is more than just a geologic wonder. Its broken country harbors a mix of eastern and western plant and animal species, such as the Rocky Mountain juniper, left here after the Pleistocene ended and the climate warmed and dried. The Palo Duro mouse lives in the Red River canyonlands and nowhere else. Many different species of birds have been sighted here, almost 200 so far. Mule deer compete for browse with the introduced African aoudad, and before they were exterminated, wolves and bears haunted the canyon country.

Humans lived in the area as long as 12,000 years ago, hunting extinct ice-age animals such as the giant bison and the Jefferson's mammoth. Succeeding groups came and went, ending with the arrival of the Comanches in

the 1700s. For many years, Palo Duro Canyon and the surrounding plains were their domain from which they ventured forth to hunt buffalo and raid other Indian tribes, Mexicans, and Anglos. The last major Indian battle in Texas, the Battle of Palo Duro Canyon, brought the Comanches' reign to a close in 1874.

Francisco Vásquez de Coronado was probably the first European to see the canyon, when he made his epic journey through the Southwest and across the High Plains in 1541. Although hunting and trading parties, especially from New Mexico, ventured occasionally onto the plains, the canyon area was not settled until after the Comanches were defeated. Charles Goodnight established the first large cattle ranch in the area and was soon followed by others. Ranching and farming are still the predominant land uses in the area today.

The park offers much to visitors in addition to spectacular scenery. The Civilian Conservation Corps built many of the park roads and facilities during the Depression, many of which are still enjoyed today. During the summer, a large cast presents the elaborate musical drama *Texas*. The outdoor performance has been very successful since it started playing in 1966 and has drawn more than two million visitors. Horses can be rented in season to see part of the park. Hiking and mountain-bike trails lead to the Lighthouse and other back corners of the park. The scenic loop drive provides an excellent introduction to one of the largest and most famous state parks in Texas, Palo Duro Canyon.

VISITOR INFORMATION

16,402 acres. Open all year. Hot in summer during the daytime, pleasant at night. Can be quite cold and occasionally snowy in winter. Heed any park warnings on flooding of the creek; serious floods do occur. *Texas* plays nightly in summer, except on Sunday; call for exact dates, times, and prices. Relatively large number of campsites with partial hookups and showers; scattered in several locations. Primitive equestrian camp area and backpacking campsites. Fully equipped rental cabins on canyon rim with views; limited-use cabins with electricity, but no plumbing. Guided horse trips, park store, snack bar, longhorn herd. Interpretive museum, hiking, picnicking, mountain biking, equestrian trails. Full visitor services available in Canyon and Amarillo. For information: Palo Duro Canyon State Park, 11450 Park Road 5, Canyon, TX 79015, (806) 488-2227.

OPPOSITE PAGE
The Lighthouse rock formation
ABOVE
Rock spire with hiker

Possum Kingdom State Park

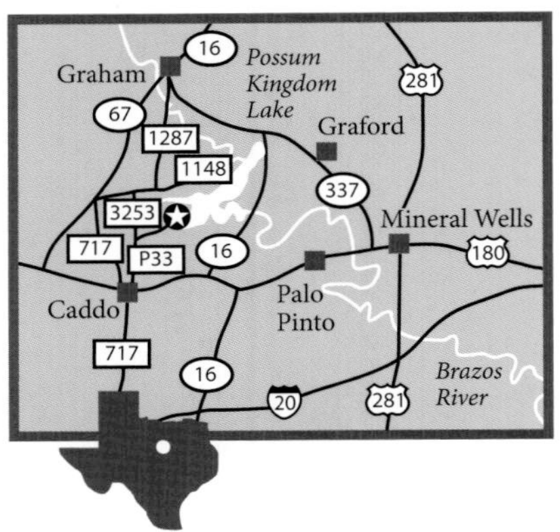

When Congress authorized the building of Morris Sheppard Dam on the Brazos River after World War II, the name of Possum Kingdom Lake was set by Congress because their legislation stated that the area was a "veritable paradise for opossums." The opossums still roam the hills of Possum Kingdom State Park, but today they are joined by thousands of people who come to enjoy the clear waters of the lake.

When the dam was built, it backed up a large 20,000-acre reservoir. Unlike many Texas lakes, Possum Kingdom winds like a snake, following the course of the meandering Brazos River. Because of its long, sinuous course, it has more than 300 miles of shoreline. The lake provides excellent opportunities for boating, swimming, and waterskiing, and the clear waters attract area scuba divers. Fishermen test their skill pursuing catfish, bass, crappie, and perch. The rocky shoreline of Possum Kingdom Lake provides a good habitat for black bass, which need such sites for spawning. Striped bass, the largest member of the bass family, is also a popular catch in the lake. Stripers normally live in saltwater, but move up rivers and streams to spawn in freshwater. By accident, it was discovered that they could survive year round in freshwater, and as a result they have been stocked in many Texas lakes.

Possum Kingdom State Park is a great access point to Possum Kingdom Lake, and offers a relaxing escape from the nearby cities of Fort Worth, Wichita Falls, and Abilene.

The state park lies on the west side of the lake on the edge of a relatively hilly area of North Texas known as the Palo Pinto Mountains. The rocks that make up the mountains, the canyons of the Brazos River, and the rocky lakeshore are limestones, shales, and sandstones. The most prominent is the Winchell Limestone, the white rock that makes up the towering cliffs at the dam and lower parts of the lake. The rocks were formed about 280 million years ago during the Pennsylvanian period, when an ancient sea filled the Permian Basin to the west. Rich deposits of petroleum, coal, and clay were created during this time, many of which are still produced in the area today.

The park lies on the western edge of the Cross Timbers area, known for its thick woods of stunted Ashe junipers, cedar elms, oaks, and mesquite interspersed with strips of prairie. Here at the drier, western side of the region, Ashe junipers seem to dominate. White-tailed deer and small mammals such as rabbits, raccoons, and of course opossums are common. Hell's Gate, a pair of tall cliffs that frame a narrow spot on the lake, hosts a noisy colony of cliff swallows that greet visitors to the lake, one of the most popular spots in North Texas.

VISITOR INFORMATION

1529 acres. Hot in summer. Large number of campsites with partial hookups and showers, plus walk-in primitive campsites. Cabins. Boating, hiking, cycling, waterskiing, picnicking, swimming, boat ramp, lighted fishing pier. Store, marina, and boat rental. All visitor services available in Breckenridge and Graham. For information: Possum Kingdom State Park, P.O. Box 70, Caddo, TX 76429, (940) 549-1803.

Waterskier on Possum Kingdom Lake

San Angelo State Park

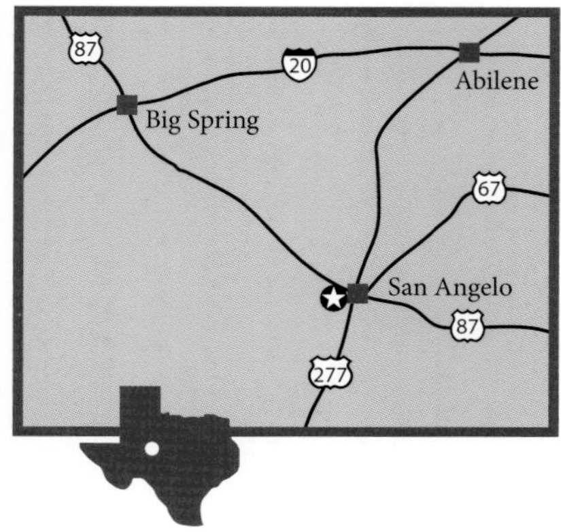

San Angelo State Park lies on the shores of O. C. Fisher Reservoir, just west of the city of San Angelo. The 5440-acre lake was created by the U.S. Army Corps of Engineers in 1952 by damming the North Fork of the Concho River. The reservoir provides flood control, water storage, and recreation.

O. C. Fisher Reservoir lies just upstream from the North Concho River's confluence with the Middle and South Concho River forks. The river, ultimately a tributary of the Colorado River, drains a large area of country in a broad arc from northwest to west to south of San Angelo. The river takes its name from the Spanish word for *shell*, because of the plentiful freshwater mussels found in its waters. These mussels sometimes produce pearls prized for their iridescent colors, particularly purple.

The park contains a mix of habitats. It is located on the far western edge of the Hill Country, with some plants and animals common to that part of the state. However, the climate this far west is considerably drier than most of the Hill Country, and is greatly influenced by the deserts of the Trans-Pecos. The oaks, pecans, and cedar elms common in most of the Hill Country become scarce here and grow mostly only in moist bottomlands. Mesquite is probably the most common tree. The Rolling Plains and High Plains to the north also contribute some plant and animal species.

Various Indian groups once dominated the area. The Spaniards were the first Europeans to arrive, as they attempted to extend their empire and convert the Indians to Christianity. Later, the area fell under the dominion of Mexico, the Republic of Texas, the Confederacy, and the United States. The first settlers in the area sustained themselves with farming and ranching. Fort Concho was established in 1867 to protect western travelers and settlers. It was decommissioned in 1889, but many of the original buildings still stand.

Today the park offers plenty of recreational opportunities. It was originally operated by the U.S. Army Corps of Engineers, but was taken over in 1995 by the Texas Parks and Wildlife Department. At present, the park offers many lake activities, including bass and catfish fishing, swimming, and boating.

VISITOR INFORMATION

7677 acres. Open all year. Hot in summer. Campgrounds with and without partial hookups and showers. Equestrian campsites with partial hookups. Primitive backpacking campsites. Limited-use cabins with heat, A/C, and electricity, but no kitchens. More than 50 miles of trails for hiking, mountain biking, horseback riding. Fishing platform, swimming, waterskiing, boat ramps, boating. Tours of petroglyphs, dinosaur tracks, longhorn herd, bison, and prairie-dog town. All visitor services available in San Angelo. For information: San Angelo State Park, 3900-2 Mercedes, San Angelo, TX 76901, (325) 949-8935.

Sunrise over O. C. Fisher Reservoir

Pineywoods

A THICK WOODLAND OF pines and hardwoods blankets the East Texas region known as the Pineywoods. Plentiful rain, as much as 50 inches or more per year, fuels lush forest growth and creates a humid climate. In the southern part of the region, near Beaumont, the land is very flat and low-lying. This area of southeastern Texas is dominated by the Big Thicket, a large ecological region that once covered 3.5 million acres but has now been reduced to less than 300,000 acres. The Big Thicket contains a variety of habitats, from cypress sloughs to grassy prairies to a climax forest of towering magnolias, beeches, and loblolly pines. An interesting mix of plants and animals from the east and west meet in the thicket. Yuccas, prickly pears, and roadrunners thrive only a few hundred feet from southern orchids and water tupelos. Much of the low lying Big Thicket is wetland, with cypress sloughs, sluggish rivers, and palmetto flats. Two state parks, Village Creek and Martin Dies, Jr., lie in or on the edge of the Big Thicket.

To the north of the Big Thicket, the land begins to roll with gentle hills. Deep woods of oaks, sweetgums, longleaf and loblolly pines, hickories, and other trees stretch north to the Red River, interrupted by cleared fields and urban areas. Wildlife is plentiful, from white-tailed deer and wild turkeys to alligators. Black bears and red wolves once roamed much of East Texas but are gone now.

Lakes attract many people to the state parks in the Pineywoods region. Some of the parks, such as Huntsville and Tyler, have small no-wake lakes perfect for canoes and paddleboats. Quite a few others, including Lake Livingston and Lake Bob Sandlin, offer vast expanses of open water perfect for sailing and waterskiing. All of the lakes, whether large or small, attract fishermen hoping to catch largemouth bass, stripers, crappie, catfish, and other species.

Caddo Lake State Park lies on the upper end of a particularly unique lake. Caddo Lake is the only significant lake in Texas that was formed naturally, although a dam now maintains the water level. A large logjam on the Red River downstream in Louisiana created the lake in about 1800. The jam, which stretched for 100 miles and was as much as 25 feet high, backed up enough water into Big Cypress Bayou to create Caddo Lake and a navigable waterway to Jefferson, upstream from the lake. Steamboats plied the lake's waters until 1874, when the Army Corps of Engineers blew the logjam apart and lowered lake levels. Today cypresses cloaked with Spanish moss grow from the lake, creating a mysterious, primeval feel. Anglers find the most diverse fishing in Texas here, with 71 different species.

A number of Pineywoods parks commemorate historic sites. Steam engines of the Texas State Railroad chug 25 miles through the lush woods between Rusk and Palestine, preserving an element of turn-of-the-century Texas life. A replica of an early seventeenth-century mission at Mission Tejas marks the unsuccessful Spanish effort to colonize East Texas. At Caddoan Mounds, Caddo Indians built three ceremonial mounds, the most southeasterly site of the Mound Builder Culture of the eastern United States.

The Pineywoods parks offer more than lake recreation and historic sites. Hiking and mountain-biking trails wind through the woods of many parks, and canoeing is possible on quiet creeks and cypress sloughs. Most of the parks provide campgrounds and picnic areas. Good fall color dots the woods of Daingerfield, and the cypresses turn burnt orange at Caddo Lake in most years. For many reasons, the East Texas parks remain popular.

1 Atlanta State Park
2 Caddoan Mounds State Historic Site
3 Caddo Lake State Park
4 Daingerfield State Park
5 Fort Boggy State Park
6 Huntsville State Park
7 Lake Bob Sandlin State Park
8 Lake Livingston State Park
9 Martin Creek Lake State Park
10 Martin Dies, Jr. State Park
11 Mission Tejas State Park
12 Starr Family Home State Historic Site
13 Texas State Railroad State Park • Rusk and Palestine State Parks
14 Tyler State Park
15 Village Creek State Park

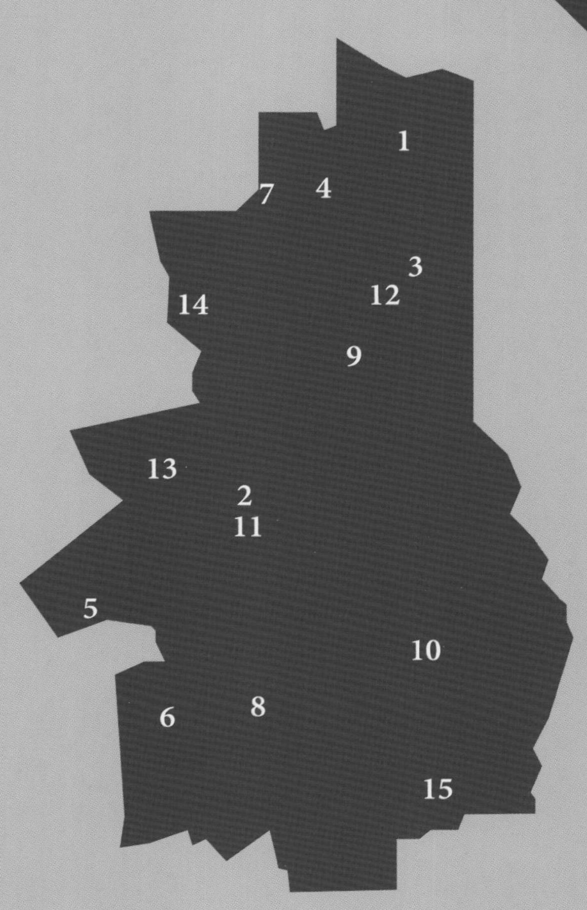

Atlanta State Park

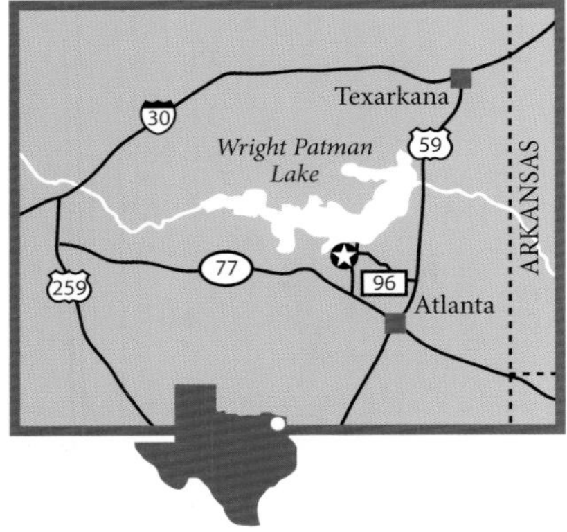

Atlanta State Park lies on the shores of Wright Patman Lake in far northeastern Texas. Hills wooded with thick stands of second-growth pines, oaks, and sweetgums tumble down to the sandy lakeshore. In fall, sweetgums, sumac, and other trees and shrubs add splashes of scarlet and gold to the dense forest.

Atlanta State Park was named for the nearby town of Atlanta, the principal city and commercial center of Cass County. In turn, Atlanta was named for the capital of Georgia, because some of its earliest settlers came from there. The town was established when the Texas & Pacific Railroad was built through the area in 1872. Farming and lumbering were the most important early economic activities, followed later by oil and gas production. Before Anglo settlers arrived in the area of the state park, Caddo Indians, the most culturally advanced tribe in Texas, lived and farmed in northeastern Texas.

Wright Patman Lake is the most popular attraction of the state park. The U.S. Army Corps of Engineers built the 20,300-acre reservoir by damming the Sulphur River. The lake is popular for fishing, sailing, waterskiing, boating, and swimming. Although the lake is the main draw at Atlanta State Park, several miles of hiking and nature trails wind through the thick forest and add another recreational activity to Texas's most northeastern state park.

VISITOR INFORMATION

1475 acres. Open all year. Hot and humid in summer. Campground with partial and full hookups and showers. Picnicking, hiking and nature trails, fishing, swimming, waterskiing, boat ramp, canoe rentals. All visitor services available in Atlanta and Texarkana. For information: Atlanta State Park, 927 Park Road 42, Atlanta, TX 75551, (903) 796-6476.

Caddoan Mounds State Historic Site

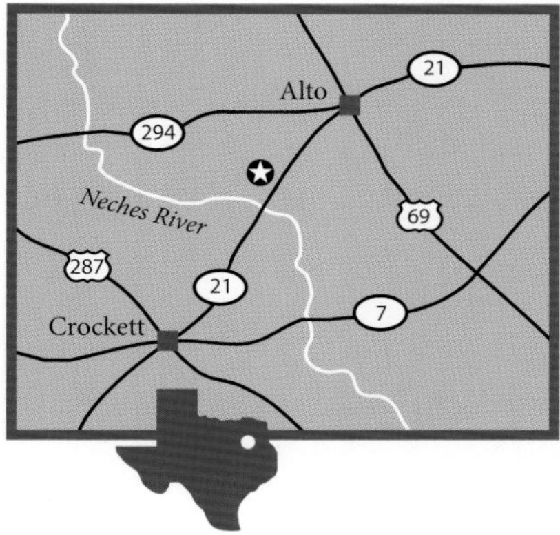

Over the course of about 2500 years, from around 1000 BC to AD 1500, the Mound Builder culture spread across the woodlands of eastern North America. In approximately AD 800, the Early Caddos, the westernmost group of Mound Builders, selected a site above the Neches River for a village and ceremonial center. The site was a frontier location for the Early Caddos, whose culture was centered farther east in the area around the Great Bend of the Red River in southwestern Arkansas. The village at what is now Caddoan Mounds State Historic Site proved to be the most southwesterly outpost of the Mound Builders.

The site was selected probably because it had good soil for agriculture, was level, had a reliable water supply in the nearby Neches River, and had abundant natural food sources in the mix of bottomland hardwoods and upland pine forests. Using wooden frames and bundles of cane for thatch, these early settlers built round, conical homes in the village area around the earthen mounds that gave their culture its name.

Archaeologists believe that the mounds were built as temple sites, for burials of members of the ruling class, and for religious ceremonies. Through careful excavation of the mounds and village, archaeologists have learned much about the Early Caddos. They appeared to have had an elite ruling class that lived in and around the temple mounds and had greater power and material wealth than average villagers. The common people lived in outer areas of the village and in outlying farming settlements.

Excavations of the burial mound uncovered remains of 14 individuals, from which archaeologists infer that about 90 were interred in the mound. Group burials suggest that servants and/or family members were sacrificed upon the death of an important member of the ruling class.

At its peak at about AD 1100, the culture of the Early Caddos was the most highly developed prehistoric culture known in Texas, with a trade network that extended from central Texas to beyond the Mississippi River. Artifacts found include Gulf Coast seashells and copper from the Great Lakes region. The people of this culture were prosperous enough and had a strong enough social organization to devote massive amounts of labor to building the large mounds.

The Early Caddos abruptly abandoned the village in the thirteenth century, probably after the ruling class lost its influence and power. War does not appear to have played a role in the abandonment. The Late Caddo culture remained in the area until Europeans arrived, but it never reached the same level of material wealth and sophistication that the earlier culture achieved.

Today, visitors can walk to the mounds and village site along a short interpretive trail. The visitor center features exhibits on the Caddo culture and many artifacts belonging to it.

VISITOR INFORMATION

94 acres. Open all year, Friday through Sunday, 9 AM to 4 PM. Museum with exhibits and audio-visual program, interpretive trail. Limited visitor services available in Alto; full services in Rusk and Crockett. For information: Caddoan Mounds State Historic Site, RR 2, Box 85C, Alto, TX 75925, (936) 858-3218.

OPPOSITE PAGE, TOP
Anole on sumac
OPPOSITE PAGE, BOTTOM
Wright Patman Lake
ABOVE
Indian mound

Caddo Lake State Park

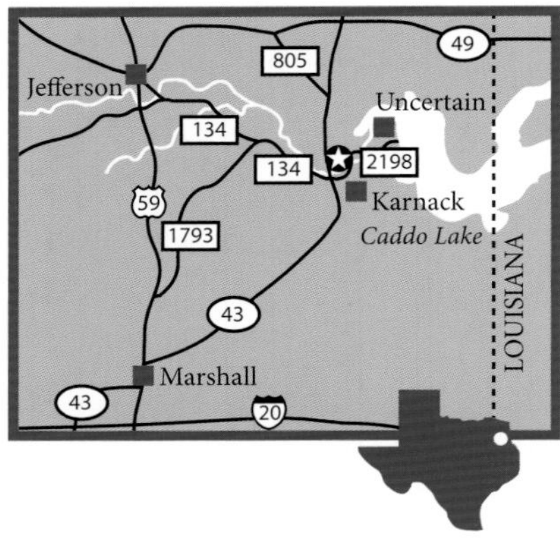

According to Caddo Indian legend, the large, mysterious body of water known as Caddo Lake had a violent beginning. After having a vision of impending disaster, a Caddo chief quickly moved his people to higher ground. The earth trembled and shook, rains fell, the ground sank, and floods drowned the tribe's former homeland. Caddo Lake was born.

The legend of Caddo Lake may be tied to the great New Madrid (Missouri) earthquake of 1811 that shook the United States from Texas to Illinois. Although the lake could have been created if the earth subsided and water filled the sunken area, researchers believe that it actually formed as the result of a huge logjam on the Red River.

Sometime around 1800, the logjam, called the Great Raft, caused water to back up into Big Cypress Bayou and create the lake. The enormous logjam stretched more than 100 miles, from Natchitoches, Louisiana, to north of Shreveport. Masses of trees piled 25 feet high and loosely cemented with roots, dirt, moss, and growing trees blocked the river's flow. Pools of still water interrupted sections of the jam. Some water flowed through the Great Raft, but most bypassed it on the Texas side, creating lakes and swamps. As the raft grew upstream, it blocked Big Cypress Bayou and formed Caddo Lake, site of the present-day state park that bears its name.

After the Louisiana Purchase of 1803, the United States and Spain disputed their mutual boundary in the Caddo Lake area. In 1806, the countries agreed to declare the area neutral ground, and to ban settlement there. Instead, the unpoliced region became a no-man's-land and attracted all manner of outlaws and renegades. The area remained lawless and disputed after Mexico gained its independence from Spain in 1821. Nor did Texas independence bring peace to Caddo Lake. From 1840 to 1844, a virtual civil war raged between two local factions called the Regulators and the Moderators.

The Regulator faction, a vigilante group organized to curtail lawlessness, committed so many crimes itself that an opposing group, the so-called Moderators, formed to curb the excesses. No one could remain neutral; all were forced to join one group or the other. At times, as many as 100 men fought in pitched battles. Texas historian Henderson Yoakum wrote that the area was a place where the "law was only a passive onlooker."

Finally, Texas President Sam Houston himself pleaded for the war to stop and sent in 500 militia men. The fighting ceased at last, and the Regulators

ABOVE
Bald cypress trees on Sawmill Pond
OPPOSITE PAGE, TOP
Cypress trees and lake in predawn light
OPPOSITE PAGE, BOTTOM
Fall leaves on forest floor

and Moderators disbanded, although personal feuds persisted for years.

In the 1830s, Captain Henry Shreve of the U.S. Army Corps of Engineers cleared the Great Raft as far north as Shreve's landing (later called Shreveport), but the jam reformed. However, steamboats found a way around the raft through Caddo Lake and Big Cypress Bayou to Jefferson, which soon became Texas's second-largest port, with overland trade arteries branching out all over northeast Texas. Even though Jefferson was far inland, only Galveston boasted a greater volume of trade in the late 1800s.

Steamboats more than 200 feet long plied the shallow, hazardous waters of Caddo Lake, carrying cargoes as large as 4500 cotton bales or 700 head of cattle. Roads leading into Jefferson were jammed with wagons. The town boomed, and palatial houses sprouted along its streets. The first gas street-lighting system in Texas was installed there, and one of the world's first ice plants was built.

Jefferson's prosperity came to an abrupt end in 1874, when the Corps of Engineers blasted loose the Great Raft, some say at the behest of railroad owners who wanted the steamboats' trade. Water levels fell, steamboat traffic ended, and Shreveport took over as the premier Red River port. In about 1914, the Corps built a dam in Louisiana to maintain the lake's lower level and to facilitate oil drilling on the Louisiana

side of the lake. A new dam replaced the old one in 1971.

The Regulators' bullets no longer fly and steamboat whistles no longer echo across Caddo Lake; today, people still come to enjoy the lake's natural beauty. Its shallow waters support thick stands of bald cypress throughout, and water lilies, duckweed, lotus, and water hyacinths also thrive in the lake waters. When combined with the Spanish moss draping the cypresses, the plants give the lake an eerie, primeval, swamp-like atmosphere.

The cypresses and other vegetation are so thick that much of the 26,800-acre lake is really more a maze of sloughs, bayous, and ponds than open-water lake. Because the twisting, intersecting channels confuse boaters, the Cypress Valley Navigation District has marked a series of boat roads. Darkness or bad weather can make it especially easy to get lost; boaters who dawdle on the lake after the sun sets may get to spend the night in the "Caddo Hotel," dreaming of Regulators and Moderators.

Caddo Lake State Park offers excellent access to the upper end of the lake. A boat ramp allows an easy put-in, and a fishing pier provides opportunities to fish without a boat. The lake offers the most diverse fishing in Texas, with 71 species of fish identified, including crappie, largemouth bass, and catfish. The prehistoric-looking alligator gar grows as long as eight feet here.

The park was developed in the 1930s by the Civilian Conservation Corps (CCC). The entrance gates, cabins, pavilions, and other facilities were built of heavy timbers and stone by the Corps. They are still in use today, a testament to the builders' craftsmanship.

Although most visitors come to the state park for lake-oriented activities, hiking and nature trails lead into backcountry areas of the park. Deep in woods of magnolia, oak, and loblolly pine, hikers can find an old CCC pavilion hidden away in thick forest and almost forgotten. In fall, the bald cypresses of Caddo Lake turn burnt orange, providing visitors with a rare opportunity to see fall color in Texas. Caddo Lake has a long, sometimes violent history, but today makes a quiet escape from city life.

VISITOR INFORMATION

468 acres. Nearby Caddo Lake Wildlife Management Area contains 8005 acres. Both are open all year. Hot and humid in summer. Busy on weekends, spring through fall. Small campground with both partial and full hookups and with showers. Cabins are popular and are booked early on weekends. Screened shelters. Picnicking, hiking and nature trails. Canoe rental in season. Small interpretive area in the headquarters building introduces lake history and biology. Limited visitor services available in Uncertain and Karnack. All services in Marshall and Jefferson. For information: Caddo Lake State Park, 245 Park Road 2, Karnack, TX 75661, (903) 679-3351.

Sawmill Pond, small boat, and bald cypresses

Daingerfield State Park

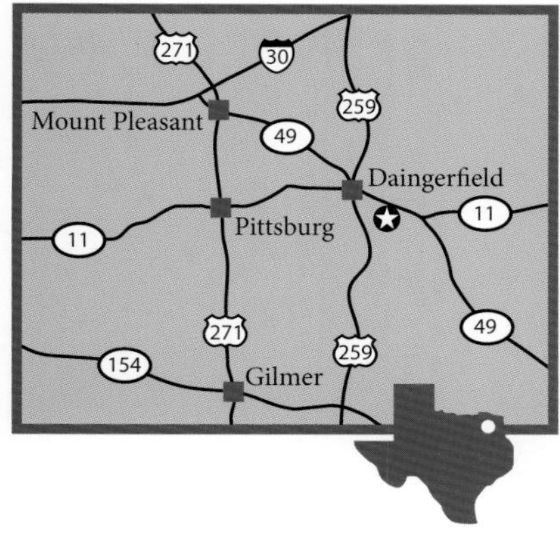

The dense mixed pine and hardwood forests of northeast Texas shelter popular Daingerfield State Park. In spring, masses of dogwoods adorn the forest with their white blooms, like some sort of strange late-season snowstorm. The forests resume their lush green appearance for the long days of summer, but in fall, as temperatures drop and days shorten, sweetgums and maples dot the park with splotches of orange and scarlet, an uncommon sight in most of Texas.

Because the park was founded in the 1930s and has been carefully protected since, the forest is mature, with towering loblolly pines, oaks, sweetgums, and other trees. During the Depression, the Civilian Conservation Corps (CCC) built many of the park facilities with its usual meticulous craftsmanship. Most of the buildings built by the Corps, including the cabins, lodge, and bathhouse, are still in use today. The most obvious CCC project is the small lake around which the park is centered. The Corps built an earthen dam to impound the spring-fed 80-acre reservoir.

Most park activities center around the small, no-wake lake, especially in summer. In warm weather, people swim in its cool waters or lounge on the grassy banks. Canoes and small sailboats glide almost silently across the lake, while paddleboats churn through the water. Fishermen pursue largemouth bass, crappie, chain pickerel, and blue and channel catfish from the fishing pier, the shore, or small boats. Winter weather cools the water enough that even rainbow trout are stocked periodically.

A 2.5-mile hiking trail circles the lake. One segment of the trail on the west side of the lake climbs to the top of a hill of a respectable size for East Texas. Although the view to the southwest from the top is somewhat obscured by trees, it is quite expansive. On parts of the hike, the rock and soil have a reddish color, having been stained by iron ore that, nearby, is rich enough to be mined and smelted for steel production.

If you can, take the hike on a quiet fall weekday. Autumn color dots the lakeshore beneath a deep blue sky. The cool, crisp air carries the distinctive, astringent smell of decaying foliage. Fallen leaves pile up on the trail, crunching noisily as you walk through them. A white-tailed deer takes flight, crashing through the brush, while a woodpecker hammers away at a tree trunk, searching for insects. Although you are still in Texas, you may feel like you have traveled to New England.

VISITOR INFORMATION

507 acres. Open all year. Hot and humid in summer, but mitigated by the lake. Very popular on weekends during warm part of year. Moderate number of sites in three campgrounds, with limited to full hookups and showers. Three cabins and larger lodge. Picnic area, hiking trail, boating, fishing, swimming. Seasonal canoe, kayak, rowboat, and paddleboat rental. Concession sells camping supplies and food from April through October. Full visitor services available in Daingerfield and Mount Pleasant. For information: Daingerfield State Park, 455 Park Road 17, Daingerfield, TX 75638, (903) 645-2921.

Sweetgum tree with fall color

Fort Boggy State Park

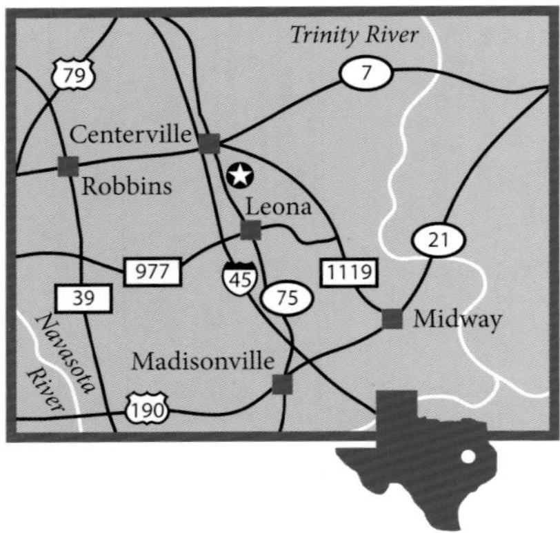

Fort Boggy State Park lies in East Texas on Boggy Creek near the small town of Centerville. The creation of the park was spurred by a generous land donation in 1985. It lies in an area of gently rolling, mostly wooded hills. The park is not quite far enough east to have pines, so its forest is dominated by oaks, elms, sweetgums, pecans, and other hardwoods.

Boggy Creek flows year round through the property, nurturing a large area of bottomland hardwoods. Beavers and their ponds are plentiful in the spring-fed creek, in addition to other wildlife such as white-tailed deer, raccoons, opossums, and armadillos.

The John Byrns and Christopher Staley families of Tennessee established the first settlement north of the Old San Antonio Road and between the Navasota and Trinity rivers in 1840. They were soon joined by John and James Erwin and their families from Mississippi, and several other families. In February of that year, Christopher Staley was killed by Indians, leading the settlers to build a fort for protection. Two Indian tribes living nearby, the Keechi and the Kickapoo, periodically raided the settlements for livestock. The palisade fort first bore the name of the Erwin family, but later became known as Fort Boggy because of its proximity to Boggy Creek. The fort enclosed two blockhouses and eleven dwellings that housed 75 people by the end of 1840. To protect the settlers, the Republic of Texas authorized formation of a military company for the fort, under the leadership of Captain Thomas Greer.

After a few years the Indian attacks lessened, and the fort fell into disuse. The site of the fort lies near the park. The land within the park was farmed for almost a century. In the 1930s the Sullivan family consolidated many of the farms and took it out of cultivation. Fifty years later it was donated to the State of Texas for a park by Eileen Crain Sullivan.

After more than 60 years of lying fallow, the parkland has regained much of its original undeveloped beauty. Only modest facilities have been developed at the park thus far. A small 15-acre lake offers swimming, fishing, and boating with canoes, kayaks, and other small no-wake boats. Two trails provide routes for hikers and mountain bikers. Eventually, the park should feature additional facilities such as campgrounds, larger picnic areas, and more trails. For now the park is open for day use from Friday through Sunday.

Visitor Information

1847 acres. Open Friday through Sunday, 8 AM to sunset. No camping. Open-air pavilion with tables, boat ramp, picnicking, fishing, swimming, boating, hiking, mountain biking. All visitor services available in Crockett. For information: Fort Boggy State Park, Route 2, Box 4994 State Highway 75 South, Centerville, TX 75833, (903) 344-1116.

TOP
Phlox and coreopsis
BOTTOM
Hiker
LOWER LEFT
Lake with morning mist

Huntsville State Park

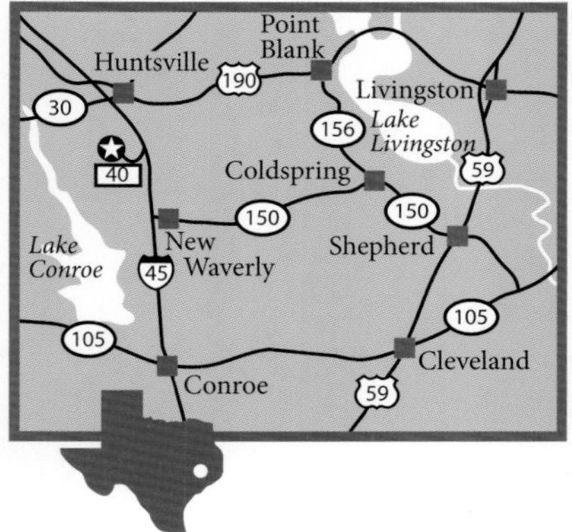

Loblolly and shortleaf pines tower over the shoreline of Lake Raven, a small impoundment that forms the heart of Huntsville State Park. As tall as the pines are, however, they are second-growth trees dating from early in the 1900s. In the period from 1880 to 1930, almost all harvestable trees were cut in the South, including those in East Texas. Much of the land in the state park and surrounding Sam Houston National Forest was devastated. Modern sustainable forestry practices were not used then; logging companies felled all the trees and moved on, doing no replanting or other reclamation work. With time, the forest has regrown, forming dense pine woodlands interspersed with hardwoods such as willow and water oak, American and cedar elm, black gum, black willow, and green ash, which are most commonly found in creek bottoms. Understory trees in the pine forests include red maple, dogwood, and sassafras.

The thick forest supports abundant wildlife. White-tailed deer, fox squirrels, raccoons, opossums, and armadillos are commonly seen. Creatures such as bobcats roam the woods also, but are reclusive and rarely observed. Occasionally alligators can be seen in the lake, floating motionless and almost completely submerged. Many species of birds flit through the forest canopy, especially during spring and fall migrations. Some birds make their presence obvious—crows squawk loudly over the lake, and pileated woodpeckers hammer away at tree trunks.

The park and nearby town of Huntsville were named after Huntsville, Alabama, because an early trader and settler from there believed that the area resembled his home. Sam Houston, commander-in-chief of Texas forces during the war for independence, first president of the Republic of Texas, and governor of the State of Texas, bought a plantation near Huntsville in 1844. Houston had grown up with neighboring Cherokees in

TOP
Lake Raven, fall color
MIDDLE
Canoeists
BOTTOM
Swimmers at Lake Raven

Tennessee and later married a Cherokee woman. He named the plantation Raven Hill in reference to "Colonneh," the name given him by the Cherokees. Raven is the English translation of this Cherokee word. Within the park, Lake Raven was named after Sam Houston, not the raucous crows that frequent the area.

The park offers plenty of recreational opportunities. Canoes, kayaks, paddleboats, and small, no-wake fishing boats float on the lake's three arms, and buoys mark off an unsupervised lake-swimming area near the bathhouse. Boats and fishing piers let anglers pursue largemouth bass, crappie, and flathead and channel catfish. Many miles of trails challenge hikers, cyclists, and mountain bikers. The trails will soon be undergoing a major upgrade with improved maintenance and signage, along with connections to trails in the city of Huntsville and the Lone Star Hiking Trail of the Sam Houston National Forest.

Like many other Texas state parks, some of Huntsville's facilities were built during the Depression by the Civilian Conservation Corps of durable native materials. Many of these structures are still used today by people seeking a quiet escape in the Pineywoods of East Texas.

VISITOR INFORMATION

2083 acres. Open all year. Hot and humid in summer. Very popular, especially in summer and on spring and fall weekends. Large campgrounds with partial hookups and showers; reservations recommended during popular times. Screened shelters. Interpretive center; nature, hiking, equestrian, surfaced cycling, and mountain-bike trails; fishing, swimming, and no-wake boating, fishing piers, and boat ramp. Seasonal park store and canoe, kayak, paddleboat, and flat-bottomed boat rental. All visitor services available in Huntsville. For information: Huntsville State Park, P.O. Box 508, Huntsville, TX 77342, (936) 295-5644.

Lake Bob Sandlin State Park

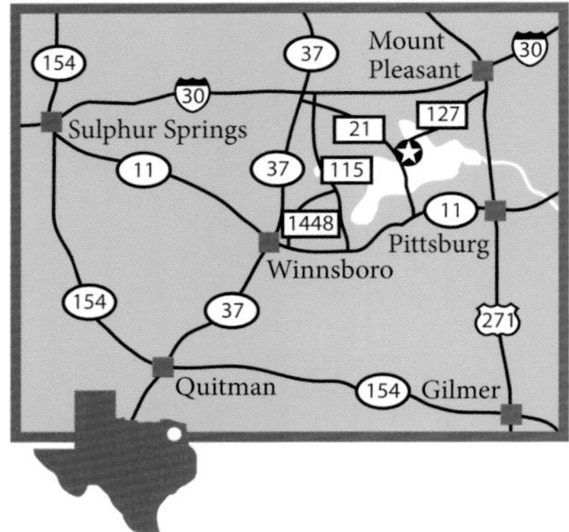

Lake Bob Sandlin State Park provides easy access to the great bass-fishing waters of Lake Bob Sandlin, a 9460-acre reservoir in northeast Texas. The lake has a long, sinuous shoreline, with deep coves and bays. Two other small lakes, Cypress Springs and Monticello, adjoin Lake Bob Sandlin on two of its arms. The three are sometimes referred to as the Tri-Lake Area. A power plant warms the waters of 2000-acre Lake Monticello, improving its bass fishery.

Lake Bob Sandlin was completed in 1977 by damming Lake Fork Creek and was named for a Mount Pleasant businessman who tirelessly lobbied

Small park pond

for the construction of reservoirs in Titus County. In its early years the lake was heavily stocked with Florida bass and channel catfish. A large amount of timber was left standing in the lake to provide habitat for small forage fish, and so provide food for the larger bass. Regular stocking, an ideal habitat, and good reproduction have made Lake Bob Sandlin and the two adjoining reservoirs famous for their bass fishing.

Within the state park, a boat ramp, a lighted fishing pier, and the shoreline offer good access for anglers. Swimmers, water skiers, and boaters also enjoy the open lake waters away from the areas of flooded timber. Inland from the lake, most of the park is heavily wooded with a mixed forest of loblolly pine, sweetgum, black hickory, and various species of oak. Wildlife includes armadillos, white-tailed deer, bobcats, opossums, and many other creatures. Several miles of hiking trails wind through the lush forest, past two ponds and several primitive campsites. A small cemetery in the day-use area is a remnant of Fort Sherman, built in the 1840s to protect settlers from Indian attack.

In spring, wildflowers blanket open fields in the park, while in fall, sweetgums, maples, and other trees add splashes of color to the woods. Lake Bob Sandlin State Park offers a quiet escape in East Texas for fishermen, campers, and other outdoor enthusiasts.

VISITOR INFORMATION

640 acres. Open all year. Hot and humid in summer. Campground with partial hookups and showers. Backpacking campsites. Shelters with closable windows in addition to screens. Limited-use cabins with heating, A/C, and electricity, but no plumbing. Lighted fishing pier, boat ramp, hiking, mountain biking, picnicking, boating, waterskiing, swimming. All visitor services available in Mount Pleasant. For information: Lake Bob Sandlin State Park, 341 State Park Road 2117, Pittsburg, TX 75686, (903) 572-5531.

Lake Livingston State Park

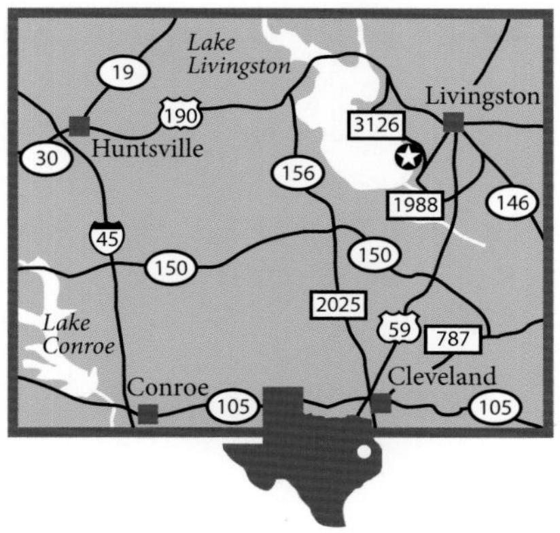

The shores of Lake Livingston provide the setting for Lake Livingston State Park. The huge 84,800-acre reservoir was created in 1969 by damming the Trinity River. The lake sprawls across four counties and has a 450-mile-long shoreline. The state park contains about 2.5 miles of the lakeshore.

Lake Livingston lies in the thick Pineywoods of East Texas about 75 miles north of Houston. Tall loblolly pines and water oaks shade the lakeshore park, and are mixed with bottomland hardwood species such as willow oak and elm. Park wildlife is typical for East Texas: white-tailed deer, swamp rabbits, and raccoons roam the park woodlands browsing plants and brush or searching for prey; pileated woodpeckers hammer away at tree trunks, hunting for grubs; and frogs and other amphibians favor the moist areas along creeks and around ponds.

Fish are probably the most popular wildlife attraction at the state park. Boat ramps and fishing piers attract anglers year-round. Native and Florida largemouth bass have long been popular at the lake, but the white bass-spawning run is probably the lake's most famous fishing activity. Every spring, the white bass swim up the Trinity River from the lake, attracting thousands of fishermen. Not only are the bass plentiful, but they are particularly large, sometimes as big as four pounds.

Another popular fish is the striped bass, an introduced saltwater fish that does well in the lake's fresh water. Flathead, channel, and blue catfish thrive in the lake as well. In 1976, a 114-pound flathead catfish was pulled from the lake, setting a state record.

Other attractions include more than four miles of nature and hiking trails that wind through the backcountry and developed areas of the state park. A swimming pool with bathhouse allows visitors to cool off on hot summer days. Finally, an observation tower offers great views of the park and the sprawling waters of Lake Livingston, one of the largest reservoirs in Texas and a popular escape for residents of Houston and other cities.

VISITOR INFORMATION

636 acres. Open all year. Hot and humid in summer. Large number of developed campsites with partial hookups and showers spread across several areas. Screened shelters. Horseback rides with Lake Livingston Stables horses. Fishing piers, boat ramps, boating, waterskiing, picnicking, swimming, and nature, hiking, and mountain-biking trails. Seasonal park store. All visitor services available in Livingston. For information: Lake Livingston State Park, 300 State Park Road 65, Livingston, TX 77351, (936) 365-2201.

Lake Livingston shoreline

Martin Creek Lake State Park

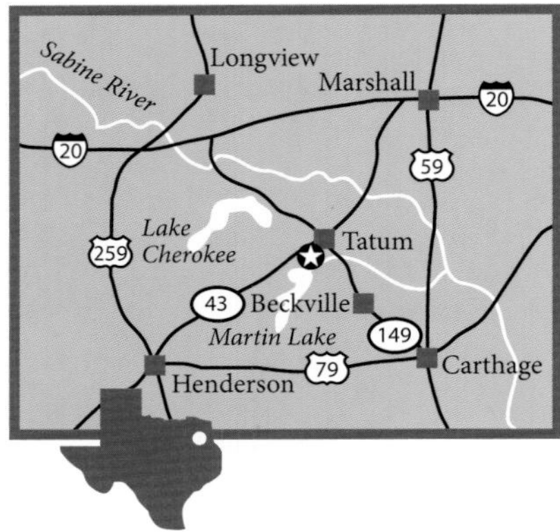

The site of Martin Creek Lake State Park, deep in the forests of East Texas, has been popular with humans since prehistoric times. Although the park itself does not have any significant archaeological sites, the Caddo Indians occupied villages in the area long before the first settlers arrived.

In the late 1600s, Spanish explorers began crossing the area. By the end of the eighteenth century, American settlers moving west had begun to displace Cherokees, Choctaws, Chickasaws, and other tribes from their eastern homelands, and some of them moved to East Texas. The Caddos also gave up their eastern lands and moved into their remaining lands in East Texas. Part of present-day Rusk County was a land grant promised to the Cherokee Nation by the Mexican government. After Texas gained its independence from Mexico, Sam Houston granted land rights in the area to the Cherokee tribe, but the Texas Senate did not ratify the treaty despite his insistence. In 1838, Mirabeau Lamar, newly elected president of the Texas republic, initiated an effort to remove the Indians from East Texas. While Sam Houston was away in 1839, Lamar sent troops to remove the Cherokees and their allied tribes from Texas. The action led to a period of hostilities and displacement of the Indians.

A historic trail, Trammel's Trace, is still visible in the park near the fishing pier. It was initially created by local Indians, who used it as a travel route. Later it was widened into a wagon path and became an important route used by settlers traveling into Texas from Arkansas. Parts of it and other old roads make up some of the park's hiking trails today.

Martin Creek, formerly known as Hogan's Bayou, was renamed for Daniel Martin who settled with his family near the bayou in 1833. His lands included the present-day park and most of the area now occupied by the reservoir. He and John Irons built a small fort and made a living through trade and hunting.

A small town named Harmony Hill was established near the park entrance in the mid-1800s. The settlement prospered as a farming and trading center until 1882, when it was bypassed by a railroad. The town quickly declined, leaving little more than a cemetery and a lone building today.

Martin Creek Lake was created in the 1970s to provide cooling water for a Texas Utilities power-generating plant. The 5000-acre lake is relatively shallow, so boaters and water skiers need to watch for tree stumps and other hazards. The power plant warms the lake in winter, providing fine year-round fishing for crappie, largemouth bass, sunfish, and channel catfish. Two boat ramps and a lighted fishing pier give easy lake access to anglers.

The park lies on the lakeshore in gently rolling terrain wooded with loblolly and shortleaf pine, mixed with hardwoods such as post oak, red oak, blackjack oak, sweetgum, elm, and river birch. A small island connected to the mainland by a footbridge is one of the park's more interesting features; at its east end is a primitive campsite for backpackers and boaters.

Visitor Information

287 acres. Open all year. Hot and humid in summer, sometimes cold in winter. Moderate number of developed campsites with partial hookups and showers. Primitive campsites for boaters and backpackers. Screened shelters. Cabins with heat, A/C, kitchen, and bathroom. Limited-use cabins with heat, A/C, and electricity, but no plumbing. Lighted fishing pier, boat ramp, picnicking, swimming, boating, waterskiing, and hiking and mountain-biking trails. Limited visitor services available in Tatum, all services in Henderson and Longview. For information: Martin Creek Lake State Park, 9515 County Road 2181D, Tatum, TX 75691, (903) 836-4336.

Boat docks

Martin Dies, Jr. State Park

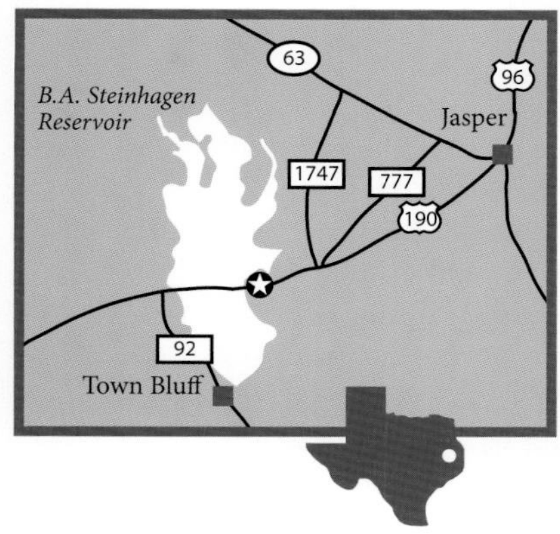

The popular Martin Dies, Jr. State Park lies on the shore of B. A. Steinhagen Reservoir deep in East Texas. Named for a U.S. Congressman, it is located on the northern edge of the Big Thicket, a vast, heavily wooded area with a unique mix of habitats. The Big Thicket forms a biological crossroads between eastern and western species of plants and animals. Visitors to the state park and surrounding areas in the Thicket might see both roadrunners and alligators, prickly pears and palmettos. Beech trees, common here, are actually at the southeastern limit of their range. The sugar maple and northern red oak are also found here, but usually grow farther north. At one time, even the tropical jaguar and ocelot roamed as far northeast as the Big Thicket.

Slight changes in elevation and moisture create very different habitats within the Big Thicket. Swampy, primeval-looking cypress sloughs wind through lush floodplains, yet dry, sandy bluffs a hundred yards away may contain a mix of longleaf pine, post oak, and yucca.

At one time, the Big Thicket covered more than three million acres, but logging, agriculture, and urbanization have destroyed most of it. Today, remnants of the thicket are protected in parks like Martin Dies, Jr. State Park and Big Thicket National Preserve.

TOP RIGHT
Shoreline campsite
BOTTOM RIGHT
Bald cypresses

The three units of the state park lie on an old river terrace of the Neches River, which was dammed just below its confluence with the Angelina River to create the reservoir. Much of the lake is very shallow, and bald cypresses dot the water, as in Caddo Lake in northeastern Texas. Narrow sloughs lined with cypresses and willows wind up into the two largest units of the park on the eastern shore of the reservoir. The park has not been logged for many years, so massive loblolly pines, beeches, magnolias, and oaks tower over the campgrounds and picnic areas. In spring, azaleas and dogwoods dot the forest understory and attract many park visitors. In fall, blackgums and oaks add splotches of color to the woods.

Many people come to Martin Dies, Jr., to try their luck with a rod and reel in the lake. Various species of bass, crappie, and catfish all make popular catches. Other visitors enjoy canoeing through the backwaters of the 15,000-acre lake or simply relaxing under the tall pines and hardwoods that shade the state park.

VISITOR INFORMATION

705 acres. Open all year. Hot and humid in summer. Mosquitoes can be pesky in warm weather. Most popular in spring, especially on weekends. Large number of campsites with partial hookups and showers, split into several areas. Screened shelters. Limited-use cabins with heat, A/C, and electricity, but no plumbing. Hiking, mountain-biking, and nature trails, picnicking, lighted fishing piers, swimming, boat ramps, waterskiing. Seasonal kayak, canoe, and flat-bottom boat rental. All visitor services available in Jasper and Woodville. For information: Martin Dies, Jr. State Park, Route 4, Box 274, Jasper, TX 75951, (409) 384-5231.

Mission Tejas State Park

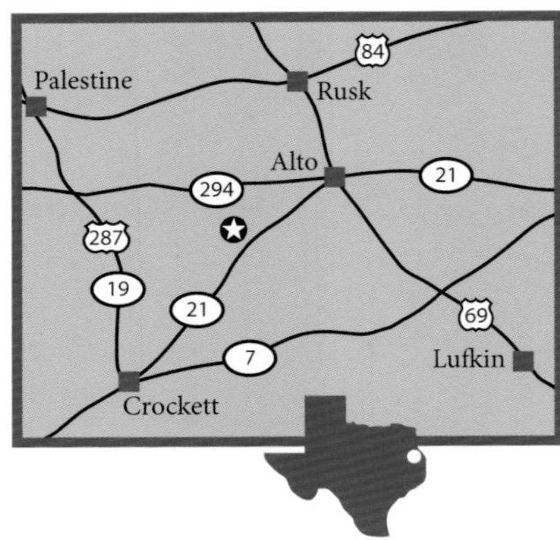

Today picnickers and campers relax under the tall pines of Mission Tejas State Park where, 300 years ago, priests and Indians toiled. In the 1600s, the Spaniards laid claim to vast areas of land northeast of Mexico, including Texas, but made little effort to colonize it. In 1685, a Frenchman, Robert Cavalier, Sieur de La Salle, established a small settlement on what is today Matagorda Bay. The Spaniards, worried about losing territory, began an effort to secure their claimed area. By the time an expedition led by Alonso de Leon found the French settlement in 1689, La Salle had died and only two members of his command remained.

The following year, de Leon set out from Monclova, Mexico, with a large expedition to establish a mission in East Texas. In May, the expedition met a group of Caddoan-speaking Indians, the Nabadache. The Spaniards used *tejas*, the Caddoan word for friends, as the name for the Caddos and their land. Later, *tejas* became Texas. The Nabadache invited the Spaniards to their homeland on the Neches River. In their villages of conical, thatched huts, the Nabadache raised crops of corn, beans, melons, and squash and hunted in the surrounding country. The Franciscan priests accompanying the expedition built a cluster of rough wooden buildings for a mission and dedicated it on June 1, 1690, as San Francisco de los Tejas.

The missionaries settled in to learn the Caddo language, improve the Indians' agricultural methods, and foster Christianity. Initially all went well, and a second mission was established a few miles away. Unfortunately, the following winter brought a smallpox epidemic that killed several thousand people in the missions and surrounding villages. The Nabadache believed that the Spaniards' Holy Water of Baptism was causing the disease. One of the priests, Father Casanas, worsened the situation by ridiculing the Indians'

Spanish mission replica

religious practices and their leaders. The summer of 1691 brought drought and increasing enmity. Spanish reinforcements and supplies arrived in August, but a second drought in 1692 worsened the missionaries' plight. In the spring of 1693, floods washed away the second mission. That fall another priest, Father Massanet, received word of an impending attack, so the missionaries loaded supplies, burned the mission, and fled to Mexico under the cover of night.

Domingo Ramón returned with an expedition to reestablish the mission in 1716, but lack of success, plus conflict between the French and Spanish, led to its abandonment only three years later. The Spaniards tried once again in 1721, but food and supplies continued in short supply, and few Indians joined the mission and converted to Christianity. Finally, in 1730, the mission was moved temporarily to a site to the west, on the Colorado River. The next year, it was moved to the San Antonio River and named San Francisco de la Espada; it thrived there for many years.

By modern times, nothing remained of the original mission buildings. During the Depression, the Civilian Conservation Corps built a wooden chapel to commemorate the original Spanish mission, plus constructed roads, trails, a pond, and a picnic area. In 1974, the home of the Rice family, early settlers in the region, was moved to the park from its original site 16 miles to the southwest. It was built between 1828 and 1838, and is one of the oldest structures in the area.

Today the park showcases the two historic buildings, the chapel and the Rice home, and offers a quiet retreat in the tall pines of the uplands above the Neches River. Campers, picnickers, hikers, and fishermen enjoy the shady woods where the Spaniards once tried to colonize East Texas.

VISITOR INFORMATION

659 acres. Open all year. Hot and humid in summer. Small campground with partial and full hookups and showers. Historic buildings, hiking, picnicking, limited fishing in pond. Limited visitor services available in Alto, full services in Crockett and Rusk. For information: Mission Tejas State Park, Route 2, Box 108, Grapeland, TX 75844, (936) 687-2394.

Dogwood fall leaves and pond

Starr Family Home State Historic Site

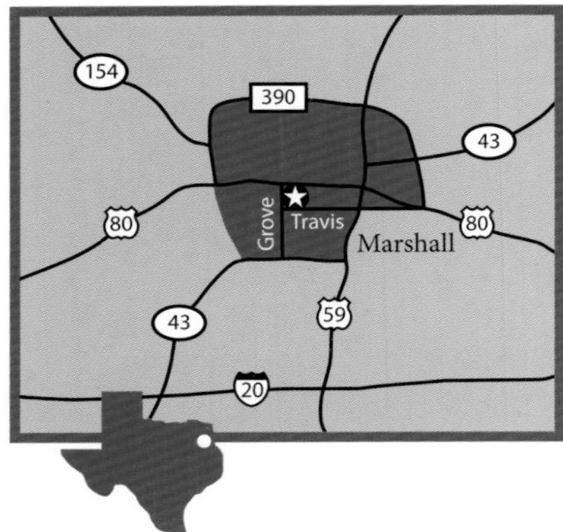

The Starr family had its start in Texas when Franklin J. Starr arrived in the state in 1834. He joined the volunteers fighting for Texas independence, but saw little action and settled in Nacogdoches with his wife after the fighting ended. His brother, Dr. James Harper Starr, and his brother's wife soon joined him in Nacogdoches. Sadly, Franklin Starr died of a fever in July 1837, saddling his brother with the responsibility of looking after his family and property.

Dr. Starr became active in the affairs of the new republic and was appointed President Mirabeau B. Lamar's Secretary of the Treasury in 1839. In 1844 he resigned and formed a very successful land agency with a partner in Nacogdoches. During the Civil War, Starr opposed secession, but supported the Confederacy by sending supplies to Southern troops. His eldest son, James Franklin (Frank) Starr, joined the Confederate Army in 1861 and served until the South was defeated.

After the war, Frank Starr attended the University of Virginia and then married Clara Fry Clapp in 1868 in New Orleans. He returned to Nacogdoches with his new wife to join his family's land business. In 1870, the family moved their home and business to Marshall, a thriving town served by the railroad and telegraph. Dr. Starr purchased a house called Rosemont on a large lot on the southwest side of town and retired from active business affairs. By the end of 1873, his son Frank was managing the family land and money while his youngest son, Amory, handled the land agency. The Starr family acquired and sold lands the State of Texas had granted as incentives for railroad construction, helping to open the western part of the state to settlement.

The Rosemont house was the beginning of a large family compound, which eventually included several homes. Frank Starr purchased the southwest corner of the compound from his parents and built his home with the financial assistance of his father-in-law. His house, Maplecroft, is the centerpiece of the park today, and fittingly, red maples still shade the grounds of the historic home. It was originally built in a transitional Italianate style, a precursor to the Victorian style. It contained four rooms on each of its two floors and had a detached kitchen and servant's room connected by a covered passageway. Most structural materials were acquired locally, but much of the trim and furnishings were shipped from New Orleans.

Over the years, the house was modified, modernized, and enlarged. A schoolhouse, barn, and other outbuildings were added to the grounds. In 1925, Ruth Starr Blake inherited the house from her mother, Mrs. Frank Starr, and in the 1930s she modified Maplecroft and the schoolhouse to reflect the Colonial Revival style of architecture. Other modifications were made to the internal layout of the home. When Ruth Blake died in 1969, the property passed to Clara Starr Pope Willoughby, the only surviving great-granddaughter of Dr. James Harper Starr. The home was acquired by the Texas Parks and Wildlife Department in 1976 and opened to the public in 1986. Today the park offers tours of the home, plus overnight stays at Rosemont Cottage, the surviving wing of the original family home. The historic cottage has four rooms and is furnished with period antiques.

VISITOR INFORMATION

3.1 acres. Open all year, Friday through Sunday. Call for tour times. Wear flat-soled shoes to avoid carpet and floor damage. Historic structure with interpretive exhibits. Bed and breakfast in Rosemont Cottage. All visitor services available in Marshall. For information: Starr Family Home State Historic Site, 407 W. Travis, Marshall, TX 75670, (903) 935-3044.

Starr family home

Texas State Railroad State Park • Rusk and Palestine State Parks

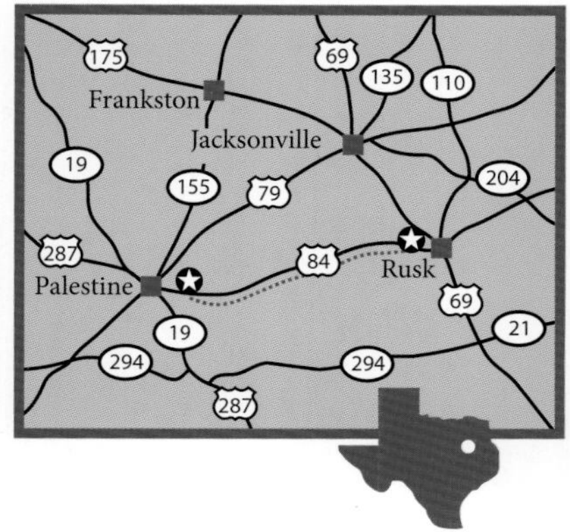

Deep in the Pineywoods of East Texas, the past still lives on, where the steam trains of the Texas State Railroad carry passengers along 25 miles of track between Rusk and Palestine state parks. Construction of the railroad was begun in 1896 by the state prison system in an effort to make the prisons self-supporting. Using penitentiary money, bonds, and legislative appropriations, the railroad was built between Palestine and Rusk. The Rusk prison built a foundry to make pig iron and pipe for the state, and the railroad was used to haul hardwood from Palestine to make coke for the iron plant.

In 1913, the iron plant in Rusk was closed, and the penitentiary was converted into a mental hospital four years later. After that the railroad was used only intermittently. In 1921, the railroad was taken from the Prison Commission's jurisdiction and placed under a separate board of managers. The state ceased regular railroad service and leased the line to the Texas & New Orleans, part of the Southern Pacific Railroad.

In the early 1960s the railroad lease was transferred to the Texas Southeastern Railroad. At the end of 1969, the railroad terminated freight operations and removed its rolling stock. In 1972, most of the railroad was transferred to the Texas Parks and Wildlife Department to preserve a part of the age of steam locomotives and railroading in Texas. A short 3.7-mile stretch of track is still used commercially by the Missouri Pacific Railroad to serve a meat-packing plant near Palestine.

Steam train at Rusk Depot

Today, passengers board the train at depots in either Rusk or Palestine State Park at each end of the line. The stations are not original, but were built to resemble railroad architecture at the turn of the century. Food, drinks, and gifts are available at both depots; the one at Rusk also has a small theater with film presentations of the railroad's history.

For each run, steam locomotives dating from 1901 to 1927 chug out of both stations pulling a string of open-air passenger cars. The route passes through 25 miles of thick East Texas woods, crossing 24 bridges. The longest bridge, over the Neches River, is 1100 feet long. Near the halfway point, the east- and westbound trains pass each other on a siding. At the stations, each train pauses for an hour and a half so passengers may eat lunch and stretch their legs before starting the return trip to the originating station. The railroad is the only one to have two steam trains operating simultaneously.

Rusk and Palestine state parks are located at each end of the Texas State Railroad. The two park units were designed to serve the passengers of the railroad plus provide additional recreational activities. Both park units lie in the thick mixed pine and hardwood forests of East Texas. Loblolly pines, oaks, sweetgums, elms, and other trees dominate the forest canopy. Smaller trees and shrubs, such as dogwood, sumac, and sassafras, create an understory.

The area was settled in the early part of the nineteenth century; Palestine was founded in 1835 to succeed Fort Houston as the Anderson County seat, and Rusk followed soon after. Rusk was named after Thomas Jefferson Rusk, a signer of the Texas Declaration of Independence and inspector general of the Texas revolutionary army. The town is probably best known as the birthplace of Texas's first two native-born governors, James Stephen Hogg and Thomas Mitchell Campbell. Palestine, the larger of the two towns, was created when Fort Houston was found not to be in the center of Anderson County as directed by the legislature in creating county seats. Thus the new town was created and named after Palestine, Illinois.

Although the terrain in the two

parks units and along the railroad line consists of gentle, unassuming hills with few rocks or minerals visible, the area is important geologically. Underlying the area are thick beds of sedimentary rock containing enormous reserves of oil and gas. Some of the oil fields are found near salt domes, a number of which lie near Palestine. Near Rusk, shallow layers of iron-bearing rock were once mined and smelted for iron.

The Rusk park is the larger of the two parks, with a small 15-acre lake with rental paddleboats, campground, and picnic area. The Palestine unit has picnicking and a small, less-developed camping area. Both units center around the depots of the Texas State Railroad, a living remnant of the past.

ABOVE
Paddleboat at Rusk unit
OPPOSITE PAGE, TOP
Stormy sunset over lake
OPPOSITE PAGE, BOTTOM
Canoeists

VISITOR INFORMATION

Texas State Railroad: 499 acres. Trains run all year on weekends, except December, January, and February, when the railroad closes for maintenance; trains run on additional days during busy times of the year. Trains depart at 11 AM and return at 3:30 PM at both stations. Ice chests and food may be brought on the train; food service is available at each depot. Call ahead for reservations and current dates, times, and ticket prices. Texas State Railroad State Park, P.O. Box 39, Rusk, TX 75785, (903) 683-2561 or (800) 442-8951.

Rusk and Palestine state parks: 136 acres. Rusk unit open all year; Palestine unit closes from December through February, matching the railroad's winter maintenance closure. Hot and humid in summer. Campgrounds and picnic areas adjoin railroad depots. Campsites with partial and full hookups and showers at Rusk unit, and with water hookups at Palestine unit. Fishing, paddleboat rental at Rusk unit. All visitor services available in Rusk and Palestine. For information: Rusk and Palestine State Parks, Route 4, Box 431, Rusk, TX 75785, (903) 683-5126.

Tyler State Park

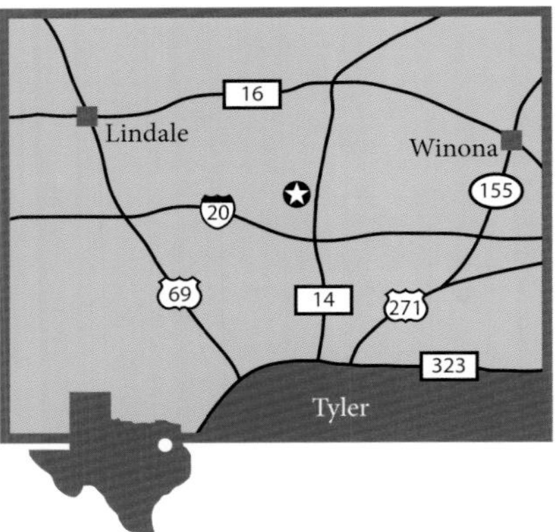

Tyler State Park is a popular, long-time retreat deep in the Pineywoods of East Texas. Heavily wooded hills surround a small 64-acre lake, the centerpiece of the park. The park site was purchased in the mid-1930s and, like many of Texas's older parks, developed initially by the Civilian Conservation Corps during the Depression.

The park lies in dense forest in gentle hills north of the city of Tyler. A mix of loblolly and shortleaf pines, sweetgums, oaks, elms, eastern red cedars, and hickories create a tall forest canopy, while smaller trees, such as sassafras, dogwoods, and redbuds, create a lower understory. In spring, the dogwoods and redbuds sprinkle the forest with white and red blooms, and in fall, trees such as the sweetgum and sassafras splash red and gold across the forest.

The lake hosts most activity at the park. A five-mile-per-hour speed limit makes the small body of water ideal for small boats, such as canoes. The park concession rents paddleboats and canoes and sells snacks and fishing bait. The nearby swimming beach is usually crowded on hot days.

Fishing piers and a boat ramp cater to anglers who, because the park is very popular, usually prefer to test their skill on weekdays and early in the morning or late in the evening. Several varieties of fish can be caught in the lake, including crappie, perch, largemouth bass, and catfish.

For those wishing to learn more about the park's natural history, a three-

quarter-mile nature trail winds through the woods near the headquarters. For hikers desiring a longer walk, the park also has a 2.5-mile hiking trail that circles the lake. An excellent 13-mile combined hiking and mountain-biking trail winds through the park's woods.

VISITOR INFORMATION

986 acres. Open all year. Hot and humid in summer. Campground with full and partial hookups and showers. Screened shelters. No-wake boating, fishing piers, hiking, nature and mountain-biking trails, picnicking, swimming. Seasonal concession store with canoe, kayak, fishing boat, and paddleboat rental and snacks. All visitor services available in Tyler. For information: Tyler State Park, 789 Park Road 16, Tyler, TX 75706, (903) 597-5338.

Village Creek State Park

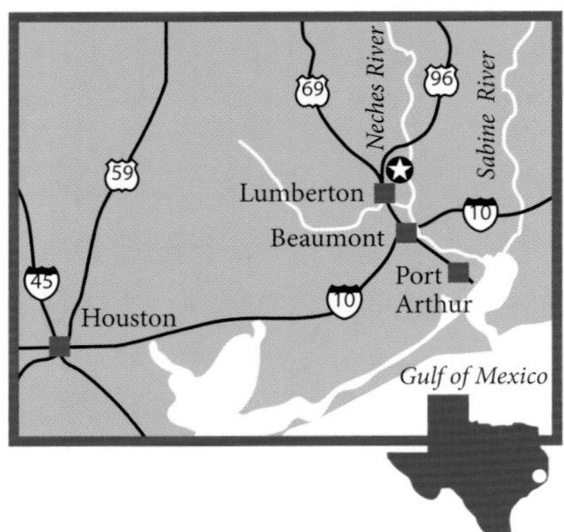

OPPOSITE PAGE
Canoeists on Village Creek
BELOW
Cypress-tupelo slough

Village Creek winds through the heart of the Big Thicket of East Texas, its clear, tea-colored waters flowing through dense forest to its confluence with the Neches River. The boundaries of the Big Thicket through which the creek flows are not easily defined. A 1970 ecological survey defined an irregular band stretching from Conroe to part of the Sabine River near Newton, and extending from Woodville and Jasper in the north to Beaumont. Researchers used a type of mixed pine and hardwood forest, particularly the beech-magnolia-pine association, as the defining parameter for the boundaries of the ecological Big Thicket.

The Big Thicket is a melange of many different habitats controlled by slight variations in elevation, soil type, and available water. Amid the lush woods of the thicket there are places where the soil is so poor that plants have developed carnivorous traits to survive. Yet a few dozen yards away, the soil can be rich enough to support dense forests of beech, magnolia, and loblolly pine. Although the thicket has been greatly reduced in size and heavily impacted by human activities, it still contains a tremendous number of different plant and animal species. Village Creek State Park protects some of the thicket's unique biology.

The Big Thicket's location within North America adds to its biological importance since it lies at an ecotone, or meeting place of different biological provinces. Its different soil types and moisture levels allow dry western desert plants such as yucca, mesquite, and prickly pear to thrive alongside the southeastern water tupelo and bald cypress. Southern orchids and ferns flourish alongside sphagnum moss more typical of Arctic bogs. Alligators

bask on the banks of cypress sloughs, while roadrunners pursue lizards through the yuccas and oak scrub of dry sandhills.

Eighty-five species of trees shade the forest floor, while a thousand species of flowering plants grow within the thicket. The beech tree reaches its southeastern limit of distribution here, as do trilliums and several orchid species. The northern red oak and sugar maple found in the Big Thicket grow more commonly much farther north. All four types of poisonous snakes found in the United States live here—the copperhead, the coral snake, the rattlesnake, and the water moccasin. More than 50 bird species call the Big Thicket home, and at least another 125 reside there part of the year or pass through during annual migrations. Evidence indicates that the tropical jaguar and ocelot once roamed as far northeast as the Thicket. Large temperate predators, such as the mountain lion, black bear, and red wolf, also thrived in the Thicket before being exterminated by man.

Several Big Thicket habitats occur in the state park, including floodplain forests, swampy baygalls, acid-bogs, and cypress sloughs. The baygall's wet, jungle-like habitat evokes the classic, mysterious Big Thicket image for most people. Black gum and bald cypress grow in the swampy terrain, anchored in the water and soft soil by wide buttresses. Smaller trees and shrubs, such as the black titi and red bay, create dense thickets at the edges of the bogs and baygalls. The carnivorous bladderwort plant thrives in this environment. Here and there alligators lurk deep in the swampy habitat, while water moccasins slither through the dark water in search of prey.

Close to the creeks and rivers, below the ancient waterway terraces that harbor baygalls and sandy uplands, lie the floodplain forests which, as the name implies, flood regularly. The periodic flooding produces a fertile sandy or silty loam soil, and provides additional water for the plants of the creek and river bottoms. A dense forest canopy grows in the floodplain, dominated by massive oaks and sweetgums.

Low ridges, backwater sloughs, oxbow lakes, and terraces break up the overall flatness of the floodplain. A few beeches and magnolias are found on the higher, drier areas. Bald cypresses and water tupelos grow directly out of the water in shallow sloughs and watery depressions. With thick, buttressed tree trunks and cypress knees poking out of the water, the sloughs are eerie, primeval-looking swamps. Unlike the baygalls, however, regular flooding and some water flow prevent water in the cypress sloughs from becoming highly acidic. The sloughs retain water most or all of the year, making them favorite haunts of water-dwelling animals such as alligators and water moccasins.

Of the original 3.5 million-acre Big Thicket, less than 300,000 acres remain. Of that, Village Creek State Park and Big Thicket National Preserve protect a sizeable portion. The state park does more than just preserve important habitat; it offers unique recreational opportunities. Village Creek provides one of the best canoeing experiences in Texas. The flatwater creek winds for miles past lush forest, eerie cypress sloughs, and white sandbars. With multiple access points in the state park and national preserve, as well as at highway bridges, trips of varying lengths can be arranged. Local outfitters can help with canoe rentals and car shuttles.

The park also offers fishing for catfish, largemouth bass, perch, and crappie. Hiking trails are another way to explore the dense Big Thicket forests. Whether explored by canoe, by mountain bike, or on foot, Village Creek State Park provides an excellent introduction to the unique and mysterious Big Thicket of East Texas.

VISITOR INFORMATION

1090 acres. Open all year. Hot and humid in summer. Insect repellent advised in warm months. Moderate number of campsites with partial hookups and showers. Walk-in primitive campsites. Large eight-person cabin. Hiking, mountain biking, swimming, picnicking, canoeing, fishing. All visitor services available in Lumberton and Beaumont. For information: Village Creek State Park, P.O. Box 8565, Lumberton, TX 77657, (409) 755-7322.

Prairies and Lakes

THE PRAIRIES AND LAKES region covers a broad band of land stretching from the Red River to the north, to as far south as east of San Antonio. Two major ecosystems, the Blackland Prairie and the Cross Timbers, run through the heart of the area, along with ecological elements of adjoining regions, particularly the Hill Country and the East Texas Pineywoods.

Before European settlers arrived, more than 12 million acres of tallgrass prairie stretched through the Prairies and Lakes region. The gently rolling terrain was blanketed with a thick sod of grasses and wildflowers that often grew taller than a man. Wild fires set by Indians and lightning periodically burned the prairie and prevented trees and shrubs from encroaching. Huge herds of bison crossed the Red River from Oklahoma to graze the rich grasses, and prairie wolves hunted the weak, sick, and young of the vast herds.

With the arrival of settlers, the prairie sod was cut by plows and built over with growing cities. The fertile, dark, clay-rich soils were plowed under for farmland and pastures over the years. Farming, combined with fire suppression that allowed forest encroachment, has left no more than maybe 5000 acres of original prairie today.

Within the Blackland Prairie region are north-south bands of Cross Timbers habitat. A thick, scrubby woodland of cedar elm, post oak, hackberry, and hickory grows in the thin, sandy soils of the Cross Timbers. Eisenhower and Lake Mineral Wells state parks contain particularly good examples of this ecosystem.

Visitors find this region's parks ideal for fishing and water sports. Rivers and streams wind through broad valleys in the rolling terrain, fed by plentiful rains. Dams have been constructed on many of these waterways for city water supplies, agriculture, flood control, and recreation. Not surprisingly, many state parks lie on the shores of these reservoirs and offer a broad range of activities, from fishing to waterskiing to swimming. Some of the lakes, such as those at Bonham, Cleburne, and Meridian state parks, are small, no-wake lakes ideal for quiet activities like canoeing and paddleboating, while others, such as Lake Whitney or Ray Roberts Lake, are large, sprawling impoundments of thousands of acres. Boaters with large sailboats and water skiers favor such big lakes.

Although the lake parks emphasize water recreation, many also offer other activities, such as hiking trails. Extensive hiking, mountain-biking, and equestrian trail systems make Lake Somerville and Lake Mineral Wells particularly noteworthy in this respect.

Although lakes dominate this region's parks, a number of exceptions exist, all of which have notable features. An isolated island of tall loblolly pines forms a thick forest canopy in the sandy hills of Bastrop and Buescher state parks, far to the west of the pines' normal range. At Monument Hill/Kreische Brewery, visitors enjoy one of the best views in this part of Texas from a high bluff above the Colorado River; they can also tour the ruins of one of the largest nineteenth-century breweries in the state.

Dinosaur Valley State Park is another notable exception to the parks dominated by water-related activities in this region. Dinosaurs once roamed the lands of this park, leaving the largest concentration of preserved tracks in Texas in the Paluxy River bed near Glen Rose. Fanthorp Inn preserves a prime example of an early Texas inn. Three of the parks in this region, Stephen F. Austin, Lockhart, and Bastrop, even offer golf courses in beautiful settings.

Prairies and Lakes

1. Acton State Historic Site
2. Bastrop State Park
3. Bonham State Park
4. Buescher State Park
5. Cedar Hill State Park
6. Cleburne State Park
7. Confederate Reunion Grounds State Historic Site
8. Cooper Lake State Park
9. Dinosaur Valley State Park
10. Eisenhower Birthplace State Historic Site
11. Eisenhower State Park
12. Fairfield Lake State Park
13. Fanthorp Inn State Historic Site
14. Fort Parker State Park
15. Lake Mineral Wells State Park and Trailway
16. Lake Somerville State Park and Trailway
17. Lake Tawakoni State Park
18. Lake Whitney State Park
19. Lockhart State Park
20. Meridian State Park
21. Monument Hill • Kreische Brewery State Historic Sites
22. Mother Neff State Park
23. Palmetto State Park
24. Purtis Creek State Park
25. Ray Roberts Lake State Park
26. Sam Bell Maxey House State Historic Site
27. Stephen F. Austin State Park and San Felipe State Historic Site
28. Washington-on-the-Brazos State Historic Site

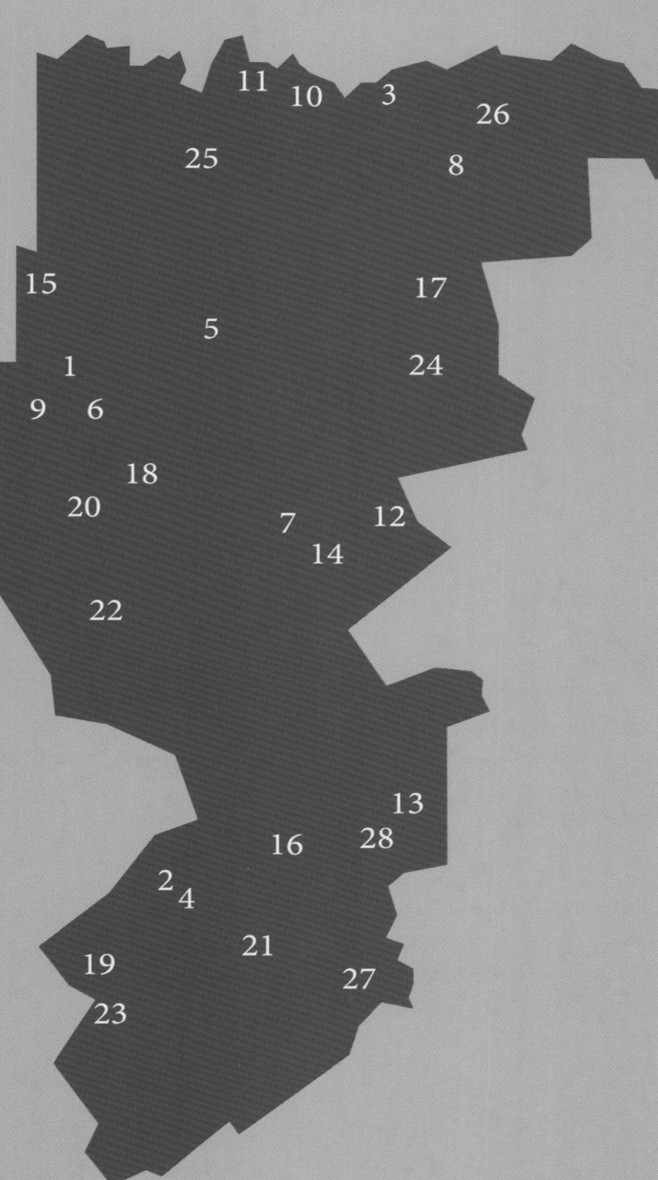

Acton State Historic Site

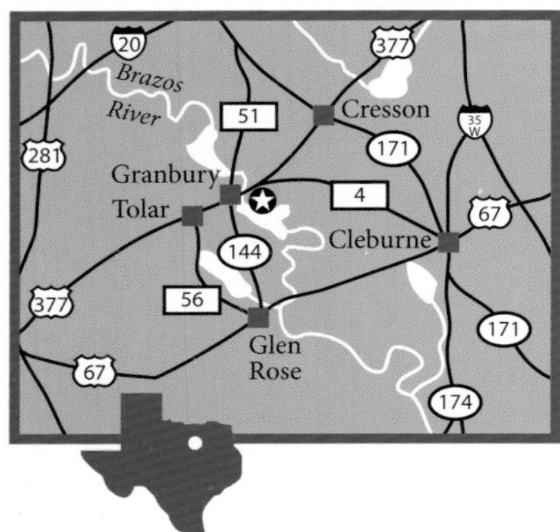

Tiny Acton State Historic Site is the smallest state park in Texas and, with dimensions of only 12 by 21 feet, it might well be the smallest park in the nation. The little-known park contains the grave of Elizabeth Patton Crockett, Davy Crockett's second wife, together with the graves of her son, Robert, and his wife, Matilda.

Davy Crockett's first wife died of an unknown illness in 1813, leaving Crockett with three young children to raise by himself. Crockett met Elizabeth Patton while exploring the Shoal Creek area in Tennessee. She was a widow with two young children, which placed her in a similar situation to that of Crockett. In 1815 they married in Lawrence County, Tennessee. They raised their separate children together, plus added three new children to the family. For many years Crockett prospered as a businessman and Tennessee Congressman. In 1835 he lost a reelection effort, and his businesses failed.

To make a new start, Crockett headed for Texas, arriving just in time for the Texas war of independence. Sadly, a few months later he lay dead after the Battle of the Alamo. Soon after, 20-year-old Robert Patton Crockett traveled to Texas to join the Texas troops to avenge Davy Crockett's death. He later returned to Tennessee to live, and married in 1841. In 1854 he moved his wife and mother to Texas, ultimately settling on land in Hood County that was granted to Davy Crockett's wife by the Texas state government.

In 1860 Elizabeth Crockett died, and was followed soon after by her daughter-in-law Matilda. Robert lived many more years, finally dying in 1889. All three were buried at the same site near the town now known as Acton. In 1911, the legislature authorized a memorial to Elizabeth. A stone shaft, capped by a marble statue of a pioneer woman searching the western horizon, marks the burial site. Tall oak trees and other graves surround the peaceful memorial to the widow of Davy Crockett.

VISITOR INFORMATION

0.006 acre. Open all year. Day use only. The state park lies within the Acton Cemetery—ask for directions in the town. Historic memorial site. All visitor services available in Granbury. For information: Acton State Historic Site, c/o Cleburne State Park, 5800 Park Road 21, Cleburne, TX 76031, (817) 645-4215.

RIGHT
Grave of Elizabeth Crockett
FAR RIGHT
Pine-forested golf course

Bastrop State Park

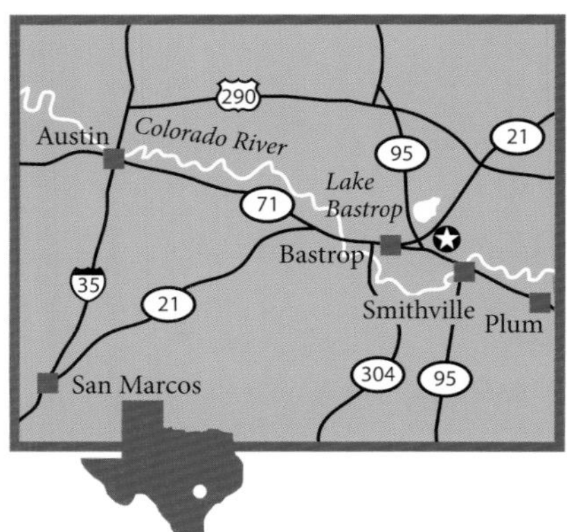

To the surprise of many, thick stands of loblolly pines thrive on sandy hills above the Colorado River only 30 miles southeast of Austin. Called the Lost Pines, they are isolated from the East Texas pine forests by more than 60 miles of post-oak woodland. During the wetter and cooler times of the last ice age, pine forests grew in an uninterrupted blanket from East Texas to the Bastrop area and westward. As the climate warmed and dried, the trees retreated eastward, leaving an isolated, 70-square-mile pocket of pines just east of the town of Bastrop, part of which is contained within

Bastrop State Park. The Carrizo and Reklaw sandstone formations created soil conditions that allowed the pines to survive in the drier climate.

The sandstones are rich in iron oxide, giving them a yellowish to reddish-brown color. The sandy land at Bastrop State Park has eroded into an area of small, steep hills and ravines. Pines dominate the forest canopy, but a mix of post oaks, blackjack oaks, junipers, and other trees adds variety.

Many mammals, such as the raccoon, opossum, bobcat, and fox, are common at Bastrop State Park. Lack of browse in the thick pine forest discourages the existence of large numbers of deer, however. A little known creature, the endangered Houston toad, lives in the park. Like the pines, a number of creatures reach the westernmost limit of their range at Bastrop, including the flying squirrel and the pine warbler.

Bastrop and its sister park, Buescher, attract many birders every year. More than 200 species have been recorded at the two parks, both migrants and residents. The parks' location on the migratory Central Flyway, plus the unique pine-forest habitat, contributes to the high bird count.

Bastrop State Park was named for the town of Bastrop, which in turn was named for Felipe Enrique Neri, Baron de Bastrop. The baron was actually a commoner named Philip Hendrik Nering Bogel, who was wanted in Holland for embezzlement. Apparently he fled Holland, changed his name, and came to the New World. He became friends with Moses Austin, Stephen F. Austin's father, and helped him gain an audience with the Mexican governor of Texas. Austin's petition to settle 300 families in Texas was granted, in part through Bastrop's negotiating efforts. In 1829, the first settlement of Stephen F. Austin's "Little Colony" was founded on the banks of the Colorado River at the western edge of the Lost Pines. Originally named Mina, the town's name was changed to honor Bastrop.

The state park was established in 1938 when the City of Bastrop donated part of the land to the state. During the Depression, the Civilian Conservation Corps (CCC) built many of the park facilities using native stone and timber. The enduring craftsmanship of the CCC is first apparent at the park entrance, whose reddish-brown stone gates were built with the native, iron-rich sandstone. The workers used the same materials to build a large dining hall and 13 rustic cabins. Because the park has so many original CCC-built structures, it earned a national historic landmark award in 1997, one of only five state parks in the nation to do so. One of the park's most popular developments is the 18-hole golf course, a rarity in the Texas state parks. The 6152-yard course, one of the most scenic in Texas, winds through the lush pine forest and attracts golfers year round.

In summer, a large swimming pool draws crowds of people to Bastrop State Park. The small park lake offers fishing, kayaking, and canoeing opportunities. Hikers come to walk the 8.5-mile-loop hiking trail or the park's other 3.5 miles of trail through the park's backcountry. Backpackers can hike to primitive forest campsites along the trail. The 12-mile scenic drive between Bastrop and Buescher state parks makes a scenic but challenging ride for cyclists. The park road goes up and down many small hills, providing a good workout. Stephen F. Austin's first colonists settled at the edge of the Lost Pines; today, thousands of people come every year to relax under the tall pines of Bastrop State Park.

VISITOR INFORMATION

5926 acres. Open all year. Hot and humid in summer. Moderate number of developed campsites in two areas with partial hookups and showers. Primitive camping for backpackers. Cabins—reserve well ahead. Groups may rent barracks buildings and dining hall. Swimming pool, picnicking, hiking trails, fishing, cycling, no-wake boating, scenic drive. Golf course open all year. Park concession store in season with canoe rental. Full visitor services available in Bastrop. For information: Bastrop State Park, P.O. Box 518, Bastrop, TX 78602, (512) 321-2101.

Small lake and pines

Bonham State Park

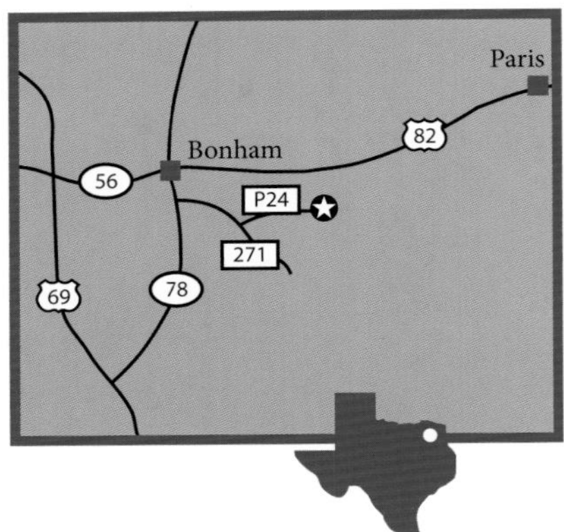

A small 65-acre lake is the centerpiece of heavily wooded Bonham State Park. Canoes slide quietly through its waters, while kids splash noisily in the shallows by the grassy shore of the swimming beach. The park lies in a gently rolling area of farms and grazing land south of the town of Bonham. Because the park has been protected since its acquisition in the 1930s, tall, mature stands of trees cover much of its area. Stately Shumard oaks, green ashes, cottonwoods, hackberries, pecans, and American elms line the lakeshore. Eastern red cedars are also common, especially in drier upland areas. Although much of the park is heavily wooded, wildflowers display their colors every spring in open grassy areas around the small earthen dam that impounds the lake.

The park was initially acquired from the town of Bonham in the 1930s and developed by the Civilian Conservation Corps (CCC). The CCC was established during the Depression of the 1930s to provide jobs for unemployed young men. Corps work crews built and improved state and national parks all across the United States, including many in Texas. At Bonham, the CCC built the dam, roads, bridges, picnic areas, and the boathouse. The combined headquarters and bathhouse building is probably the most prominent structure built by the CCC. The durable, attractive building was constructed of locally quarried limestone.

Because the lake is small, boats must observe a five-mile-per-hour speed limit. Quiet activities—fishing, canoeing, and picnicking—predominate at Bonham State Park which, as it has done for years, continues to attract families seeking a cool escape in the woods of East Texas.

VISITOR INFORMATION

261 acres. Open all year. Hot and humid in summer. Small number of campsites with partial hookups and showers. Eleven-mile hiking and mountain-biking trail, picnicking, swimming, lighted fishing pier, boat ramp, boating. All visitor services available in Bonham. For information: Bonham State Park, 1363 State Park 24, Bonham, TX 75418, (903) 583-5022.

Buescher State Park

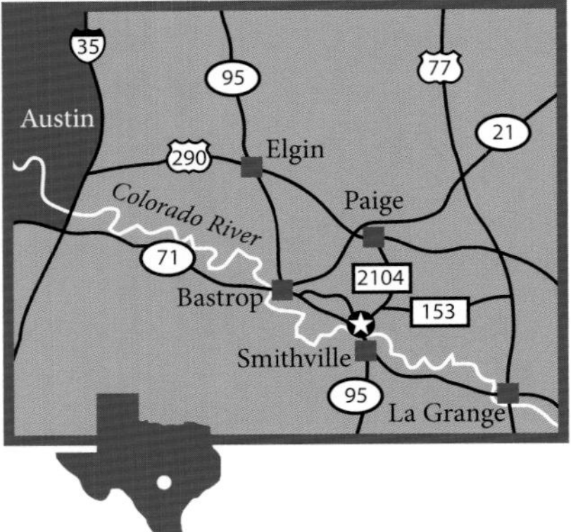

Buescher State Park lies in the Lost Pines of Texas, like its better-known sister park, Bastrop. Scenic, hilly Park Road 1C connects the two woodland parks. The fresh scent of loblolly pines wafts through the air, reminding visitors of the East Texas pine forests. Surprisingly, though, these pines are located on some hilly uplands only about 30 miles southeast of Austin.

During the wetter, cooler period of the Pleistocene, pine forests stretched uninterrupted westward from East Texas to and beyond the Bastrop area. As the ice-age glaciers melted and the climate warmed and dried, the pines slowly retreated east, leaving an isolated 70-square-mile stand in central Texas near Bastrop and Smithville. The Reklaw and Carrizo sandstone formations create a sandy soil conducive to the growth of loblolly pines, despite the drier climate.

The north end of Buescher State Park, along with Bastrop State Park, lies in the Lost Pines. Toward the south end of Buescher State Park, the pines thin, and post oaks, cedar elms, live oaks, hackberries, and other trees become more common. Buescher also has a large area of bottomland deciduous forest along drainages and around small Buescher Lake. This habitat helps attract more than 200 species of birds, including many types of waterfowl that may be seen on the 25-acre lake. Because Buescher has more varied habitat than Bastrop State Park, it tends to attract more bird species

and attendant birders. However, both parks, aided by their location on the Central Flyway, draw many migrant species at various times of year.

Buescher Lake lures fishermen hoping to catch largemouth bass, crappie, and catfish. In winter, the lake gets cold enough that the Parks and Wildlife Department stocks the popular rainbow trout. Unfortunately, the water gets too warm in summer for a year-round population to survive and reproduce.

Because of its small size, the lake is suitable only for non-motorized boats, such as canoes and kayaks. The 7.8-mile Buescher hiking trail winds through dense stands of loblolly pine and deciduous forests of oak and cedar elm. The scenic 12-mile road connecting Bastrop and Buescher state parks provides a good workout for cyclists willing to tackle its hilly terrain. If Bastrop State Park is too crowded on a given weekend, try its attractive but less well-known sister park, Buescher.

ABOVE
Buescher Lake at dawn
RIGHT
Sunset, Joe Pool Reservoir
OPPOSITE PAGE
Swimmers at Bonham Lake

VISITOR INFORMATION

1017 acres. Open all year. Hot and humid in summer. Moderate number of developed campsites with partial hookups and showers. Screened shelters. Limited-use cabins with heat, A/C, electricity, refrigerator, and microwave, but no plumbing. Picnicking, cycling, hiking, fishing, boating. Trout fishing in winter and early spring requires a trout stamp in addition to regular state license. Canoe rentals. Limited visitor services in Smithville; full services in Bastrop. For information: Buescher State Park, P.O. Box 75, Smithville, TX 78957, (512) 237-2241.

Cedar Hill State Park

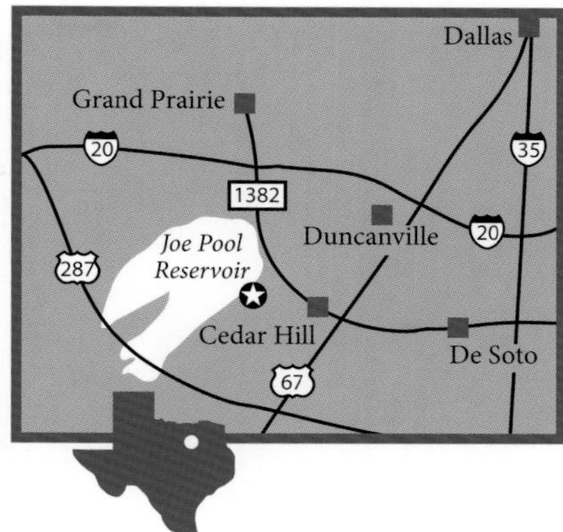

Cedar Hill State Park, one of the newest state parks in Texas, quickly became one of the most popular. Its location in southwest Dallas County makes it a convenient escape for residents of the Dallas–Fort Worth metropolitan area. The park, which opened in 1991, prepared for the expected large influx of visitors by building elaborate facilities on the shore of Joe Pool Reservoir. Among other features, it boasts a marina, two four-lane boat ramps, and 355 developed campsites, more than any other state park but Garner.

To the surprise of first-time visitors, the park lies on the edge of a particularly hilly area of North Texas sometimes known as the Cedar Mountains. The waters of Joe Pool Reservoir lap

at the western slopes of these hills. A thick blanket of junipers, cedar elms, mesquites, and other trees covers the slopes, reminiscent of the Hill Country many miles to the southwest. Skunks, raccoons, coyotes, bobcats, and armadillos all make their homes on the steep, wooded slopes above the lake.

John Anderson Penn was an early settler in the area, establishing a homestead in 1854. In 1859 his son, John Wesley Penn, inherited property in what would become the park and constructed the first buildings. At one time his farm occupied more than 1100 acres. Bottomlands along Mountain Creek, now under the waters of the lake, were farmed, while upland areas were used for grazing and haying. As the years went by, the Penn family added more structures. The farm was operated by the family until 1970. The Parks and Wildlife Department has restored the farm buildings to the 1950s era as important relics of the family farms that once occupied this area of Dallas County. The buildings, built over the course of more than 100 years, provide an architectural record of changes in construction techniques and building materials.

ABOVE
Marina at Joe Pool Reservoir
OPPOSITE PAGE
Indian blankets

Joe Pool Reservoir, opened to the public in 1989, attracts many park visitors. Its 7500 acres beckon to water skiers, weekend sailors, and swimmers, and fishermen are drawn by healthy bass, crappie, and catfish populations. Fishing jetties and boat ramps, plus a long shoreline, provide plenty of lake access. Mountain bikers built a 15-mile trail, one of the best in North Texas, in the park. The park's proximity to the Metroplex and its many recreational facilities are sure to draw large numbers of visitors for years to come.

VISITOR INFORMATION

1826 acres. Open all year. Hot and humid in summer. Large number of campsites with partial hookups and showers, primitive backpacking campsites. Picnicking, hiking and mountain-biking trails, lighted fishing jetties, boating, boat ramps, waterskiing, swimming, historic structures at Penn Farm. Joe Pool Marina rents ski boats, pontoon boats, and other boats, plus has a store, snack bar, and grill. All visitor services available in Cedar Hill, Duncanville, Grand Prairie, and other Metroplex cities. For information: Cedar Hill State Park, 1570 W. FM 1382, Cedar Hill, TX 75104, (972) 291-3900.

CLEBURNE STATE PARK

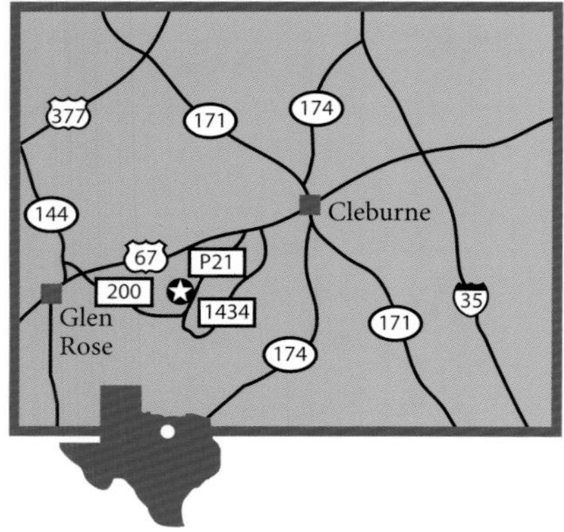

Springs feed the clear, cool waters of Cedar Lake, the centerpiece of Cleburne State Park. The 116-acre lake is tucked away in a small valley in the breaks lining the broad Brazos River Valley. In 1934, local businessmen pushed the site as a suitable location for a state park. Like many of Texas's older state parks, Cleburne was built in the 1930s by the Civilian Conservation Corps (CCC). The CCC was created to employ young men during the Depression. Both the nearby town of Cleburne and the park were named for Confederate General Pat Cleburne.

The CCC built the earthen dam that impounds Cedar Lake. Several springs, now underwater, provide the primary water source for the lake. Because springs feed the lake, its waters tend to be a little cooler than stream-fed lakes. Popular sport fish include largemouth bass, crappie, and catfish.

The narrow valley in which the lake lies is lined with bluffs of white limestone. Much of the uplands above the valley are open, grassy ranchland, but the valley slopes are densely wooded, particularly with Ashe juniper trees, commonly called cedar. Along creeks in the valley bottom, hardwoods such as elms and oaks grow tall and thick. Wildflowers often blanket open, grassy areas near the park headquarters in spring. Deer, armadillos, raccoons, opossums, and squirrels are frequently seen.

Because the lake is small, the park enforces a five-mile-per-hour speed limit for boats. The low speeds not only keep the lake very quiet, they make it ideal for canoeing, paddleboating, and fishing. Swimming, hiking, and shady campgrounds are several more reasons that Cleburne State Park makes an ideal retreat from the busy cities of Fort Worth and Dallas to the northeast.

VISITOR INFORMATION

528 acres. Open all year. Hot in summer. Moderate number of campsites with partial and full hookups and showers. Screened shelters. Boating (low-speed), fishing, swimming, picnicking, hiking and mountain-biking trails, boat ramp. Seasonal store with rental of paddleboats, canoes, fishing boats. All visitor services available in Cleburne and Glen Rose. For information: Cleburne State Park, 5800 Park Road 21, Cleburne, TX 76031, (817) 645-4215.

Confederate Reunion Grounds State Historic Site

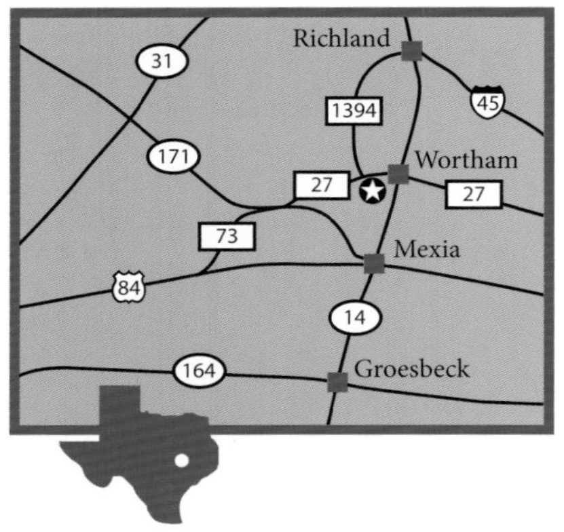

In spite of the hardships of Reconstruction after the Civil War, many Confederate veterans still retained a strong sense of brotherhood. In 1889, veterans in Limestone and Freestone County formed Joe Johnston Camp No. 94 and established a constitution for their organization. Their stated purpose was to perpetuate the memories of fallen comrades, aid disabled survivors and indigent widows and orphans of deceased Confederate soldiers, and preserve the fraternity that grew out of the war.

Reunions were held almost every year in late summer for 57 years. Over time, the organization purchased land at the confluence of the Navasota River and Jack's Creek. Some years as many as 5000 people congregated at the site to socialize, hold memorial programs, and listen to speeches. The reunion grounds were donated to the state in 1983.

Several historical items are displayed on the park grounds. In 1862, the Confederates captured six brass cannons from Union troops at the Battle of Val Verde in New Mexico. The cannons were assigned to a Texas artillery brigade led by Captain T. C. Nettles. Several other cannons captured in Louisiana were added to his brigade. After the war ended, Nettles hid the guns rather than surrender them to the Union. Later they were dug up; one is at the park. Other historical items include the 1872 Heritage House, the 1893 dance pavilion, and Miss Mamie Kennedy's 1914 Confederate Flirtation Walk along the Navasota River.

In addition to the historical sites, the park features picnicking and a variety of other outdoor activities in a peaceful woodland setting of gently rolling hills.

VISITOR INFORMATION

77 acres. Open all year. Hot and humid in summer. Day use only. Historic structures. Picnicking, hiking, fishing, swimming, short hiking trail. Canoes and other small boats on Navasota River. All visitor services available in Mexia. For information: Confederate Reunion Grounds State Historic Site, c/o Fort Parker State Park, 194 Park Road 28, Mexia, TX 76667, (254) 562-5751.

TOP
1893 pavilion
BOTTOM
Flirtation Walk footbridge, Navasota River

Cooper Lake State Park

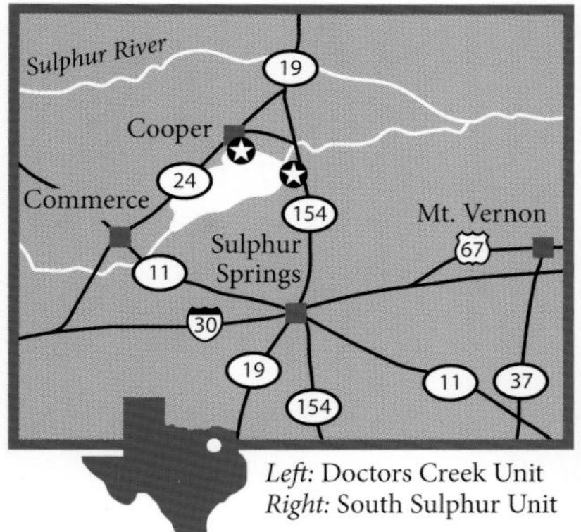

Left: Doctors Creek Unit
Right: South Sulphur Unit

Lake sunset

Cooper Lake State Park is a fairly new park in northeast Texas with extensive facilities for everyone from fishermen to campers to horse lovers. The two main units of the park lie on the shores of Cooper Lake, itself a relatively new reservoir. The Army Corps of Engineers began construction on the five-mile-long earth-fill dam in 1986 and began filling the 19,280-acre reservoir in September 1991. A little more than a year later, the lake was opened to boats. The main lake tributary is the South Sulphur River, although a number of other waterways add significant flows.

Cooper Lake was built primarily as a water-supply reservoir for Dallas, Sulphur Springs, and other communities, but has important secondary uses for recreation and flood control. Unlike other lakes, the Texas Parks and Wildlife Department controls the entire shoreline and lake, except for dam and water-supply functions. Most of the lakeshore lies within a wildlife management area; the rest is occupied by the two main units of the state park and the dam.

Cooper Lake lies in a mixed-habitat area a little west of the Pineywoods of East Texas. The gently rolling terrain is a mix of post-oak woodland—oaks, elms, hackberries, eastern red cedars, and other trees—and prairie. The most common wildlife include white-tailed deer, opossums, armadillos, cottontails, and raccoons. Interesting, but less common, wildlife include wild turkeys, falcons, and bald eagles. A lot of timber was left standing in the lake to provide fish habitat, but it has proven to be valuable for waterfowl as well. Fishing on the lake has already showed good success, due in large part to heavy initial stockings of Florida largemouth bass. Other species caught in the lake include catfish, crappie, and striped bass.

The park has two main units, Doctors Creek and South Sulphur. Both units have camping with partial hookups, picnic areas, fishing piers, and boat ramps. Doctors Creek has screened shelters, and South Sulphur has cabins and an equestrian camping area. Because the two units adjoin a wildlife management area, the combined large area allows long horse, hiking, and mountain-biking trails. Two boat ramps, separate from the main units, are also available.

VISITOR INFORMATION

3026 acres. Open all year. Hot and humid in summer. Camping with partial hookups and showers at both units. Walk-in tent sites and equestrian campground (at South Sulphur). Screened shelters at Doctors Creek and cabins (both fully furnished and limited use—heat, A/C, and electricity, but no plumbing—cabins) at South Sulphur. Lighted fishing piers, boat ramps, picnicking, waterskiing, swimming. Hiking, mountain-biking, nature, and equestrian trails. All visitor services available in Paris and Sulphur Springs; limited services available in Cooper. For information: Cooper Lake State Park, Doctors Creek Unit, 1664 FR 1529 South, Cooper, TX 75432, (903) 395-3100; South Sulphur Unit, 1690 FM 3505, Sulphur Springs, TX 75482, (903) 945-5256.

Dinosaur Valley State Park

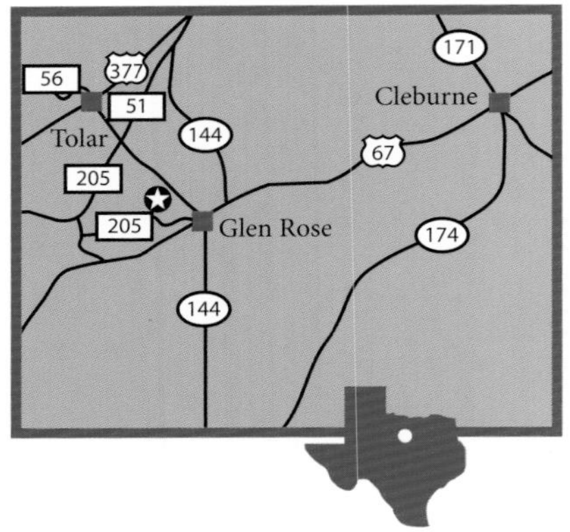

About 113 million years ago, during the early Cretaceous period, shallow seas washed over much of Texas. On mudflats near the shore of one of these seas, a giant sauropod called the *Pleurocoelus* or another similar dinosaur grazed on evergreen foliage. A hungry, carnivorous *Acrocanthosaurus* spied the larger herbivore and began pursuit, leaving a trail of footprints across the soft mud. The final outcome of the fight is unknown; only the tracks remain, preserved in a process beginning when the sun started to dry and harden these prints. Tides from the sea then washed in sediment that covered them. Over time the mud hardened into rock, with the track-bearing layer becoming limestone. The Paluxy River eroded away the softer, overlying sediments, leaving the tracks exposed today in Dinosaur Valley State Park.

The tracks were first discovered in 1903, but were not widely known until Roland Bird of the American Museum of Natural History investigated the site in 1938. The tracks described above were excavated and are now displayed at the American Museum of Natural History in New York and the Texas Memorial Museum in Austin. Since the discovery, at least 1000 tracks have been found in the riverbed of the Paluxy. The most common track is that of the three-toed *Acrocanthosaurus*. The footprints measure as much as 24 inches long and 17 inches wide. The 20- to 30-foot-long carnivore belonged to the same group as the later, and larger, *Tyrannosaurus rex*.

The second type of track uncovered in the park belonged to one of the *Acrocanthosaurus*'s prey animals, the 30- to 50-foot-long sauropod. This massive animal weighed as much as 40 tons and left tracks as large as three feet long and two feet wide. It was related to the even larger *Apatosaurus*, one of a group of the biggest land animals of all time. Two full-size models of the *Apatosaurus* and *Tyrannosaurus rex* are displayed in the park.

The third type of track found in the park is much rarer than the other two and harder to identify. Researchers believe that it may be from a 30-foot, three-ton dinosaur called the *Iguanodon* or from a theropod. It was a plant-eating creature, as was the big sauropod, and like the latter, it was probably pursued by the carnivorous *Acrocanthosaurus*.

Dinosaur Valley State Park contains one of the best displays of dinosaur tracks in the world. Other such sites are scattered throughout central Texas, from Glen Rose to Utopia, but they lie mostly on private land. The state park's headquarters building has exhibits that explain much about the giant reptiles.

The dinosaur tracks are visible in several areas of the Paluxy River bottom. Hiking trails lead from the river to overlooks and primitive campsites in the hills to the north. The upland terrain, wooded with Ashe junipers, live oaks, Texas red oaks, and other trees, is similar to that of the Hill Country to the southwest. In the creek bottoms, cedar elms, American elms, green ashes, and other trees dominate. In the deep, moist soils along the river, pecans, cottonwoods, sycamores, black willows, and walnuts thrive.

Many different animals inhabit the park, from wild turkeys to armadillos, and from raccoons to coyotes. They too leave tracks in the mud, but unless certain conditions act to preserve them, their prints will quickly disappear, unlike those of the dinosaurs that roamed this area millions of years ago.

VISITOR INFORMATION

1580 acres. Open all year. Hot and humid in summer. Relatively small, developed campground with partial hookups and showers. Primitive campsites for backpackers. Picnicking, hiking, mountain biking, swimming, fishing, equestrian area for horseback riding, interpretative museum at visitor center. All visitor services available in Glen Rose, Cleburne, and Granbury. For information: Dinosaur Valley State Park, P.O. Box 396, Glen Rose, TX 76043, (254) 897-4588.

Eisenhower Birthplace State Historic Site

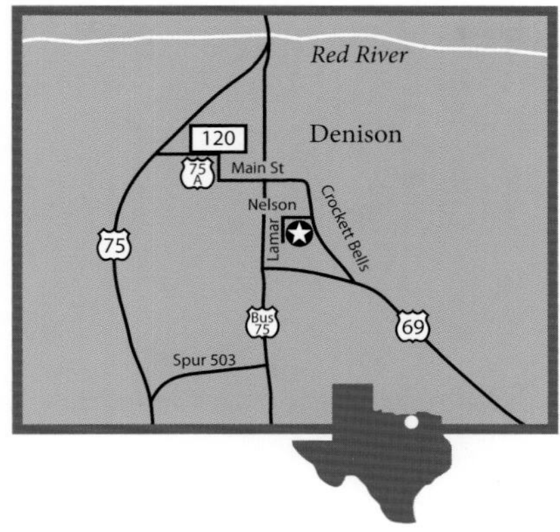

On October 14, 1890, Dwight David Eisenhower was born in a white, two-story frame house at 208 E. Day Street in Denison, Texas. His father worked in the yards of the Missouri, Kansas, and Texas Railroad, known as the Katy. His parents lived in Denison for only three years; they moved to Abilene, Kansas, in the spring after the birth of Dwight, who was their only child born in Texas.

Eisenhower later became a five-star general of the United States Army and led the Allies to victory in Europe in World War II. Publicity surrounding his success in Europe spurred the memories of Jennie Jackson, the principal of Lamar Elementary School in Denison. She remembered an Eisenhower family that lived in Denison and a baby named David. (The future president's mother only later changed the order of the baby's given names to avoid confusion with his father, also named David.) Jackson wrote General Eisenhower in an attempt to verify her memories. The general was at that time unaware of the house in Denison, believing that he had been born in Tyler. He gave Jackson his mother's address, however, and she confirmed that he had indeed been born in Denison.

Jennie Jackson formed a group to preserve the home of one of America's most prominent generals. The group raised funds to purchase the house and donated it to the City of Denison. Jackson's interest was well-placed; in 1952, Eisenhower was elected President of the United States. On October 14, 1953, the President's birthday, the Eisenhower Birthplace Foundation was established with the purpose of restoring the house and converting the surrounding property into a park. In 1958, the property was conveyed to the Texas State Parks Board.

VISITOR INFORMATION

6 acres. Open all year, except on Mondays, with guided tours of restored home. Call for hours. Historic home, visitor center, garden, short hiking trail, interpretive exhibits on the life of President Eisenhower, plus some of his personal effects. Store with Eisenhower and Texas history books and other items. All visitor services available in Denison. For information: Eisenhower Birthplace State Historic Site, 609 S. Lamar Ave., Denison, TX 75021, (903) 465-8908.

OPPOSITE PAGE, TOP
Fossil dinosaur footprint
OPPOSITE PAGE, BOTTOM
Paluxy River
RIGHT
Dwight D. Eisenhower statue

Eisenhower State Park

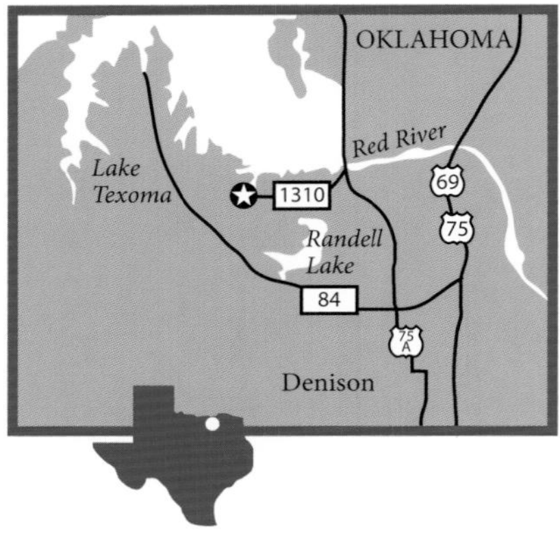

Although an early government report once described the area around Eisenhower State Park as "uninhabitable to man or beast," modern-day visitors and residents would hardly agree. The park, named for President Dwight D. Eisenhower, who was born in nearby Denison, lies on the shores of Lake Texoma in the heart of the Cross Timbers region. The Cross Timbers is a north-south belt of gently rolling land forested with a thick growth of shrubs and stunted trees, such as cedar elms, blackjack oaks, post oaks, hackberries, and hickories. Unlike the fertile Blackland Prairie soil to the east, Cross Timbers soil is thin and sandy and easily washes away, exposing rock and clay outcroppings.

The thick woods of the Cross Timbers were a major barrier to travel and culture for both Indians and settlers, despite the determined efforts of both to eradicate it. They were such a formidable obstacle that in 1832 Washington Irving described travel through it as "like struggling through a forest of cast iron." Although modern civilization has made many inroads, much of the tenacious forest still exists.

In 1944, the U.S. Army Corps of Engineers created Lake Texoma by building the earth-fill Denison Dam on the Red River just north of Denison. The 89,000-acre impoundment, the tenth largest man-made reservoir in the United States, lies on the boundary of Texas and Oklahoma and has a sinuous 580-mile shoreline. The Red

River, named for its heavy burden of red silt and clay, is the lake's principal water source, but the Washita River in Oklahoma also makes a significant contribution. The two rivers and numerous smaller tributaries give the lake a watershed of almost 40,000 square miles.

Eisenhower State Park perches on rocky bluffs above the lake on the south shore. The rocks were created 90 million years ago during the Cretaceous period, when seas covered what is now North Texas. The rocks are called marl, and are made of interbedded layers of limestone and shale. Ammonoids and other fossils are common in these bluffs.

The area had a colorful history long before the creation of the lake. In the 1850s, the Butterfield Overland Stage had several water stops in the area. The Chisolm and Shawnee cattle-drive trails crossed the Red River nearby. Indians, Fort Washita soldiers, outlaws, settlers, and cattle crossed the river at Colbert's Crossing, a busy ford just below the dam. Later, a ferry replaced the ford, and eventually a bridge replaced the ferry.

Fishing attracts many people to Eisenhower State Park today. Fishing piers, a boat ramp, and a marina all make lake access easy. Introduced striped bass are probably the most popular and successful fish at the lake. The striper, a saltwater fish, reproduces and does well in the slightly saline water of the Red and Washita rivers. One bass caught in 1984 weighed 35 pounds 2 ounces. Although they are not heavily fished, catfish lurk deep in Lake Texoma waters. In 2004, an angler pulled a record 121.5-pound blue catfish from the reservoir.

Another introduced fish, the smallmouth bass, favors rocky habitat such as that found under the bluffs of the state park. Although Texas's record-largest smallmouth was caught at Lake Whitney, the Oklahoma record smallmouth, weighing six pounds eight ounces, was caught in Lake Texoma. Other popular fish caught at Lake Texoma include black and white crappie, largemouth bass, spotted bass, white bass, and alligator gar. Even the rare paddlefish is found in the lake.

The massive lake attracts more than just fishermen. Sailboats glide across the lake, pushed by North Texas breezes. Powerboats zip over the waters, often towing water skiers. The marina at the state park, along with several others, provides slips for permanent mooring. Some boats in the lake approach 60 feet in length.

Swimmers can paddle around a protected cove in the state park, while hikers and mountain bikers can traverse a six-mile trail that winds along the bluffs and through the campgrounds, providing excellent lake views. Campers can relax in shady campsites and escape fast-paced modern life, at least for a while.

VISITOR INFORMATION

423 acres. Open all year. Very busy on weekends, spring through fall. Hot and humid in summer, but the lake is available for cooling off. Several large campgrounds, with partial to full hookups with showers. Screened shelters. Swimming, picnicking, lighted fishing pier, boat ramp; hiking, mountain-biking, and nature trails. Marina has boat rentals, store, fuel, and other services. The park does not allow fossil collecting. Fishermen with only a standard state fishing license must stay on their respective state's side of the lake. A special license is available that allows fishing anywhere on the lake. All visitor services available in nearby Denison. For information: Eisenhower State Park, 50 Park Road 20, Denison, TX 75020, (903) 465-1956.

OPPOSITE PAGE, TOP
Jet skiers
OPPOSITE PAGE, BOTTOM
Lake Texoma
LEFT
Purple coneflowers

Fairfield Lake State Park

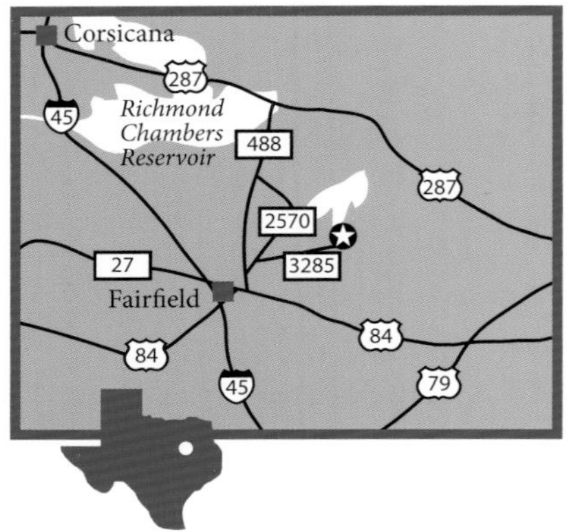

Fairfield Lake State Park lies in a transition zone known as post oak savannah between the pine forests of East Texas and the Blackland Prairies to the west. The area surrounding Fairfield Lake consists of gently rolling woodland with scattered farms. Trees such as post oaks, eastern red cedars, elms, white ashes, and hickories dominate the forest. In spring, wildflowers dot scattered open fields within the park.

The park hugs the shoreline of 2400-acre Fairfield Lake, a reservoir that was built to provide cooling water for a Texas Utilities electrical generating plant. The power plant keeps the lake water warmer than normal all year, extending the season for swimming and waterskiing further into spring and fall than at other area lakes.

Because they are suitable for other fish than those usually found in the waters of this region, the warm lake waters allow a unique fishing experience. Red drum, commonly called redfish, is a saltwater species from the Gulf of Mexico that has been stocked in this freshwater lake where, surprisingly, it has done quite well. The state-record inland redfish, 36.83 pounds, was caught at the lake. Unlike on the coast, there is no maximum-length limit on redfish catches in Fairfield Lake.

Other fish also thrive in the reservoir. Another non-native fish, the blue tilapia, or African perch, flourishes in the warm lake waters. Unlike the redfish, however, the tilapia was introduced by accident and is unwelcome because it tends to dominate and overpopulate reservoirs. However, it does provide a good sport and eating fish. Because the fish are plankton feeders, they are not normally caught with a hook and line. Instead, bowfishing gear used in shallow waters is usually the most effective method.

Despite the presence of tilapia, largemouth bass do very well at Fairfield, in part because of the abundance of smaller prey fish, such as threadfin shad, in the warm water. Bass as large as 13 or 14 pounds have been caught there. Other popular fish include hybrid striped bass, crappie, and both channel and flathead catfish.

The state park attracts more than just fishermen. Swimmers enjoy the warmer water at a sandy, buoyed swimming area. Boat ramps provide easy access for water skiers and sailboats. Away from the lake, 15 miles of hiking, mountain-biking, and equestrian trails lead to quiet areas of the park. The long trail leads to a primitive camping area for backpackers which, despite its designation, is not too primitive: it has water, flush toilets, and charcoal grills. A two-mile nature trail and one-mile bird-watching trail offer other recreational opportunities.

Visitor Information

1460 acres. Open all year. Hot and humid in summer. Busiest on weekends, spring through fall. Large developed campground with showers; most sites have partial hookups. Primitive camp area for backpackers. Lighted fishing pier, boat ramps, picnicking; hiking, nature, and mountain-biking trails; swimming, fishing, boating. Limited visitor services in nearby Fairfield; all services available in Palestine and Corsicana. For information: Fairfield Lake State Park, 123 State Park Road 64, Fairfield, TX 75840, (903) 389-4514.

Fanthorp Inn State Historic Site

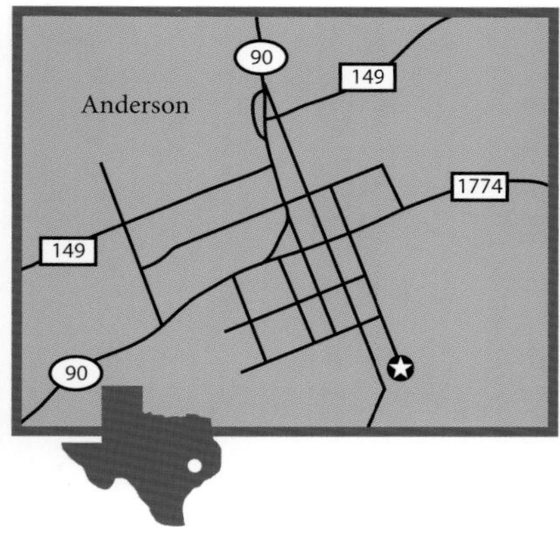

Travelers in the early days of the Texas Republic generally found accommodations to be either rough or nonexistent. Usually they ended up staying in the tiny, primitive houses of settlers. As time passed, however, roadside inns developed to serve the needs of travelers. Initially, the Fanthorp Inn was little more than a small log house shared with travelers, but it later became a sizable, prosperous inn.

Henry Fanthorp, an Englishman, purchased land on which the inn was built in 1832 from one of Stephen F. Austin's first colonists. Initially he built a corncrib and dealt in corn, buying when prices were low and selling when they were high. He soon built a two-room dogtrot log home and married Rachel Kennard in 1834, having been widowed twice before. They had three children over the next few years.

The Fanthorp home was well-located on busy roads and became a popular stopping place for travelers. Several stage lines passed through, providing a steady flow of customers. Fanthorp charged $1.00 to $2.00 per night for food and accommodations for one person and a horse. The food served was basic: beef, pork, cornbread, and sweet potatoes enlivened at times with chicken, turkey, and apple pie. One boarder described the coffee as "strong enough to bear up an iron wedge." Although the food received mixed reviews, it must have been better than the alternatives, because the inn grew in popularity.

To accommodate the increasing trade, Fanthorp steadily enlarged the inn. He built additions and a second story with an upstairs gallery, so that the building ultimately ended up with 18 rooms. To lessen the risk of fire and to keep the main building cooler, the kitchen was built as a separate structure in back. A barn boarded travelers' horses. Quite a few famous people, such as Sam Houston, Anson Jones, and Henderson Yoakum, stayed at the establishment over the years. Others rumored to have visited include Jefferson Davis, Robert E. Lee, Ulysses S. Grant, and Zachary Taylor. Kenneth Anderson, the last vice president of the Republic of Texas, died at the inn on July 3, 1845, and was buried in the Fanthorp family cemetery. The town developing around the inn was named Anderson in his honor.

The inn prospered during the Civil War, but Henry and Rachel Fanthorp died of yellow fever soon thereafter, in 1867, and their one surviving heir, daughter Mary Fanthorp Stone, soon closed the inn. She and her descendants used the hotel as a residence and kept it in the family until it was conveyed to the Texas Parks and Wildlife Department in 1977. The department has done a meticulous job restoring the inn to its appearance during its heyday from 1850 to 1867. For six generations, the historic inn remained in the Fanthorp family; today, it provides a glimpse of the early days of Texas history.

OPPOSITE PAGE
Sunrise over Fairfield Lake
ABOVE
Fanthorp Inn

VISITOR INFORMATION

1.4 acres. Open all year for tours Saturday and Sunday, 9 AM to 3:30 PM, and Wednesday through Friday for group tours by reservation. Stagecoach rides in replica of 1850 Concord coach offered on the second Saturday of each month. Historic structure with exhibits, picnicking. Food and gas in Anderson. Full visitor services available in Navasota and Bryan. For information: Fanthorp Inn State Historic Site, P.O. Box 296, Anderson, TX 77830, (936) 873-2633.

Fort Parker State Park

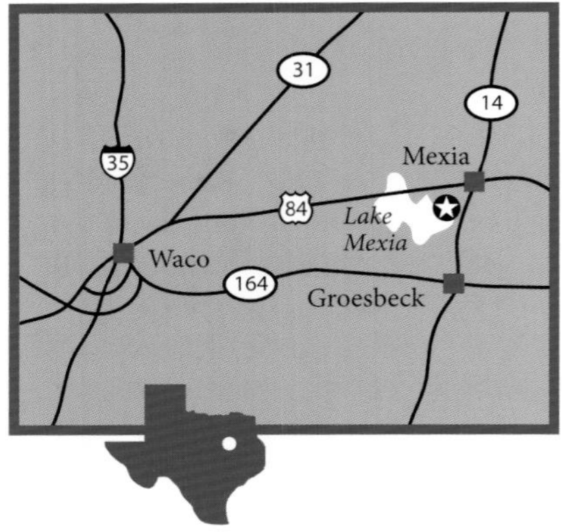

Fort Parker State Park lies in lush, gently rolling terrain in east-central Texas south of Mexia. Its wooded facilities line the shore of 750-acre Lake Fort Parker. The small reservoir was created by the Civilian Conservation Corps (CCC) in the 1930s by building an earth-fill dam on the Navasota River. The CCC was established during the Depression of the 1930s to provide jobs for unemployed young men. Its workers were responsible for the construction at many state parks and other public facilities in Texas, as well as in the rest of the country. At Fort Parker State Park, the CCC built roads and buildings in addition to the dam.

The park was named after nearby Fort Parker, a historic settlement founded in 1833. The settlement was built within the walls of a wooden stockade to protect against Indian attacks. In a Comanche raid on May 19, 1836, five settlers were killed and five were captured, including nine-year-old Cynthia Ann Parker. She was adopted by the Comanches, later married Chief Nacona, and bore three children. In 1860 she and her infant daughter were recaptured by Captain Sul Ross and some Texas Rangers and returned to relatives in East Texas. She readjusted poorly to Anglo-American life and died four years later, shortly after the death of her daughter. Her two sons remained with the Comanches; one of them, Quanah Parker, became a famous chief of the tribe.

The park rests in an area with characteristics of both the post oak savannah and the Blackland Prairie. Because the park was established many years ago, a tall canopy of oaks, cedar elms, pecans, hickories, and other trees has grown up. The thick woods shelter wildlife such as white-tailed deer, armadillos, opossums, raccoons, and many bird species. A short hiking trail provides good opportunities to view some of the park's wildlife, especially early and late in the day.

The waters of Lake Fort Parker hide some of the park's most popular wildlife. Fishing piers, a boat ramp, and an extensive shoreline provide excellent lake access for fishermen. Popular catches include largemouth and white bass, crappie, and channel, blue, and flathead catfish. Small boats can travel upstream on the Navasota River, adding more fishing options.

In winter, the Texas Parks and Wildlife Department stocks rainbow trout in tiny Lake Springfield, located just north of the Lake Fort Parker dam. Cool spring water feeding Lake Springfield, plus colder winter weather, allows the cold-water fish to survive. The lake is reached via a short hiking trail that starts near the group camp area.

Because Lake Fort Parker is small and shallow, it is better suited to canoes and small fishing boats than large, fast boats and water skiers. From March through November, the park offers canoe rentals and prearranged shuttles on weekends to Confederate Reunion Grounds State Historic Site for the three-mile canoe trip down the Navasota River to the lake. Although the lake's small size restricts some activities, it makes it a quiet retreat from everyday life, and one that continues to attract visitors, as it has been doing for more than 60 years.

Visitor Information

1448 acres. Open all year. Hot and humid in summer. Small campground with partial hookups and showers. Screened shelters. Fishing piers, boat ramp, short nature, hiking and mountain-biking trails, swimming, picnicking, seasonal canoe rental. All visitor services available in Mexia and Groesbeck. For information: Fort Parker State Park, 194 Park Road 28, Mexia, TX 76667, (254) 562-5751.

LEFT
Lake Fort Parker fishing pier
OPPOSITE PAGE
Sunrise over Lake Mineral Wells

Lake Mineral Wells State Park and Trailway

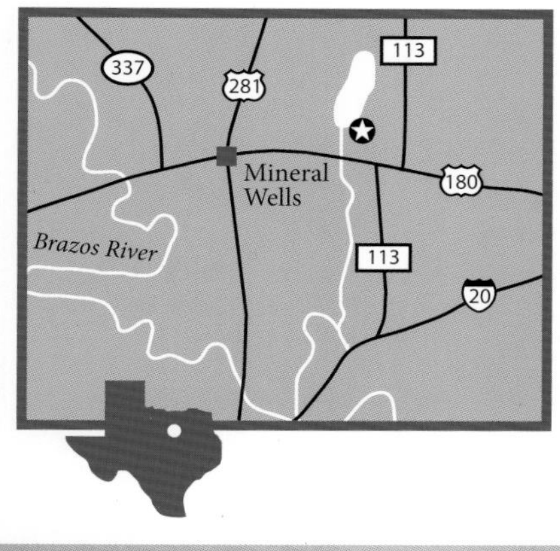

Lake Mineral Wells State Park has some of the most diverse recreational opportunities of any state park in Texas. The 646-acre lake offers swimming and boating, although waterskiing and jet skis are not allowed because of its small size. Several fishing piers and boats allow easy access for fishermen. Extensive hiking, mountain-biking, and equestrian trails lead to primitive campsites deep into the park's backcountry. At the trailhead, there is even a developed equestrian campground with 20 campsites. The Lake Mineral Wells State Trailway passes right by the park, offering miles of scenic trail for hikers, mountain bikers, and equestrians.

Most surprising to first-time park visitors are the rock-climbing opportunities on bluffs on the east side of the lake. Only three other state parks in Texas, Enchanted Rock, Hueco Tanks, and Caprock Canyons, offer the sport.

Much of the park's soil has a reddish color, due to the presence of iron. Coal was mined in the area, as close as six miles north of the park. The ghost town of Thurber, 30 miles to the southwest, depended for years on mining that began in the 1880s. The nearby town of Mineral Wells got its start in 1885, when the Crazy Well was dug and discovered to produce highly mineralized water. The town became an important health spa by the early twentieth century, with 400 wells producing mineral water said to cure mental illness and a host of other maladies. Today, the state park is probably the largest draw in the Mineral Wells area.

The park is particularly popular with climbers from the Dallas–Fort Worth area. As would be expected in the rolling North Texas terrain, the cliffs are not high, generally no more than 35 to 40 feet high. However, the sheer rock faces and overhangs offer plenty of challenges to climbers.

Most of the climbing activity happens in Penitentiary Hollow, a small but scenic maze of cliffs, narrow canyons, and massive boulders. Tall cedar elms and other trees dot the area, reaching toward the sun from deep, shaded canyon bottoms. The rock is a firm, durable conglomerate, which provides an excellent climbing surface. Climbs are rated on a scale of increasing difficulty, from 5.1 to 5.14. Climbs at Penitentiary Hollow rate as difficult as 5.10 to 5.11.

During World War II, the hollow was the boot-camp training center of nearby Fort Wolters. The difficult, punishing military training that troops underwent there left less fond memories of the place than those modern-day rock climbers have.

The Lake Mineral Wells State Trailway, once a busy railroad line, opened in 1998 with 20 miles of trail. It begins northwest of Weatherford, and travels west to downtown Mineral Wells. The trailway has four trailheads, including one at the state park. It winds gently through farm and ranchlands, crossing numerous creeks on 16 bridges. Because the country is relatively flat and railroads must have gentle grades, the route is easy with no steep climbs.

The railroad was built in the late 1800s, and stayed active as a freight line until 1992. After abandonment, the tracks were removed, the bridges were decked and railed, and the railroad bed was surfaced with crushed limestone and, on the two miles leading into Mineral wells, paved with asphalt. A 500-foot-long bridge allows the safe crossing over U.S. Highway 180.

The state park lies within the Cross Timbers region. Rolling hills of sandstone and shale are covered with thick, stunted woods of cedar elm, post oak, blackjack oak, Ashe juniper, and mesquite, interspersed with occasional grassy prairies. The dense woods made travel difficult in the early days. Pecans and cottonwoods thrive in the moister bottomlands along creeks and rivers. The lake was created by damming Rock Creek, a large tributary of the Brazos River.

Common wildlife includes white-tailed deer, wild turkey, and many bird species.

VISITOR INFORMATION

3283 acres. Open all year. Hot in summer. Large campground with partial hookups and showers. Screened shelters. Developed equestrian campground. Primitive campsites for backpackers. Hiking, mountain-biking, and horse trails; boat ramp, fishing piers, picnicking, and swimming. Park concession store rents canoes, paddleboats, kayaks, and fishing boats. Rock climbers must register at park headquarters; there are restrictions on bolts, pitons, and other rock-damaging equipment. Full visitor services available in Mineral Wells. For information: Lake Mineral Wells State Park, 100 Park Road 71, Mineral Wells, TX 76067, (940) 328-1171.

ABOVE
Lake Mineral Wells
OPPOSITE PAGE, TOP
Lake Somerville Trailway
OPPOSITE PAGE, BOTTOM
Lake Somerville

Lake Somerville State Park and Trailway

Top: Birch Creek Unit
Bottom: Nails Creek Unit

Lake Somerville State Park contains a surprisingly large undeveloped tract of land in the middle of the state, on the shores of Lake Somerville. In 1962, the U.S. Army Corps of Engineers began building Somerville Dam to control flooding and provide municipal water. The dam was constructed on Yegua Creek, about 20 miles upstream from its confluence with the Brazos River. The two main units of the state park, Nails Creek and Birch Creek, lie across the lake from each other and are connected by the extensive Lake Somerville Trailway that loops around the undeveloped west end of the lake.

Each unit contains boat ramps, picnic and swimming areas, and nature trails. From these two areas, boaters and water skiers can set out on the 11,630-acre lake. Fishermen try their luck from shore or the fishing pier at Birch Creek, or else launch boats and search for a favorite fishing hole. Popular catches include white bass, crappie, largemouth bass, and catfish. Children splash around in the lake, keeping cool on hot days.

The park's real jewel is the trailway, which contains almost 22 miles of trail. The main trail is 13 miles long and connects the two park units; spurs and side loops make up the rest of the trailway. The broad trail is open to hikers, equestrians, and mountain bikers. Because some of the side trails have small bridges that cannot handle the weight of a horse, a few of them are not open to equestrians. The park has built a specially developed equestrian campground at Birch Creek at the start of the trail, and along the way there are several primitive campgrounds with pit toilets for equestrians and backpackers.

The trail passes through a mix of two habitats, the Blackland Prairie and the post oak savannah. Lush meadows, carpeted with wildflowers in the spring, line some of the trail and offer broad views of the lake and surrounding country. Hillsides often contain a mix of yaupons, post oaks, blackjack oaks, and other plants. In creek bottoms, a dense canopy of water oaks, elms, hickories, and other trees shades the trail. Waterfowl and wading birds favor Flag Pond, near the Nails Creek end of the trail. The large undeveloped area encourages abundant wildlife; raccoons, white-tailed deer, coyotes, rabbits, and many other creatures are commonly sighted.

Lake Somerville State Park contains a broad mix of recreational activities, from boating and waterskiing on the lake to backcountry hiking and horseback riding. There is an activity at Lake Somerville to fit every taste.

VISITOR INFORMATION

5520 acres. Open all year. Hot and humid in summer. Large number of developed campsites with partial hookups and showers at Birch Creek. Equestrian campground at Birch Creek. Primitive campsites for backpackers and equestrians. Hiking and nature trails, picnicking, waterskiing, swimming, boat ramps at both units. Fishing pier at Birch Creek. Extensive hiking, mountain-biking, equestrian trail system connects units. All visitor services available in Brenham, Giddings, Caldwell. For information: Lake Somerville State Park and Trailway, Birch Creek Unit: 14222 Park Road 57, Somerville, TX 77879, (979) 535-7763; Nails Creek Unit: 6280 FM 180, Ledbetter, TX 78946, (979) 289-2392.

Lake Tawakoni State Park

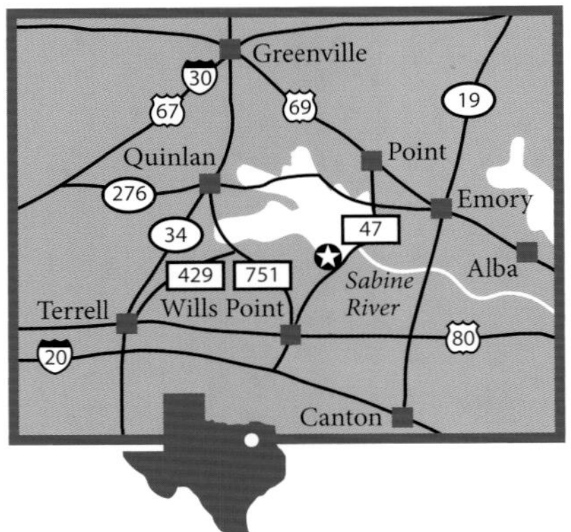

Lake Tawakoni State Park is a relatively new park lying on the south shore of Lake Tawakoni. The lake is a large 36,700-acre reservoir created by the U.S. Army Corps of Engineers when it built Iron Bridge Dam on the upper reaches of the Sabine River east of Dallas. It was constructed primarily as a water supply for Dallas and other area communities, and was named for an early Indian tribe. Before the land was flooded by the lake's creation, it was used primarily for farming and ranching. The park contains about five miles of shoreline out of the approximately 200 miles of total lakeshore. Fishermen visit the lake in large numbers, hoping to catch striped bass, largemouth bass, crappie, and catfish. Large areas of submerged timber encourage good fish populations.

The park and surrounding terrain is relatively flat, typical for the area. Post oak savannah is the dominant habitat in the park, with a mix of woodland and open meadows. Post oaks, along with cedar elms, red oaks, hackberries, eastern red cedars, and hickories, make up the forested sections. The park contains a 40-acre patch of native tallgrass prairie, a habitat that has become quite rare in East Texas.

VISITOR INFORMATION

351 acres. Large number of campsites with partial and full hookups and showers. Hiking and mountain-biking trails, boat ramp, picnicking, swimming, fishing, boating, waterskiing. All visitor services available in Greenville. For information: Lake Tawakoni State Park, 10822 FM 2475, Wills Point, TX 75169, (903) 560-7123.

RIGHT
Sunset over Lake Tawakoni
OPPOSITE PAGE
Lake Whitney campsite

Lake Whitney State Park

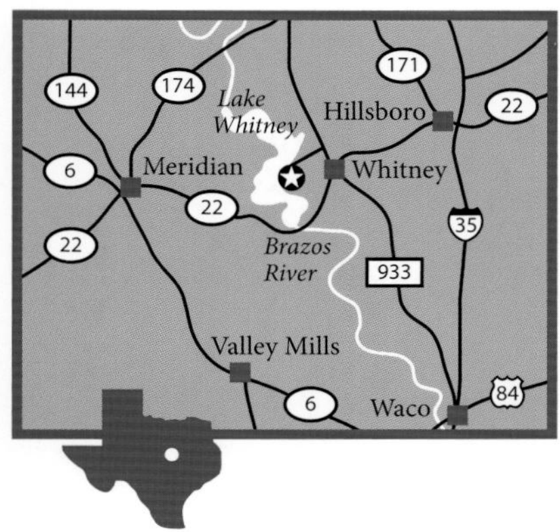

Lake Whitney State Park lies on a peninsula on the east shore of 23,560-acre Lake Whitney, created in 1951 when the U.S. Army Corps of Engineers completed a two-mile-long dam on the Brazos River for flood control and power generation. The large lake winds upstream from the dam for 45 miles, providing plenty of room for large numbers of boaters, fishermen, and water skiers.

Without a doubt, the lake is the main draw of the popular state park, especially in summer and on warm weekends in spring and fall. Most camping and picnic sites lie near the lakeshore, within sight of water. The large, deep lake has no restrictions on the size of boats or motors used, and boat ramps in the park make launching easy. Water skiers love the broad open lake and zip back and forth across the water. The wide expanse of water also provides plenty of room for sailboats to glide across.

Lake Whitney is noted for its varied fishing opportunities. Excellent smallmouth bass fishing can be found along rocky sections of shore; the bass favor rocky areas under cliffs because they need such habitat to spawn. The lake is so conducive to the smallmouth bass that the state's largest smallmouth was caught here.

Largemouth bass, another popular Whitney catch, favor a different type of habitat, shallow areas with aquatic vegetation and submerged trees and brush. The striped bass, a saltwater fish that lives mostly in the ocean but breeds in freshwater rivers and streams, was introduced into Lake Whitney in 1973. It has done well there, and has even spawned, although stocking still continues. Catches of 20 pounds or more have not been uncommon. Other popular fish include white bass, crappie, and catfish.

The park lies above the lake, on gently rolling slopes covered with a mix of oak woodland and grasslands. The habitat is a mix of Blackland Prairie and Hill Country species. In spring, blankets of wildflowers, particularly favorites like the bluebonnet and Indian paintbrush, attract large numbers of visitors. Frequently seen wildlife include white-tailed deer, squirrels, armadillos, rabbits, raccoons, and opossums.

When the dam was built, the lake flooded the early Texas settlement of Towash. The village was named for a chief of the Hasinai Indian tribe that moved into the area in 1835. A marker commemorating the village has been built in the park.

While most state parks in Texas can be reached only by car, Lake Whitney State Park also caters to visitors wishing to fly there; it has a paved airstrip that can accommodate small planes.

VISITOR INFORMATION

955 acres. Open all year. Hot and humid in summer. Large number of campsites with partial or full hook-ups and showers. Screened shelters. Hiking and mountain-biking trails, picnicking, swimming, boating, boat ramps, waterskiing, fishing, paved air-strip. Limited visitor services available in Whitney; full services in Hillsboro and Waco. For information: Lake Whitney State Park, P.O. Box 1175, Whitney, TX 76692, (254) 694-3793.

Lockhart State Park

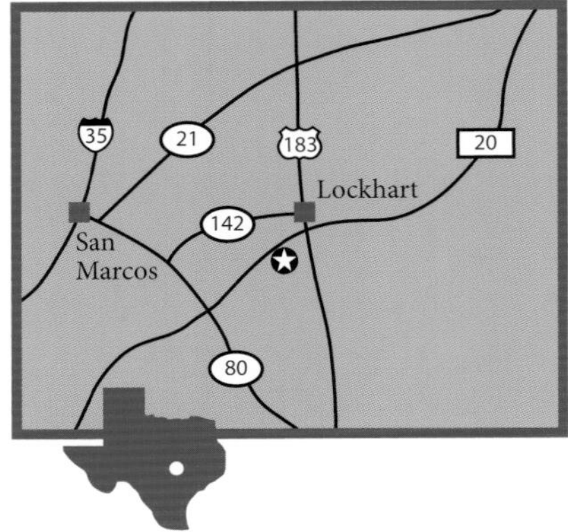

Lockhart State Park is a small, quiet retreat in the Blackland Prairie region of central Texas. An attractive golf course, of which there are few in the state-park system, draws both local golfers and many people from farther away. Its nine holes follow the slopes along and above Clear Fork Creek, crossing it more than once. Hole distance ranges from about 150 yards to more than 500, with a total of 3000 yards, and a par of 35.

Tucked deep in the trees on a bluff above the golf course is a recreation hall built by the Civilian Conservation Corps (CCC) in the 1930s. The CCC was started during the Depression to create jobs for unemployed young men. The men of the CCC constructed the improvements at this park and many other state and national parks across the country during the dark economic days of the Depression. Until the late 1940s, the park was leased to a local country club, but since then it has been managed by the state. An adjoining rodeo arena is part of the park, but is leased to and managed by the Lockhart Kiwanis Club.

A swimming pool provides an opportunity to cool off after a round of golf or other park activities. Other popular recreational pursuits include picnicking, camping, and fishing for bass, catfish, or sunfish in the creek.

VISITOR INFORMATION

264 acres. Open all year. Hot and humid in summer. Small number of campsites have both partial or full hookups. The swimming pool is open during the summer months; call for hours and fees. Golf carts can be rented at park headquarters. Picnicking, fishing, hiking. All visitor services available in Lockhart. For information: Lockhart State Park, 4179 State Park Road, Lockhart, TX 78644, (512) 398-3479.

Walkers

Meridian State Park

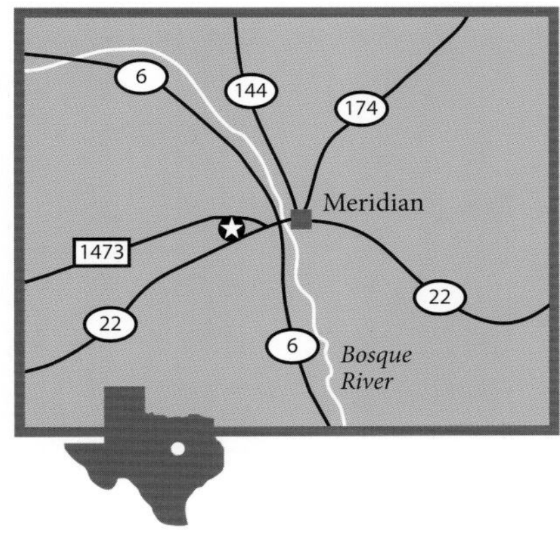

Meridian State Park lies in an area of gently rolling hills northwest of Waco. A mix of several Texas habitats covers the terrain, including elements of the Edwards Plateau, Blackland Prairie, and Cross Timbers regions. Ashe juniper, commonly called cedar, is the dominant tree, particularly on drier hillsides. Other trees include live oaks, post oaks, and blackjack oaks. In moist areas, trees such as the cottonwood, pecan, and cedar elm thrive.

A small 72-acre lake, created by a dam built across Bee Creek, forms the centerpiece of the park. The dam and other park facilities, including an attractive, solidly built refectory, were built by the Civilian Conservation Corps during the Depression in the 1930s. Bee Creek originates in the hills a short distance north of the park and, downstream from the dam, flows into Meridian Creek. A short distance farther, the combined creek joins the North Bosque River, a larger watercourse that flows through the town of Meridian just east of the park.

The thick woods of Ashe juniper within the park attract a rare bird, the golden-cheeked warbler. The endangered warbler arrives early in the spring to build its nests using bark from the Ashe juniper. Probably because of its need for the juniper bark, it nests nowhere in the world but the Edwards Plateau area of Texas.

Because it offers a variety of recreational opportunities, as well as a quiet retreat, the park attracts a wide variety of people. In spring, birders come, hoping to catch a glimpse of the golden-cheeked warbler or another rare bird, the black-capped vireo. Several miles of hiking trails wind through the woods and around the lake, providing excellent access for birders. In good years, wildflowers blanket the roadsides and open areas of the park. During the hot days of summer, the lake is the park's main draw. Swimmers paddle through the cool waters, and fishermen cast their lines, hoping to hook bass, crappie, or catfish. Boating is allowed, but only at speeds of less than five miles per hour.

VISITOR INFORMATION

505 acres. Open all year. Hot and humid in summer. Small campground with partial hookups and showers. Screened shelters. Hiking and nature trails, picnicking, swimming, no-wake boating, boat ramp, fishing, birding. Limited visitor services available in Meridian; full services in Waco. For information: Meridian State Park, 173 Park Road 7, Meridian, TX 76665, (254) 435-2536.

Meridian State Park lake

Monument Hill • Kreische Brewery State Historic Sites

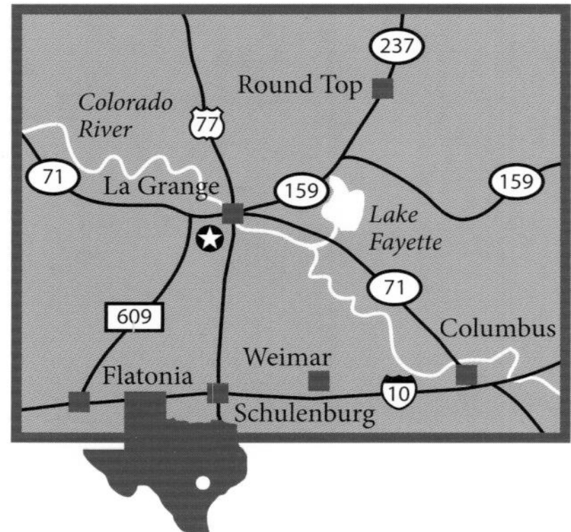

On top of a high bluff on the south side of the Colorado River across from La Grange are two important Texas historic sites. One is an early Texas brewery, and the other is a tall granite monument that marks the tomb of Texans who died at the Battle of Salado Creek and on the ill-fated Mier Expedition.

After Texas won its independence from Mexico in 1836, ownership of the land between the Rio Grande and Nueces River was hotly disputed by Texas and Mexico. In February 1842, General Rafael Vásquez led Mexican troops on a raid of San Antonio and then retreated back to Mexico. Some months later, on September 11, a large body of Mexican troops under General Adrian Woll captured San Antonio. The next day, news of the attack reached Gonzales, and Mathew Caldwell assembled Texas troops to go to San Antonio.

Three days after the attack, news reached La Grange, and a small group there assembled and marched on San Antonio as well. Others joined along the way, so that by the time it reached San Antonio, the group comprised 54 men. During the trip, Nicholas Dawson was elected captain. On September 18, Dawson's men reached the San Antonio area, but were intercepted by 500 Mexican troops about two miles from Caldwell's position on Salado Creek. The outnumbered Texans were defeated, with 36 killed, 15 captured, and 3 who escaped. The next day, Caldwell's men buried Dawson's men at the battlefield. Caldwell and his men pursued Woll's troops back toward Mexico, but the Mexicans were able to retreat largely unscathed.

After learning of the Mexican raid, President Sam Houston assembled troops under Brigadier General Alexander Somervell and sent them to San Antonio. On November 25, Somervell and his men marched to the Rio Grande, but failed to find the enemy troops. Some of the Texans returned to San Antonio, but more than 300 remained on the border under Captain William Fisher. On December 25, they attacked the Mexican town of Mier after learning that it was defended by General Pedro de Ampudia and 350 men. The battle raged into the next day, with the Texans having the advantage. Ampudia, who was about to retreat, bluffed, claiming that he had 1700 troops in the city and 800 nearby. Even though they were unknowingly on the verge of victory, the Texans fell for the ruse and surrendered.

The captured Texans were marched toward Mexico City. At Rancho Salado, 188 Texans escaped, but 176 were recaptured within two weeks. General Santa Anna ordered that one-tenth of the recaptured escapees be shot. Seventeen black beans were put into a pot with 159 white beans. Those who drew the black beans were summarily executed, and the others were jailed until September 12, 1844.

In 1847, during the Mexican-American War, American troops exhumed the remains of the Texans buried at Rancho Salado and shipped them to La Grange. Shortly thereafter, the remains of Captain Dawson's party were retrieved from near Salado Creek and also brought to La Grange. On September 18, 1848, the remains of the men were given a full military burial in a tomb on the bluff overlooking the Colorado River above La Grange. Sam Houston and other dignitaries attended the ceremony.

In 1849, Heinrich Kreische purchased the property upon which the tomb lay. At the time he purchased the property, a Fayette County committee agreed to buy ten acres of land that included the tomb from him and build a monument. It failed to follow through, however, and the tomb deteriorated over time. Finally, in the 1930s, a new granite vault was built around the tomb, and a 48-foot marker was erected. The land around the tomb was finally purchased by the state in 1907, and in 1956 additional land was donated to the state.

In 1977, the state also acquired adjoining land that included the old Kreische holdings. In the 1870s, Kreische built a brewery near the tomb, and by the late 1870s his brewery was the third largest in Texas. It was a large three-story structure constructed of locally quarried sandstone and wood framing. Kreische built his home in several sections above the brewery between 1855 and 1882, the year he died. Although the brewery seems to have been prosperous at the time of his death, it declined and went out of business soon thereafter. Family descendants continued to live in Kreische's home until 1952, but the brewery fell into ruin. Today visitors can tour the brewery, the Kreische home, and the old tomb and its marker, and enjoy the sweeping view from the top of the bluff.

VISITOR INFORMATION

40 acres. Monument, tomb, and interpretive trails open all year, Thursday through Monday. Brewery and Kreische home tours are usually conducted on weekends; call ahead for dates and times. Day use only. Historic structures and exhibits, nature trail, picnicking. All visitor services available in La Grange. For information: Monument Hill/Kreische Brewery State Historic Sites, 414 State Loop 92, La Grange, TX 78945, (979) 968-5658.

OPPOSITE PAGE
Historic Kreische home
RIGHT
Limestone rock shelter

Mother Neff State Park

Mother Neff State Park, a quiet retreat on the shady banks of the Leon River, is the first state park in Texas. In 1916, Isabella Eleanor "Mother" Neff donated the use of six acres of land along the Leon River bottom for community meetings. She and her husband Noah were early settlers of the region, arriving from Roanoke, Virginia, in 1855. One of her sons, Pat Neff, was governor of Texas from 1921 to 1925. During his tenure, he created the Texas State Parks Board and arranged for his mother's donated property to become the first state park in Texas.

Governor Neff was a tireless supporter of the parks system, traveling often and making many speeches in support of the program. In the 1930s, when Neff was chairman of the State Parks Board, he donated the remainder of the land that makes up the park.

Mother Neff's legacy remains a popular retreat today. Most recreational opportunities are concentrated in the rich bottomland lining the Leon River. During the Depression, the Civilian Conservation Corps developed the park, building attractive, durable stone structures, including a pavilion called the tabernacle and the headquarters building, in the bottomland area. Tall pecans, sycamores, elms, oaks, and other trees thrive in the rich soil and shade the developed area along the river.

A short loop drive leads north away from the river along a narrow rocky ravine to the prairie uplands. Dense stands of Ashe juniper cloak the rocky slopes between the prairie and the river. A hiking trail winds through the ravine area and leads to a limestone rock shelter once used by Indians, and to a pool called the Wash Pond, thought to have been used by Indians and early pioneers. In spring, wildflowers blanket the upland prairie, a small remnant of the prairies that once covered much of central Texas.

The park lies at the extreme northeastern edge of the Edwards Plateau, the massive uplift from which the Hill Country was formed. It contains a mix of plants from the Edwards Plateau to the southwest, the Blackland Prairie to the east, and the Cross Timbers region to the north. Although Mother Neff State Park is small, it contains a variety of natural features and offers a range of recreational opportunities to visitors.

VISITOR INFORMATION

259 acres. Open all year. Hot in summer. Small number of campsites with partial hookups and showers. Primitive backpacking campsites. Hiking, picnicking, fishing. Limited visitor services available in Moody; all services in Temple and Waco. For information: Mother Neff State Park, 1680 State Highway 236, Moody, TX 76557, (254) 853-2389.

Palmetto State Park

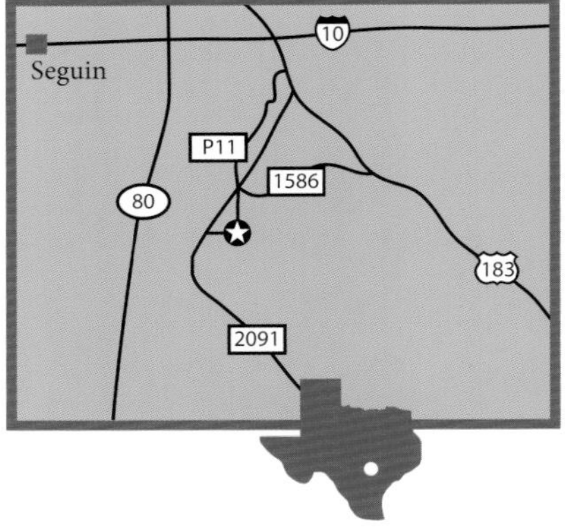

Palmetto State Park provides a surprising contrast to the gently rolling hills of post oak woodland that surround it. The lush, tropical-seeming Ottine Swamp lies on a terrace of the San Marcos River valley, nourished by underground water and intermittent flooding. The water feeds a boggy oasis most notable for the thick understory of dwarf palmettos, a plant that usually grows farther east in wetter climates. A tall forest of green ash, Lacey and burr oak, sycamore, and other trees creates a thick canopy of foliage. Two species of iris, a purple native and a yellow import, add splashes of color to the margins of ponds.

Native iris in Ottine Swamp

The lush vegetation that is now limited to the small swamp at Palmetto probably covered a much larger area during the cooler, wetter ice age 12,000 years ago. As the climate became warmer and drier, the greenery at Palmetto was able to survive only in its present isolated location, fed by springs and flooding.

The springs that feed the swamp issue out of Carrizo sands that are exposed at the base of the bluff that lines the river valley. At one time, thermal springs and mud volcanoes fed by underground water and natural gas existed in the park and, with the unusual swamp, were a major draw for visitors in the late 1800s and early 1900s. Unfortunately, extensive groundwater pumping and other changes wrought by humans have caused them to mostly dry up. If the Civilian Conservation Corps (CCC) had not put in a well to provide supplementary water to the swamp, the remaining bog might have disappeared by now. A faint sulfur smell rises from the water pumped from this well.

Adolph Otto and his family settled in the area in 1879 and built a cotton gin and sawmill nearby. Because there was already a post office named Otto in the state, and the postal service would not allow two post offices to have the same name, the village was named Ottine, a name created by combining Otto with Christine, the name of the wife of one of his sons.

The unusual swamp, plus the mud volcanoes and thermal springs, has attracted tourists for many years. Before the park was established, the San Antonio and Aransas Pass Railroad offered weekend excursion trips to Palmetto. In 1933, the State Parks Board acquired part of the Ottine Swamp and established Palmetto State Park. During the Depression, the CCC helped build park facilities. The most notable structure is the large refectory, built from heavy blocks of reddish, iron-rich native sandstone and large wooden timbers.

Today the park still attracts visitors. Birders frequent Palmetto, hoping to see some of the 240 species recorded there. In the spring, the area in and around the park is excellent for wildflowers. Two nature trails, one in the swamp and the other in floodplain woodland of the San Marcos River, introduce the unique swamp of Palmetto State Park to visitors.

VISITOR INFORMATION

270 acres. Open all year. Hot and humid in summer. Small number of campsites in two areas with partial hookups and showers. Fishing in river and small oxbow lake, picnicking, swimming, hiking and nature trails, canoeing on San Marcos River, paddleboat and canoe rentals. All visitor services available in Luling and Gonzales. For information: Palmetto State Park, 78 Park Road 11 South, Gonzales, TX 78629, (830) 672-3266.

ABOVE LEFT
Native iris
ABOVE RIGHT
Tree frog on palmetto frond

Purtis Creek State Park

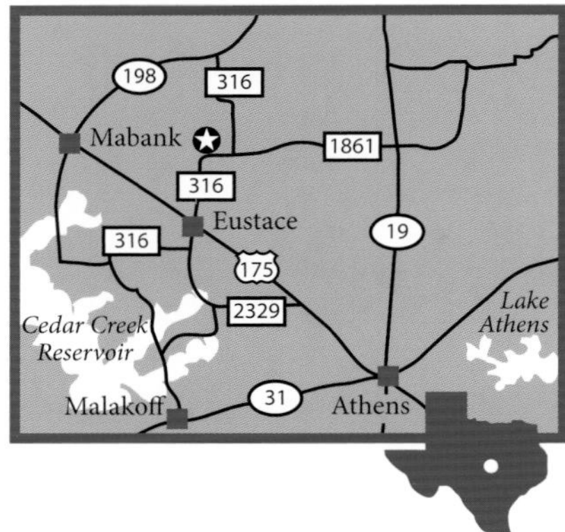

Purtis Creek State Park was literally built for fishermen. The land was purchased in the late 1970s, and dam construction began in 1981. As soon as the 355-acre reservoir filled, the Texas Parks and Wildlife Department began stocking Florida largemouth bass, channel catfish, coppernose bluegills, shad, and redear sunfish. Before stocking began, all other fish were removed to ensure a pure strain of Florida bass. When the lake was filled, timber was left standing to create a good fish habitat.

To provide a pleasant fishing experience, the park allows no more than 50 boats on the small lake at one time and enforces a no-wake rule. Bass fishing is restricted to catch and release in order to allow a healthy population of large fish to develop. Other fish, such as catfish, crappie, and bluegills, may be taken within size and bag limits.

Although the park lies in East Texas, it is not quite far enough east to have pines. Instead, it lies in post-oak habitat, with woods of post oaks, red oaks, white oaks, cedar elms, eastern red cedars, pecans, and other trees. Although fishing is the main draw of the park, others come to camp and relax along the quiet lakeshore. A short hiking trail leads to a number of primitive backpacking campsites, allowing an easy escape from modern life.

Visitor Information

1582 acres. Open all year. Hot and humid in summer. Campground with partial hookups and showers. Walk-in and primitive backpacking campsites. Lighted fishing piers, boat ramp, picnicking, hiking, swimming. Canoe, paddleboat, and kayak rental. All visitor services available in Athens. For information: Purtis Creek State Park, 14225 FM 316, Eustace, TX 75124, (903) 425-2332.

Ray Roberts Lake State Park

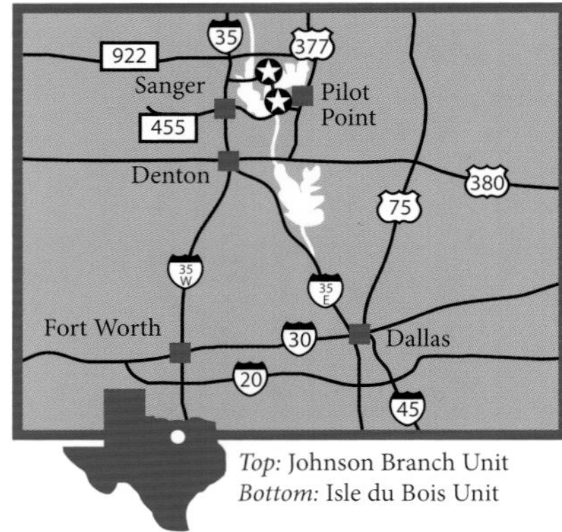

Top: Johnson Branch Unit
Bottom: Isle du Bois Unit

Ray Roberts Lake State Park is one of the newest additions to the state-park system in Texas. The large 29,350-acre lake was authorized in 1965 to provide water to Denton and Dallas, but obtaining funding for and building the reservoir took many years. In 1980, the lake was named for Congressman Ray Roberts of Denton. In the mid-1980s the lake began to fill, helped along by several major floods.

The lake was created when a dam was built to impound the Elm Fork of the Trinity River below its confluence with Isle du Bois Creek. The Texas Parks and Wildlife Department began raising fish in brood ponds to stock the lake before it was filled, and today the lake is known for its largemouth bass, white bass, crappie, and catfish. Today the lake draws many thousands of people every year, who come to fish its fertile waters, sail, swim, or water-ski. With further exploration, visitors find a luxurious lodge; many miles of hiking, mountain-biking, and equestrian trails; and a great canoeing river.

The Isle du Bois Unit was designed for large numbers of people from the start and has elaborate facilities, including large campgrounds, paved hike and bike trails, and a multilane boat ramp. The unit is set in the wooded hills of a large peninsula that juts into the eastern side of the lake. The hills lie in Cross Timbers woodland on the edge of the Blackland Prairie. The Cross Timbers is a narrow band of terrain heavily wooded by post

and blackjack oaks, black hickories, winged elms, and other trees. Rust-colored Woodbine Sandstone underlies the dense Cross Timbers forest. Commonly found wildlife include white-tailed deer, armadillos, rabbits, opossums, raccoons, and skunks. A high point of this wooded terrain to the east of the lake became a landmark to early travelers in the area and became known as Pilot Point.

The large Isle du Bois Unit is only part of the park. Across the lake, the other main park unit, Johnson Branch, has camping, trails, a boat ramp, and many other facilities. Jordan Park has a lodge perched high on a ridge with great lake views. It not only offers lodging for people, but has stalls for horses. It is connected to the Isle du Bois Unit with a 12-mile hiking, mountain-biking, and equestrian trail system. Sanger Park offers a full-service marina, store, and restaurant. The other four satellite parks around the lake—Pond Creek, Elm Fork, Buck Creek, and Pecan Creek—have boat ramps and restrooms.

The Ray Roberts Lake/Lake Lewisville Greenbelt Corridor begins at the Ray Roberts dam and ends at the headwaters of Lake Lewisville. Its 12 miles of equestrian trail and 10 miles of hiking and biking trail meander through the lushly wooded floodplain of the Elm Fork of the Trinity River. The trail system can be accessed at three trailheads: Elm Fork Park, FM 428, and U.S. 380. Canoeists can float the river through the greenbelt, using the same access points as other users. When the corridor is combined with the other lengthy park trails, Ray Roberts Lake offers one of the most extensive state-park trail systems in Texas. Much of the rest of the undeveloped land surrounding the lake is maintained by the Texas Parks and Wildlife Department as a wildlife management area.

VISITOR INFORMATION

5849 acres total for park, split among two main units (Isle du Bois and Johnson Branch) and six satellite parks. Open all year. Hot and humid in summer.

Isle du Bois Unit: Large number of campsites with partial hookups and showers. Developed walk-in and equestrian campsites. Hiking, mountain-biking, and equestrian trails; swimming, boat ramp, boating, waterskiing, fishing pier. All visitor services available in Denton. For information: Ray Roberts Lake State Park, Isle du Bois Unit, 100 PW 4137, Pilot Point, TX 76258, (940) 686-2148.

Johnson Branch Unit: Large number of campsites with partial hookups and showers. Developed walk-in campsites. Hiking and mountain-biking trails, swimming, boat ramp, boating, waterskiing. All visitor services available in Denton. For information: Ray Roberts Lake State Park, Johnson Branch Unit, 100 PW 4153, Valley View, TX 76272, (940) 637-2294.

Jordan Park: Lodging, restaurant, horse boarding, boat dock, boat ramp; hiking, mountain-biking, and equestrian trails. Lantana Lodge, 2200 FM 1192, Pilot Point, TX 76258, (940) 686-0261, (866) 526-8262.

Sanger Park: Lake Ray Roberts Marina. Boat slips, fuel, boat rental and sale, restaurant, store. Lake Ray Roberts Marina, 1399 Marina Circle, Sanger, TX 76266, (940) 458-7023.

TOP
Ray Roberts Lake sunset
ABOVE
Ray Roberts Lake fishing pier
OPPOSITE PAGE
Fisherman

Sam Bell Maxey House State Historic Site

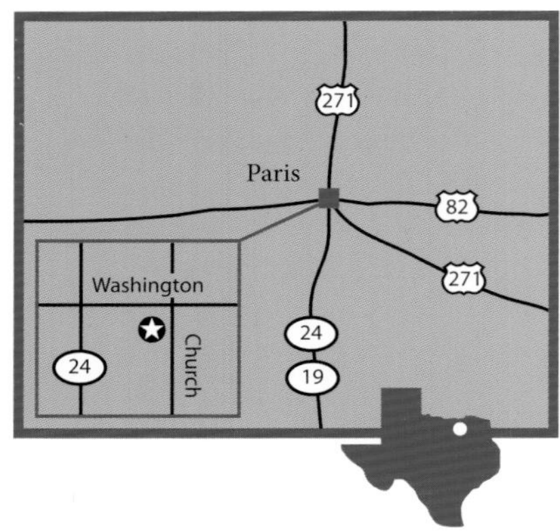

Samuel Bell Maxey was born in 1825 in Tompkinsville, Kentucky, to a socially prominent family. He attended West Point and, although he ranked near the bottom of his class, he found that he liked military life. After graduating in 1846, Maxey served with distinction in several battles of the Mexican War.

In 1849 he resigned his army commission and moved back to Kentucky, where he studied law under his father and became involved in state politics. In 1853 he married Marilda Denton.

The family law firm became unprofitable, so in 1857 Maxey and his father moved their families to Paris, Texas. They settled on five acres just south of the town and opened a new law office. Soon thereafter, Sam Bell Maxey became the county district attorney, and in 1861 he was elected to the Texas Senate.

The outbreak of the Civil War prevented Maxey from taking office. He volunteered his services to the Confederacy, and during 1861 he organized the Ninth Texas Infantry Division, numbering 1120 men. He was promoted to brigadier general in April 1862 and was detached from the Ninth Texas. He spent most of the first two years of the war in Tennessee and Mississippi. In December 1863, he assumed command of Indian Territory (later to become Oklahoma) to prevent any Union invasion into North Texas. After he helped capture a 170-wagon Union supply train in 1864, he was advanced to the rank of major general. During the war, the Maxeys adopted seven-year-old Dora Rowell after her father, one of Maxey's men, was killed at Shiloh. In February 1865 he asked to be relieved, as the war was obviously coming to a close, and returned to Paris.

After two years of effort, Maxey obtained a presidential pardon for his services as a high-ranking Confederate officer with the help of West Point classmate Ulysses S. Grant. In 1867 he resumed his law practice in Paris with his father and completed plans for a new home on his five-acre tract. In late 1868, the Maxey family moved into their new house. The home was built as a two-story frame structure in High Victorian Italianate style. It was designed to be very symmetrical, with a central hall dividing each floor in half.

After failing to win a House seat in 1872, Maxey was elected to the United States Senate by the Texas legislature in 1874. During his Senate tenure, he worked hard to advance projects of benefit to Texas. In 1887, he lost his bid for a third term and returned to his law practice and family in Paris.

During the Senate years, the Maxey household expanded, with various relatives and in-laws living in the family home over the years. At an uncertain date a large rear wing was added to the house. Maxey died in 1895 in Eureka Springs, Arkansas.

Indirect descendants of Maxey inherited the house in 1908, after Marilda died. They undertook a major remodeling of the home in 1911, the last major changes made to the house. Members of the Maxey family lived in the property until 1966; a year later, it was donated to the Lamar County Historical Society. In 1976, the Maxey home was conveyed to the Texas Parks and Wildlife Department. The historic house and its furnishings are now open to guided tours.

VISITOR INFORMATION

0.4 acre. Open all year, except Christmas Day and New Year's Day. Tours on Friday 1–4 PM, Saturday 8 AM–4 PM, and Sunday 1–4 PM, and by reservation for groups on Wednesday and Thursday. Day use only. Historic structures and exhibits. All visitor services available in Paris. For information: Sam Bell Maxey House State Historic Site, 812 S. Church Street, Paris, TX 75460, (903) 785-5716.

Sam Bell Maxey House

Stephen F. Austin State Park and San Felipe State Historic Site

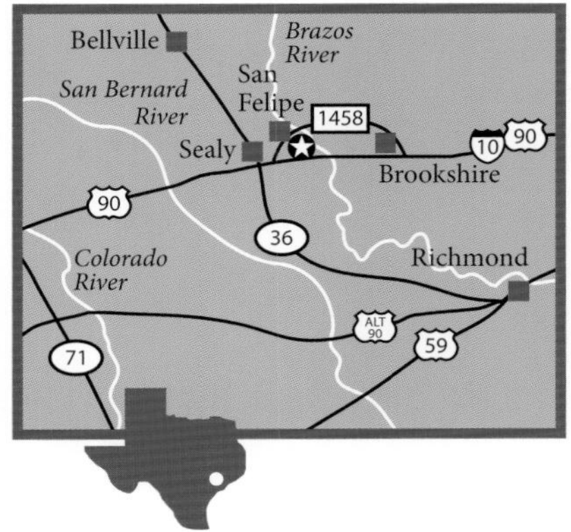

Early in the nineteenth century, Stephen F. Austin brought the first 300 families from the United States to colonize Texas under contract with the Mexican government. He obtained a land grant along the Brazos River from the Mexican government and founded San Felipe de Austin in 1828. Today, Stephen F. Austin State Park and San Felipe State Historic Site mark the location of part of the original grant.

Austin lived in the settlement, along with other early Texas heroes, such as Sam Houston and William Travis. Initially the settlement worked relatively well, with Austin working to smooth over cultural, political, and religious differences between the Americans and the Mexican government. However, tensions increased and finally came to a head when General Antonio Lopez de Santa Anna came to power as Mexico's president and dictator. Santa Anna's army was soon marching on the upstart immigrants to enforce his unquestioned authority. The Texans declared independence on March 2, 1836, during the Alamo siege. The fall of the Alamo was followed by the surrender and subsequent massacre of Colonel James Fannin's troops by Mexican forces.

Word reached San Felipe de Austin of the disasters and the continuing advance of Santa Anna's army. On March 29, the settlers of San Felipe packed what they could carry and burned their settlement to leave nothing for Santa Anna. With Santa Anna in pursuit, the Texans, under General Sam Houston, crossed the Brazos River and fled east, taking their provisional government with them. Houston realized that he and his troops were greatly outnumbered, so he continued to retreat eastward, hoping to find some way to gain the advantage on the battlefield. Finally, on April 21, when he found that Santa Anna had split up his troops and left himself with a much smaller numerical superiority, Houston attacked. The Battle of San Jacinto was a rout for the Texans. In 18 minutes, they overwhelmed the Mexican force, killing 630 Mexican soldiers while losing only nine of their own. Santa Anna surrendered, and independence was won.

The park is much more peaceful today, with little to break the quiet than the sound of children playing or a golf club striking a ball. The park hugs the Brazos River, occupying both floodplain and upland areas of coastal plain. It is divided into two segments. The smaller historical section, San Felipe State Historic Site, memorializes

TOP
Golfers
ABOVE
Historic J. J. Josey General Store

Stephen F. Austin and the early Texas settlers. Attractions include the old J. J. Josey General Store, which contains many items found in early general stores, plus other objects of historical interest. There is also a dogtrot cabin, hand-dug water well, and a statue of Austin.

The 18-hole golf course is the most prominent feature of the recreational area in Stephen F. Austin State Park. The beautiful fairways wind through lush woods draped with Spanish moss. During the summer, the park swimming pool is the main attraction for kids.

To get a feel for how the land appeared when the colonists first arrived, take the hiking trail in the back part of the park. Lush forests of oaks, pecans, cottonwoods, elms, and other trees arch over the trail as it drops down through the floodplain to the banks of the muddy Brazos River. The river slides quietly by, much as it did for Austin's first Texans.

VISITOR INFORMATION

663 acres. Open all year. Hot and humid in summer. Moderate number of campsites with partial or full hookups and showers. Screened shelters. Eighteen-hole golf course with pro shop, seasonal swimming pool, picnicking; hiking, mountain-biking, and interpretive trails; historic structures and exhibits, fishing. All visitor services available in Sealy and Houston. For information: Stephen F. Austin State Park and San Felipe State Historic Site, P.O. Box 125, San Felipe, TX 77473, (979) 885-3613.

Washington-on-the-Brazos State Historic Site

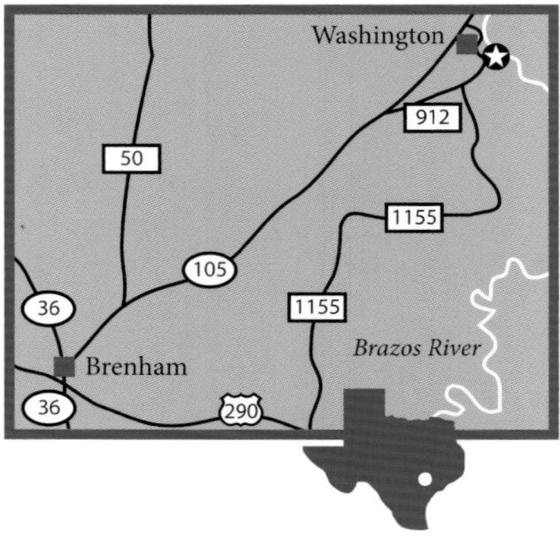

Although Washington was never a big town, it looms large in Texas history. In 1821, Andrew Robinson and his family first settled the site, when they joined Stephen F. Austin's colony. They farmed and raised livestock on the west bank of the Brazos River and operated a ferry at the La Bahia river crossing of the old Spanish road between Goliad and East Texas.

In 1835, Robinson's son-in-law John Hall purchased the property and, with partners, laid out the town site of Washington. The lots were sold at a public auction on January 8, 1836, on the eve of the Texas revolution. Even though the new town was rough and ragged, the provisional government of Texas designated it as the site of the convention that was to meet to determine Texas's fate. A Virginian visiting Washington in February was less than impressed:

Left Washington at 10 o'clock. Glad to get out of so disgusting a place. It is laid out in the woods; about a dozen wretched cabins or shanties constitute the city; not one decent house in it and only one well-defined street, which consists of an opening cut out of the woods. The stumps still standing. A rare place to hold a national convention. They will have to leave it promptly to avoid starvation.

Poor conditions or not, the delegates convened in Washington on March 1, 1836, in an unfinished frame building. As Santa Anna's Mexican forces besieged the Alamo, the delegates declared Texas's independence from Mexico, wrote a constitution for the Republic of Texas, and organized a government. On March 17, the newly formed government and the citizens of Washington fled east, ahead of the advancing Mexican army.

After the victorious Battle of San Jacinto on April 21, the residents of Washington returned home, finding the town little disturbed. Town citizens fought to retain its status as the Texas capital, but lost out, first to Houston and then to Austin. In 1842, however, Mexican troops captured San Antonio, giving President Sam Houston an excuse to move the capital back to Washington, owing to its greater distance from San Antonio. After a major political fight, Houston moved the capital to Washington in the fall of 1842, bringing new life to the town. Although accommodations had improved there since 1836, they were still crowded and spartan.

The Republic of Texas was in poor financial condition and subject to invasions by Mexican troops. To help shore up the Republic, the new government worked to gain recognition and diplomatic relations with the United States and other countries. Many Texans thought that the way to solve their problems with Mexico was to be annexed by the United States. After extended negotiations, annexation was approved by the U.S. Congress and the people of Texas. On December 29, 1845, Texas officially joined the Union. The capital moved back to Austin, which remains the state capital today.

Washington prospered for some years after it lost its status as the capital, but it was dealt a mortal blow in the mid-1850s when the railroad bypassed it, and it was finished by the Civil War. At some point the town became known as Washington-on-the-Brazos.

Today the state park contains the

old town site and several museums. The building where the Declaration of Independence was signed on March 2, 1836, has been reconstructed. Extensive exhibits chronicling the history of Washington and Texas are displayed in the interpretive center and the Star of the Republic Museum.

The home of Anson Jones, the last president of the Republic of Texas, was moved from a nearby location to the park and restored as the center of the Barrington Living History Farm. Jones named his farm Barrington after his Massachusetts home in Great Barrington. He lived on the farm with his wife Mary, their four children, his sister, his sister-in-law, and five slaves. His house is original; the outbuildings were reconstructed by the park using Jones's notes and journal as a guide. Park personnel, dressed in period clothing, recreate life on a Brazos River farm in the 1850s. They plant and harvest crops, make soap, spin yarn, and do the many other things necessary to maintain a farm of that era. Short walking trails and a pecan-shaded picnic area overlooking the Brazos River round out the opportunities available to park visitors.

VISITOR INFORMATION

293 acres. Open all year. Day use only. Historic buildings, living-history farm, museums, and interpretive exhibits, picnicking, short walking trails. All visitor services available in Navasota. For information: Washington-on-the-Brazos State Historic Site, Box 305, Washington, TX 77880, (936) 878-2214.

Anson Jones home

South Texas Plains

From the edge of the Hill Country in San Antonio, the South Texas Plains sweep south in a broad swath to the Rio Grande. The land is relatively flat, especially in the Lower Rio Grande Valley downstream of Roma. A mix of grassland and brush, particularly mesquite, characterizes the region. Along its eastern edge, near the coast, the area receives moderate rainfall, but it becomes relatively dry farther west. Even in eastern areas with moderate rainfall, however, high evaporation rates tend to make the area fairly dry.

At one time the region had less brush, but heavy grazing has encouraged shrubby plants and cacti to encroach. Wildlife is plentiful in the brushy country; white-tailed deer and javelina are particularly prolific here. Many rare forms of wildlife found along the Rio Grande, especially in the lower Valley downstream from Falcon Lake, attract many people to the parks and wildlife refuges of the region.

The Lower Rio Grande Valley, much of which is the delta of the Rio Grande, lies farther south than any other part of the United States, except Hawaii and part of Florida. Its location and weather patterns give the area a warm, subtropical climate. Winter freezes are generally rare, mild, and short-lived, allowing even citrus trees to grow.

Its subtropical climate and southerly location give the Rio Grande Valley many species of plants and animals found nowhere else in the United States. The mouth of the Rio Grande once was wooded with thousands of acres of palm trees, spurring Spanish explorer Alonso Alvarez de Piñeda to name it Río de las Palmas in 1519. Upstream from the palm woodland, the river supports a narrow forest corridor of cedar elms, ebony, huisaches, Rio Grande ashes, mesquites, anaquas, black willows, and many other trees. Away from the river, the land quickly dries and supports less lush brushlands of mesquite and other shrubs.

Small numbers of the rare ocelot and the even rarer jaguarundi live here in the thick, brushy woodlands. The elusive wildcats slip quietly through the brush, making observation difficult. Long ago, even the jaguar, North America's largest cat, roamed the Rio Grande Valley.

Many species of birds range as far north as the Rio Grande Valley and no farther. Birders come from all over the United States to see the chachalaca, green jay, Altamira oriole, pauraque, groove-billed ani, hook-billed kite, and many other species. Almost 300 species of birds have been sighted in Bentsen–Rio Grande Valley State Park alone. More than 70 other species have been recorded elsewhere in the Rio Grande Valley.

Unfortunately for the native plants and wildlife, the soil of the Valley is fertile, and the vast majority of the woodland has been cleared for farming. In addition, high birth rates and heavy immigration have increasingly urbanized the area along the river. The state parks, state wildlife management areas, and national wildlife refuges contain most of the small remaining fragments of the original habitat.

Two parks along or near the Rio Grande, Falcon and Lake Casa Blanca International, as well as Choke Canyon on the Frio River, not only protect wildlife habitat, they offer extensive opportunities for fishing and water sports.

A number of South Texas parks preserve important historic sites. The Civilian Conservation Corps reconstructed Mission Espíritu Santo, an early Spanish mission, in the 1930s at Goliad State Park. Fannin Battleground lies nearby, marking the Battle of Coleto Creek, where Colonel James Fannin surrendered to superior Mexican forces during the battle for Texas's independence. A week later, Fannin and 342 of his men were executed after being promised honorable treatment. In San Antonio, another park preserves the home of early Texas patriot José Antonio Navarro.

The state parks of the South Texas Plains not only preserve historic sites and protect unique wildlife, they also offer many recreational opportunities. Many sites offer camping, picnicking, and hiking trails, while others boast museums or water sports. The parks of the Rio Grande Valley offer something found nowhere else—the chance to see rare and uncommon species of plants and animals.

1 Bentsen–Rio Grande Valley State Park • World Birding Center

2 Casa Navarro State Historic Site

3 Choke Canyon State Park

4 Estero Llano Grande State Park • World Birding Center

5 Falcon State Park

6 Fannin Battleground State Historic Site

7 Goliad State Park • Mission Espíritu Santo State Historic Site • Zaragosa Birthplace State Historic Site • Mission Rosario State Historic Site

8 Lake Casa Blanca International State Park

9 Resaca de la Palma State Park • World Birding Center

10 Sebastopol House State Historic Site

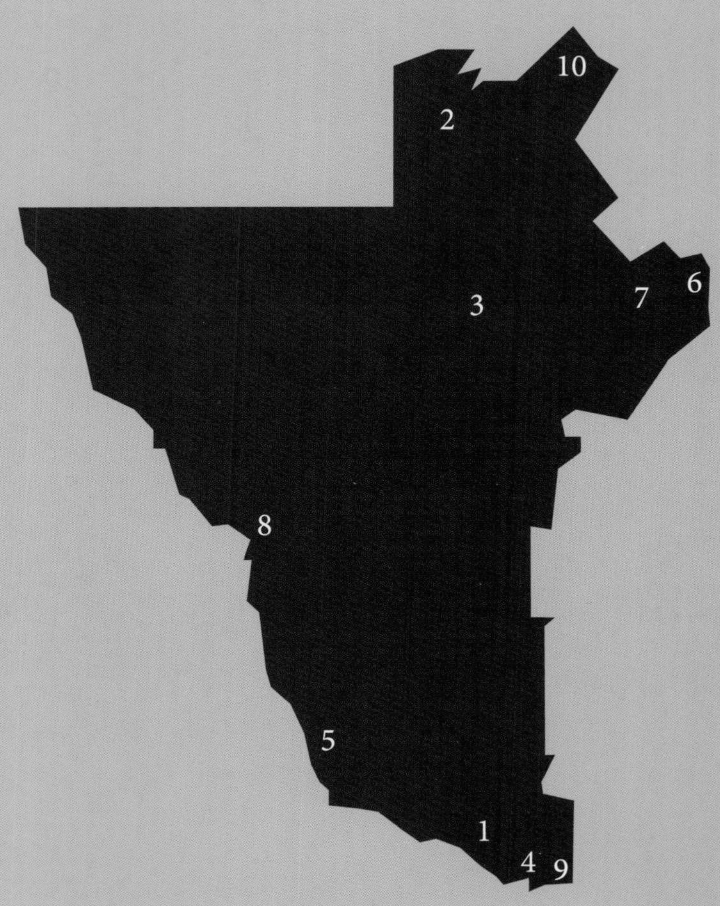

Bentsen–Rio Grande Valley State Park • World Birding Center

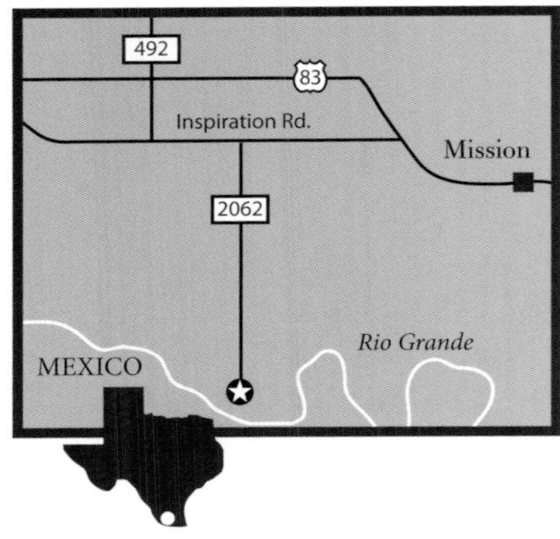

BELOW
Resaca—oxbow lake of Rio Grande—and palms
OPPOSITE PAGE
Spanish moss and woodland

Deep in the Rio Grande Valley lies one of the southernmost state parks in the United States. Bentsen–Rio Grande Valley State Park adjoins the Rio Grande, near the city of Mission in South Texas. Unusual, rarely seen animals such as the ocelot and jaguarundi roam thick, brushy woodlands of cedar elm, Rio Grande ash, black willow, anaqua, ebony, huisache, and many other species. At one time, even the jaguar, the largest cat in the Western hemisphere, stalked prey on the banks of the Rio Grande.

The park and other areas of the Rio Grande Valley provide a home for a tremendous variety of birds. About 370 species have been recorded in the state park and elsewhere in the Rio Grande Valley. Two major flyways, the Central and the Mississippi, converge here, funneling large numbers of migrants through the Valley. Many tropical species, limited by climate, reach the northern limit of their range here, and the nearby Gulf Coast draws many shorebirds. Birders come from all over the United States to see the green jay, Altamira oriole, chachalaca, white-tipped dove, pauraque, groove-billed ani, hook-billed kite, ringed kingfisher, and many other species.

The state park's unique avian life draws far more people than do the rare cats. Cementing its reputation as a premier birding site, the park was made headquarters of the World Birding Center. The headquarters' buildings have exhibits, a café, an exhibit hall, and a gift shop. The World Birding Center consists of nine state parks and other sites scattered across the Lower Rio Grande Valley that are noted for their excellent bird populations and native habitat.

The Lower Rio Grande Valley forms an ecosystem found nowhere else in

the United States. Before the area was heavily developed into farms and urban areas on both sides of the river, the Rio Grande shifted constantly, creating a broad, fertile floodplain. The Valley's southern location near the Tropic of Cancer, combined with its proximity to the warm Gulf of Mexico, creates a subtropical climate with a 320-day growing season. However, since rainfall is only moderate and evaporation is high, there is only a narrow corridor of lush woodlands fostered by the river. Away from the river, the woodland grades into brushland more adapted to dryness.

Unfortunately, urbanization and farming have destroyed virtually all of the original habitat of the Rio Grande Valley. Only a few islands remain of the once-extensive subtropical woodland. Many species, such as the ocelot and jaguarundi, have become endangered because of habitat loss and hunting. The state and federal government have an ongoing program to protect the remnants in a system of state parks, state wildlife management areas, and national wildlife refuges. The Rio Grande Valley is the highest-priority acquisition area in the United States for the U.S. Fish and Wildlife Service.

Private entities, such as the Audubon Society, the Nature Conservancy, and the Valley Land Fund, have also protected pieces of the remaining habitat. Audubon's Sabal Palm Sanctuary, for example, preserves 37 acres of original palm forest in its 527-acre refuge, a tiny remnant of the 40,000 acres that once covered part of the Rio Grande delta. As a mark of how extensive the palm forest once was, the early Spanish explorer Piñeda named the river Rio de las Palmas when he sailed up it in 1519. Today, with so little natural habitat left, it is hard to imagine that such a name was once appropriate.

Unfortunately, even native woodland protected in Bentsen–Rio Grande Valley State Park has suffered. Many trees have died, particularly cedar elms and ash trees. Dams, upstream irrigation and water use, and flood-control projects have ended periodic flooding along the river and lowered the water table, drying out areas along the river. Recently the state park and the U.S. Fish and Wildlife Service undertook a large irrigation project to water much of the park and an adjoining Fish and Wildlife tract. Not only was the vegetation watered, but one of the park's resacas, an old cutoff river channel, was refilled. With such care, the Valley's unique ecology will be protected in the state park and other refuges.

Four hiking and nature trails that wind through the state park's woodland provide an excellent introduction to the habitat of the Rio Grande Valley. Those not wanting to walk can rent bicycles or take a tram through the park. Spanish moss drapes the trees, creating a tropical, primeval atmosphere. Blinds, observation decks, and a tower help birders spot many different species. Observant visitors will see many plants, birds, and animals found nowhere else in the United States. A very lucky person might even see the beautiful spotted ocelot as it slips silently through the brush.

VISITOR INFORMATION

570 acres. Open all year. Hot and humid in summer. The park is very popular from December through April, when "winter Texans" arrive to escape harsh northern winters. World Birding Center Headquarters with exhibits, hiking trails, cycling, birding, picnicking. Full visitor services available in nearby Mission. For information: Bentsen-Rio Grande Valley State Park/World Birding Center, 2800 S. Bentsen Palm Drive, Mission, TX 78572, (956) 585-1107.

Casa Navarro State Historic Site

San Antonio
Commerce
Market Square
Dolorosa
S. Laredo
W. Nueva

Casa Navarro State Historic Site preserves the 1850s home of José Antonio Navarro (1795–1871), an important leader in early Texas history. Navarro's lifetime covered the period when Texas underwent many changes in sovereignty, starting as a Spanish colonial province and ending as a state in the United States. In 1810, when Mexico's struggle for independence from Spain began, Navarro's family supported the movement, even though doing so forced them into exile for several years. After Mexico achieved independence in 1821, Navarro served as a representative of the Mexican state of Coahuila y Texas.

In 1828, Navarro's legislative term ended, and he worked as a merchant and acquired large landholdings. In 1835, the Mexican president Santa Anna abolished the Mexican Constitution and became dictator, helping to foment the Texas revolution. Not only the Anglo settlers resisted the totalitarian moves by Santa Ana; many of the Mexican settlers did as well. A group of citizens of San Antonio elected Navarro to represent them in Washington-on-the-Brazos, at that time the state capital. There, Navarro signed the Texas Declaration of Independence on March 3, 1836. He was one of only two signers actually born in Texas. He also helped write the constitution of the new Republic of Texas and later helped revise it after Texas joined the United States. Navarro County was named in his honor.

In 1841, Navarro took part in the ill-fated Santa Fe Expedition, whose purpose was to open trade with New Mexico and take possession of lands in eastern New Mexico. He was captured by the Mexican Army and imprisoned in Mexico for three years, narrowly escaping execution.

During his life, Navarro worked to preserve the rights of the Mexican settlers of Texas, the Tejanos. He helped protect Spanish and Mexican land grants and defended Tejano rights in the Texas Constitution.

Navarro's home in downtown San Antonio has been preserved to honor his contributions to Texas history. Navarro and his wife moved to the house in about 1856, after selling their ranch near Seguin in 1853. To prevent its demolition, the San Antonio Conservation Society purchased the site in 1960 and restored the buildings—three stone and adobe buildings, tentatively identified as the residence, kitchen, and store. The site was later donated to the State of Texas. The store, a two-story building, was evidently used as a rental property. The residence does not contain any of Navarro's actual furnishings, but it does hold representative antiques from that period of Texas history. For the most part, the home and furnishings are plain and simple.

VISITOR INFORMATION

0.6 acre. Open Wednesday through Sunday, 10 AM to 4 PM. Historic structures, museum, guided tours, living-history demonstrations. All visitor services available in San Antonio. For information: Casa Navarro State Historic Site, 228 S. Laredo, San Antonio, TX 78207, (210) 226-4801.

BELOW
Restored bedroom
BOTTOM
José Antonio Navarro home

Choke Canyon State Park

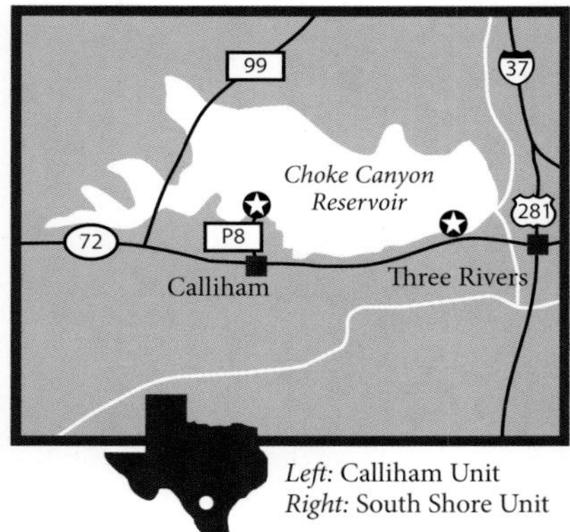

Left: Calliham Unit
Right: South Shore Unit

The two Choke Canyon State Park units, Calliham and South Shore, lie on the shores of Choke Canyon Lake, a large 26,000-acre South Texas reservoir. The dam project was initiated in the 1970s by the City of Corpus Christi and the Bureau of Reclamation to provide a water source for Corpus Christi and the surrounding area. To create the reservoir, the Frio River was dammed at a narrow "choke" point along the river. Most of the surrounding terrain consists of relatively flat grasslands invaded by brush such as mesquite and acacia.

The two park units were built within a 38,000-acre wildlife management area, resulting in plentiful wildlife within the park. Many of the animals have lost much of their natural shyness and can be viewed relatively closely, especially early and late in the day. White-tailed deer, javelina, and wild turkey are some of the most popular and frequently seen creatures.

Birders are drawn to Choke Canyon, hoping to spot some of the almost 200 species of birds that have been recorded in the park. To the surprise of many visitors to the relatively dry brushlands surrounding the lake, even alligators are found in some marshy areas on the lakeshore. Choke Canyon is the westernmost site in which alligators are commonly found.

Wildlife viewing is only one of Choke Canyon State Park's attractions. Boaters and water skiers love the vast expanse of open water, and anglers actively pursue the many species of fish found in the reservoir's depths. Some of the most popular fish include largemouth, striped, and white bass, catfish, crappie, and freshwater drum.

If wildlife viewing and lake attractions are not enough, the Calliham Unit has some of the state-park system's most elaborate facilities. A large swimming pool and bathhouse is probably the most popular attraction, especially in summer, but the park also offers basketball, tennis, volleyball, and shuffleboard courts and a baseball diamond. There is even an auditorium, complete with dressing rooms and a raised stage. A small 75-acre lake lies near the tent-camping area. The undeveloped North Shore Unit offers 18 miles of trails, and primitive equestrian and group camping.

Humans have been coming to the Frio River Valley since long before the park was built. Nomadic hunters are thought to have visited the area as long as 10,000 years ago. An archaeological survey conducted before the lake was created found a number of Archaic sites that are several thousand years old. Evidence was also discovered of more recent Indian groups that lived there prior to the arrival of the Spaniards in the 1500s. Later, in historic times, the area was settled under the jurisdictions of the Mexican, Texas, and United States governments. Then, as now, water was the primary draw for residents of and visitors to the area.

VISITOR INFORMATION

1485 acres. Open all year. Hot and humid in summer. Large number of campsites in the Calliham Unit with partial hookups and showers. Walk-in tent campsites at Calliham Unit. At present, South Shore Unit is currently open only for day use; campground is not open. Screened shelters at Calliham Unit. Boating, boat ramp, waterskiing, fishing, lake swimming, picnicking at both units. Tennis, basketball, volleyball, and shuffleboard courts, nature and hiking trails, baseball diamond, swimming pool, and store in Calliham Unit. Most visitor services available in Three Rivers. For information: Choke Canyon State Park, Calliham Unit, P.O. Box 2, Calliham, TX 78007, (361) 786-3868.

Sunset over Choke Canyon Lake

Estero Llano Grande State Park • World Birding Center

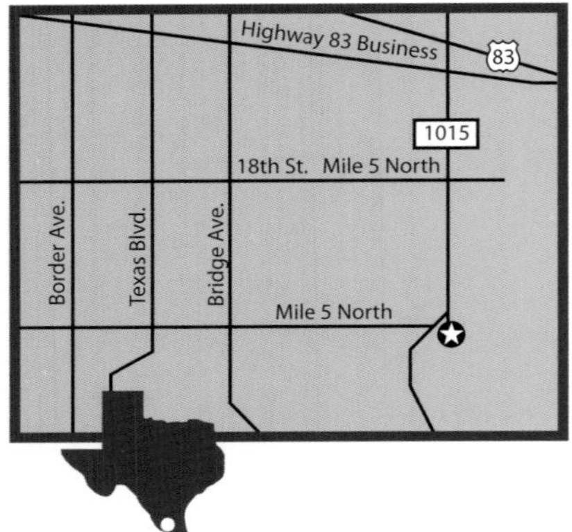

The new Estero Llano Grande State Park lies in the heart of the Lower Rio Grande Valley, and is one of nine units of the World Birding Center. The World Birding Center is headquartered at Bentsen-Rio Grande Valley State Park, near Mission. The World Birding Center works to protect increasingly rare native habitat in the Lower Rio Grande Valley. Virtually all of the Valley's native habitat has been lost to agricultural uses and to urbanization recently swelled by a flood of immigrants from Mexico. Because of the Valley's southern, subtropical location, many species of animals and plants live here and nowhere else in the United States. Federal, state, and local governments, along with several private entities, have been making an enormous effort in recent years to protect the remaining bits of natural habitat in the Valley, plus even return former farmland to its natural state.

Estero Llano Grande adds another patch of protected land to foster the existence of rare cats, such as the ocelot and jaguarundi, and birds such as the green jay, Altamira oriole, chachalaca, white-tipped dove, pauraque, groove-billed ani, hook-billed kite, and ringed kingfisher. Part of the park consists of native woodland dominated by mesquite and other hardy plants; part is former farmland converted to shallow wetland ponds and land replanted in native species; and part is a shallow marshy lake, Llano Grande. The lake is part of Arroyo Colorado, a large natural drainage in this part of the Valley that has been dammed here.

Because of all the water, the most of any World Birding Center unit, shorebirds and wading birds frequent the park. Birders commonly see the roseate spoonbill and ibis at the park. Observant visitors may even spot the rare red-crowned parrot or green parakeet, along with many other birds found only in the Valley or in neighboring Mexico. The water also attracts alligators, usually easily found in Alligator Lake via one of the park's several easy hiking trails. Other trails circle other ponds and climb the levee to overlook Llano Grande.

In addition to more than three miles of hiking trails, the park features boardwalks, a visitor center, a nature trail, and an observation deck. Estero Llano Grande State Park makes a fine new addition to the network of parks, wildlife refuges, and other areas of natural habitat that make the Valley famous with birders.

VISITOR INFORMATION

176 acres. Hot and humid April through October. Day use only. Visitor center, hiking and nature trails and boardwalks, birding. All visitor services available in Weslaco. For information: Estero Llano Grande State Park, 3301 S. International Blvd., Weslaco, TX 78596, (956) 565-3919.

BELOW LEFT
Llano Grande ponds with sunset sky
BELOW RIGHT
Wildflowers at Ibis Pond

Falcon State Park

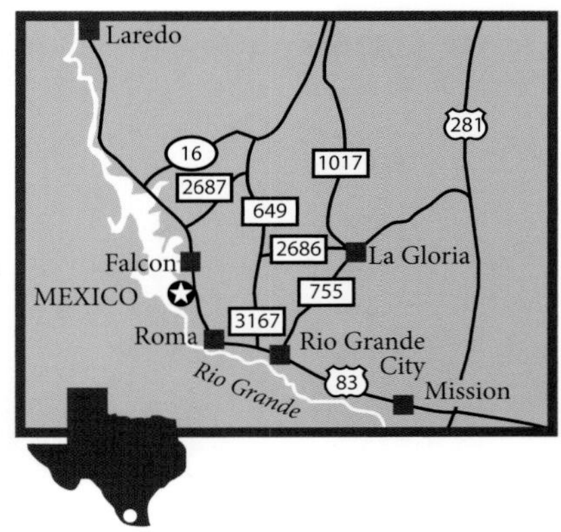

Deep in the dry brush country of South Texas lies sprawling Falcon Lake, a large reservoir fed by the Rio Grande and secondarily by the Rio Salado of Mexico. When the five-mile-long dam was completed in 1953, the lake began to fill, eventually flooding 99,000 acres and extending 60 miles upstream. The reservoir was created jointly by the United States and Mexico for flood control, power generation, irrigation, and recreation. Falcon State Park, on the east shore of the lake near the dam, provides excellent access to the enormous lake.

The brush country surrounding the lake contains many subtropical plant and animal species found only in Mexico and far South Texas. Brushy thickets of mesquite, huisache, palo verde, ebony, and other plants provide cover to birds such as the chachalaca, groove-billed ani, ringed kingfisher, and green jay.

Tropical cats are of particular interest in the Rio Grande Valley, from Falcon Lake downstream. Although they were once more common, the spotted ocelot and especially the dark, thin jaguarundi are now very rare in South Texas. Most of their habitat, the woodland and brushland that once lined the Rio Grande, has disappeared because of agricultural use and urbanization. The two cats have declined in tandem with many other plants and animals. At one time even the jaguar, the largest cat in the New World, roamed the Rio Grande Valley. Today, the Texas Parks and Wildlife Department, the U.S. Fish and Wildlife Service, and other public and private entities are attempting to preserve undisturbed tracts of habitat in the Rio Grande Valley to protect the remaining cats and other rare plants and animals. Falcon State Park is one such site.

The state park lies in an area with extensive human history. Nearby Roma was founded by the Spaniards in about 1767. It later became a trading center for steamboats that traveled up the Rio Grande from the Gulf of Mexico. Many historical buildings dating from the 1800s still stand around the town square.

Across the river and slightly upstream from Roma is the Mexican town of Mier. It was founded in the 1750s and is most famous as the site of the black-bean incident. During hostilities between Mexico and the newly formed Republic of Texas, a group of defeated Texans escaped from captivity; most were recaptured by Santa Anna and taken to Mier. As punishment, Santa Anna ordered that ten percent of the escapees be shot. To determine which of them would be executed, 17 black beans were put in a pot with 159 white beans. Those who drew the black beans were summarily executed, and the others were jailed until September 12, 1844.

Some history is visible to boaters in the lake. When the reservoir was built, it flooded the old Mexican town of Guerrero. Depending on water levels, boaters can sometimes view the ruins and foundations of a number of the town's buildings, including the old mission church that was founded in 1750. Recent droughts have often left much of the old town site and other long-flooded lands high and dry.

Falcon Lake provides the primary freshwater fishing opportunity in South Texas. Striped, white, and largemouth bass, crappie, and catfish all draw anglers to the lake. The vast expanse of open water also attracts water skiers, boaters, and swimmers. In winter, the park is particularly popular with visitors from northern states seeking to escape cold, snowy weather by coming to the warm, temperate climate of Falcon Lake.

VISITOR INFORMATION

573 acres. Open all year. Hot from April through October. Very popular in winter. Large number of campsites with partial or full hookups and showers. Screened shelters. Boating, fishing, birding, boat ramp, picnicking, swimming, waterskiing; hiking, mountain-biking, and nature trails. All visitor services available in Roma. For information: Falcon State Park, P.O. Box 2, Falcon Heights, TX 78545, (956) 848-5327.

Fishermen

Fannin Battleground State Historic Site

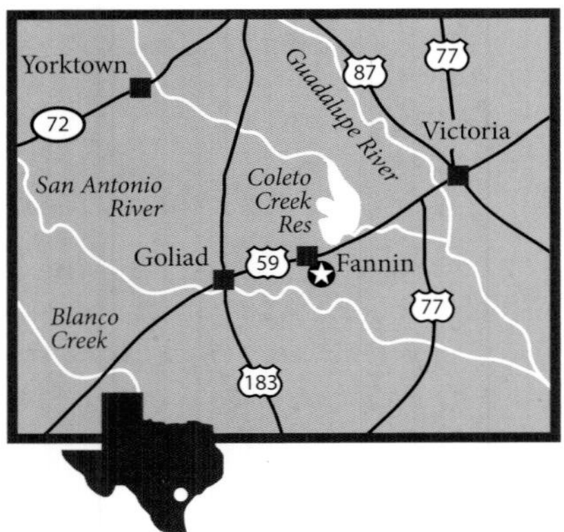

A handsome stone obelisk marks the site where Colonel James W. Fannin Jr. and his men surrendered to superior Mexican forces on March 20, 1836, after the Battle of Coleto Creek. The battle was one of a number fought during the course of Texas's fight for independence from Mexico. After the surrender, which Fannin believed was done on honorable terms, the Texans were taken to the La Bahia presidio in nearby Goliad. Against the wishes of local Mexican commanders, General Antonio López de Santa Anna ordered Fannin and his men executed. On March 27, Palm Sunday morning, Fannin and 342 of his men were slain.

Word quickly spread of the massacre, giving the Texan troops a new rallying cry during the revolution: "Remember Goliad!" Fannin and his men were buried near the presidio in a site now enclosed in a small city park and marked by a large monument, the Fannin Memorial.

The location of Fannin's surrender at the battleground is peaceful now. Landscaped grounds and a circular drive surround the stone obelisk on the flat coastal plain. A small museum tells of the battleground's history, and a pavilion shades a cluster of picnic tables.

VISITOR INFORMATION

14 acres. Open all year. Day use only. Hot and humid in summer. Historic site and museum, picnicking. All visitor services available in Goliad. For information: Fannin Battleground State Historic Site, c/o Goliad State Park, 108 Park Road 6, Goliad, TX 77963, (361) 645-3405.

LEFT
Fannin Battleground memorial
RIGHT
Mission church walls in last light with agave plant
OPPOSITE PAGE, TOP
Presidio de la Bahia with agave plant
OPPOSITE PAGE, BOTTOM
Front of mission church

Goliad State Park •

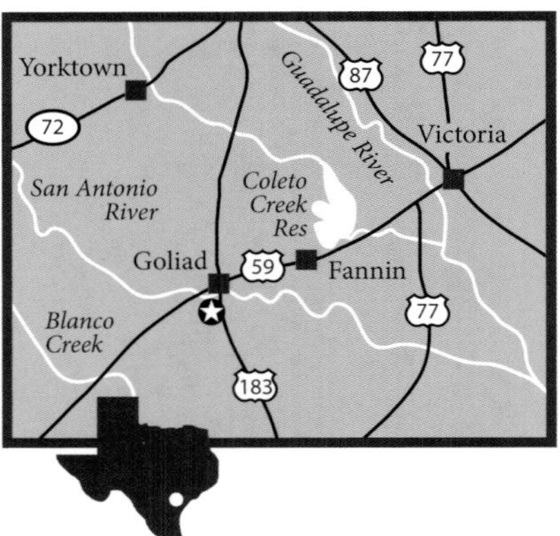

"Remember Goliad!" shouted Texans in memory of the Goliad massacre, as they fought for independence from Mexico. After a day and a half of fierce fighting at Coleto Creek, Texas forces led by Colonel James Walker Fannin Jr. had surrendered to superior Mexican forces on March 20, 1836. Expecting fair treatment, they were imprisoned at the Presidio La Bahia at Goliad. A week later, Fannin and 342 of his men were summarily executed under the orders of General Antonio López de Santa Anna. Outrage over the massacre fueled the fires of the Texas war of independence.

Today the San Antonio River slides silently by Goliad State Park. The imposing white church of Mission Espíritu Santo de Zúñiga, a state historic site, dominates the quiet 178-acre

park. In 1722, long before the Texas revolution, the mission was established by the Spaniards near Matagorda Bay to serve the Karankawa Indians and their allies. The Indians abandoned the mission in 1724, and it was moved to a site near Victoria, in the territory of the Aranama and Tamique Indians. Finally, in 1749, it was moved a last time, to a hill lying in a large loop of the San Antonio River just south of the present-day town of Goliad.

The mission lasted 108 years, longer than any other Spanish colonial mission in Texas. Sporadic rains made farming difficult at the mission, but ranching thrived. With a herd of 40,000 head, the mission operated the first large cattle ranch in Texas. Raids of the mission and its herds were common, and the mission was in poor shape when it was secularized in 1830. The mission lands were distributed to colonists, and the buildings were used for schools for a number of years. An 1886 hurricane heavily damaged the buildings, which by then were already closed and in disrepair, and they collapsed into ruin. Area settlers salvaged stone and wooden beams for building materials, leaving little of the original mission by the time the site was designated a historical park by the state legislature in 1931.

Beginning in 1935, the Civilian Conservation Corps and the Works Progress Administration excavated and reconstructed the mission. Because of a lack of photographs or drawings of the original buildings, the reconstructed mission probably differs somewhat from the original structure.

The ruins of another mission, Nuestra Señora del Rosario, lie a few miles west of Mission Espíritu Santo. The more short-lived Mission Rosario was founded by Franciscan missionaries in 1754 and abandoned in 1807. The mission ruins are a state historic site, but are not open to the public.

About a mile south of Mission Espíritu Santo lies the birthplace of

General Ignacio Zaragosa, at a small state historic site. He was born there in 1829, and after growing up in the area, he was educated in Mexico and joined the Mexican Army. On May 5, 1862, he led his troops to victory over superior French forces in the Battle of Puebla, Mexico. His triumph is celebrated every year in Mexico as Cinco de Mayo.

Next to Zaragosa's birthplace is the privately administered Presidio La Bahia, the oldest fort in the western United States. It was built to house the Spanish troops that protected the mission complex. Like Mission Espíritu Santo, it has been reconstructed. Behind the presidio lies a large granite marker that commemorates Colonel Fannin and his men, who were executed there by order of Santa Anna.

Today visitors can tour the old mission church and museum, the Presidio La Bahia, the Fannin Memorial, and Zaragosa's birthplace. A nature trail follows the banks of the San Antonio River, introducing both the lush riparian vegetation of the river corridor and the South Texas brushland. The City of Goliad operates a large swimming pool within the park during the summer. The San Antonio River offers opportunities for canoeing and fishing.

The tranquil façade of Goliad State Park and its subsidiary historic sites masks its rich history, vital to both Texas and Mexico. Listen carefully on a quiet moonlit night; maybe the sound of church bells calling the faithful to prayer at the isolated Spanish outpost can still be heard.

VISITOR INFORMATION

188 acres. Open all year. Campground with full or partial hookups. Screened shelters. Restored mission church and museum, Zaragosa's birthplace, Fannin Memorial, short nature and hiking trails, fishing, canoeing, picnicking. The City of Goliad operates a large swimming pool within the park in summer. All visitor services in Goliad. For information: Goliad State Park, 108 Park Road 6, Goliad, TX 77963, (361) 645-3405.

Lake Casa Blanca International State Park

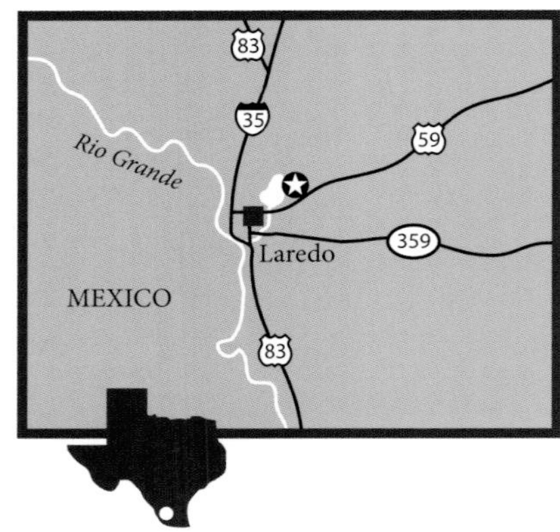

Little-known Lake Casa Blanca International State Park provides one of the few public recreational retreats near Laredo. The lake was impounded in 1946, and it was the only lake of significant size in the area until Falcon Lake was built to the south in the 1950s. Unlike Falcon Lake, however, Lake Casa Blanca was not created by damming the Rio Grande. Instead, water from Chacon and San Ygnacio creeks feeds the small 1650-acre reservoir.

The lake lies in relatively flat country on the west side of Laredo, adjoining the airport. The land surrounding the park is dry and dominated by South Texas brush country plants such as mesquite, palo verde, and prickly pear. Because the terrain has little relief, the lake averages only about 12 feet in depth. The shallow water encourages dense growth of reeds and other water plants along the lakeshore. These plants provide excellent fish habitat, a fact little known outside the Laredo area. Largemouth bass exceeding ten pounds in weight are frequently caught at the lake. Other species caught include sunfish, white and black crappie, and channel, flathead, and blue catfish.

The park was formerly managed as a county park, but operation was taken over by the Texas Parks and Wildlife Department in 1991. Early in the morning and late in the evening, fishermen practice their skills along the banks and from boats. During the middle part of the day, boats and water skiers zip across the blue waters, taking their turn enjoying the oasis of Lake Casa Blanca International State Park.

VISITOR INFORMATION

371 acres. Open all year. Hot from April through October. Moderate number of campsites with partial hookups and showers. Swimming pool, lake swimming, fishing, boat ramp, waterskiing, short mountain-bike trail, picnicking, and basketball, volleyball, and tennis courts. All visitor services available in Laredo. For information: Lake Casa Blanca International State Park, 5102 Bob Bullock Loop, Laredo, TX 78044, (956) 725-3826.

Boaters

Resaca de la Palma State Park • World Birding Center

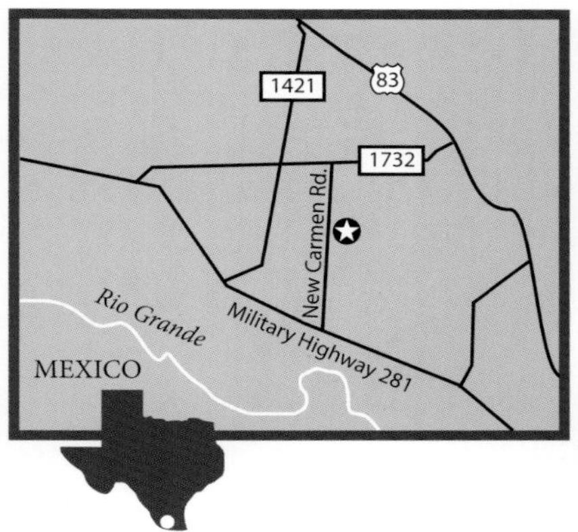

Resaca de la Palma State Park is the newest of three state parks that make up part of the World Birding Center's nine units. With 1700 acres, it contains the largest tract of native habitat in the center. The Lower Rio Grande Valley is famous nationwide among biologists and birders for its unique plants and wildlife. Because of its subtropical, southerly location on the Mexican border, many animals and plants live here and nowhere else in the United States. Lush woodlands of sabal palms, ebonies, cedar elms, anaquas, Rio Grande ashes, and many other trees once lined the Rio Grande and other waterways in the Valley. In drier areas away from the riparian zones, thick brush composed of mesquite, huisache, and other plants once dominated. Ocelots, jaguars, and jaguarundis used to roam the land. But the arrival of Spanish, Mexican, and Anglo settlers changed all of that. Over the years, almost all of the habitat was cleared for agriculture. Towns were founded and grew into cities. Today, with immigration-driven population growth, even much of the farmland is being lost to urbanization. To protect what remains of the natural habitat in the Valley, federal, state, and local governments, along with private entities, are making a concerted effort to preserve land. Resaca de la Palma State Park is one of the latest fruits of that effort.

The new park contains a mix of native woodland and farm fields that are slowly returning to their natural brushy condition. An ancient cutoff meander of the Rio Grande, commonly known as a resaca in the Lower Rio Grande Valley, winds its way across the park. It has been refilled with water to create a habitat for wildlife, particularly shorebirds and wading birds.

Birders come to the Lower Rio Grande Valley from all over the country to see birds such as the green jay, hook-billed kite, ringed kingfisher, Altamira oriole, chachalaca, white-tipped dove, pauraque, and groove-billed ani. Resaca de la Palma hosts all these birds and many other species. Although the jaguar is long gone from the Valley, the rare ocelot and very rare jaguarundi still slip silently through the remaining bits of habitat such as that found at the new park.

The park includes a paved loop road for a tram route, plus several miles of both surfaced and unsurfaced trails. The trails, plus observation decks and benches, help birders add new species to their life list. A visitor center and picnic area round out the park facilities.

TOP
Mesquite tree and grassland in last light
BOTTOM
Palmettos and other trees

VISITOR INFORMATION

1700 acres. Hot and humid April through October. Day use only. Birding, hiking trails, bicycle and tram route, picnicking, visitor center. All visitor services available in Brownsville. For information: Resaca de la Palma State Park/ World Birding Center, 2800 S. Bentsen Palm Dr., Mission, Texas 78572, (956) 585-9156.

Sebastopol House State Historic Site

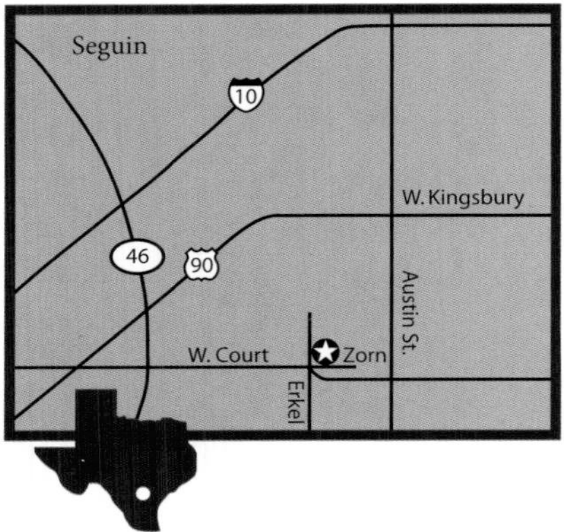

Seguin has been called the "mother of concrete cities" because of its many structures built of concrete, dating back to the 1800s. A number of concrete buildings had been built in Seguin by 1850, which was surprising because the use of concrete in wall construction was less than 20 years old. Frederick Olmstead, the famous architect of New York City's Central Park, passed through Seguin in 1854. He found it worthy of note that a small, isolated town in Texas would be using such a new building technique.

In the 1600s, the Spanish used a type of aggregate wall-construction material utilizing shells from along the coast. One of the oldest known aggregate buildings in the United States is Castillo de San Marcos in St. Augustine, Florida. However, it was not until 1819, with the building of the Erie Canal, that cements were used that hardened even when wet. Concrete soon became popular for uses such as canals and bridges that required strength and weather resistance, but it was not used in homes until the 1830s, when it was used in a New York residence. Historians are uncertain how the technique came to Seguin, but it may have been brought by Dr. John Park, who came from Georgia in about 1847. Over the years he acquired several patents on concrete use.

Seguin proved to be an ideal site for concrete—or limecrete as it was called—construction. The town lies on a thick, shallow bed of coarse gravel, ideal for use in concrete when mixed with lime and water.

In 1854, Colonel Joshua Young built a large home, which later became known as Sebastopol, using gravel dug on the site to make limecrete. Sadly, his wife died just before the home's completion; he sold it shortly afterward to his widowed sister, Catharine Young LeGette. Young's children opposed the sale, but eventually LeGette obtained the house for herself and her children. Her family lived in the house until 1874, when the property was sold to Joseph Zorn Jr., a local merchant.

Although Zorn's personal fortunes waned in the 1890s, he held prominent civic positions in Seguin, including the mayorship for 20 years. Zorn died in 1923, followed by his wife Nettie in 1937. Family members continued to live at Sebastopol until 1952. Because the house's condition had deteriorated, it was threatened with demolition in 1960, but was saved by the Seguin Conservation Society. The home was later obtained by the state and was restored.

The origin of the home's name is unknown. It may have come from the Battle of Sebastopol in the Crimean War, made famous by Tennyson's poem "The Charge of the Light Brigade," or from the Russian naval base during that war. The war took place in 1854, about the time of the house's construction.

As many as 90 limecrete buildings had been built in Seguin by 1900, although fewer than 20 still remain. The restored Sebastopol house is an important site that exhibits both an early innovative construction technique and a window into the lives of the home's past residents.

VISITOR INFORMATION

2.2 acres. Day use only. Open Friday through Sunday, 9 AM to 4 PM. Guided tours. Call ahead to check days and hours. Historic structure with interpretive exhibits and period furnishings. Picnicking. All visitor services available in Seguin. For information: Sebastopol House State Historic Site, P.O. Box 900, Seguin, TX 78156, (830) 379-4833.

Sebastopol home

Index